SAVING DESIRE

SAVING DESIRE

The Seduction
of Christian Theology

Edited by

F. LeRon Shults *&* Jan-Olav Henriksen

WILLIAM B. EERDMANS PUBLISHING COMPANY
GRAND RAPIDS, MICHIGAN / CAMBRIDGE, U.K.

© 2011 William B. Eerdmans Publishing Company

All rights reserved

Published 2011 by

Wm. B. Eerdmans Publishing Co.

2140 Oak Industrial Drive N.E., Grand Rapids, Michigan 49505 /
P.O. Box 163, Cambridge CB3 9PU U.K.

Printed in the United States of America

17 16 15 14 13 12 11   7 6 5 4 3 2 1

Library of Congress Cataloging-in-Publication Data

Saving desire: the seduction of Christian theology /
    edited by F. LeRon Shults & Jan-Olav Henriksen.
        p.   cm.
    ISBN 978-0-8028-6626-4 (pbk.: alk. paper)
    1. Emotions — Religious aspects — Christianity.
    2. Desire — Religious aspects — Christianity.
    3. Theology.   I. Shults, F. LeRon.   II. Henriksen, Jan-Olav.
    III. Title: Seduction of Christian theology.

    BV4597.3.S28   2011
    233′5 — dc22

                                    2011005871

www.eerdmans.com

Contents

Contents

Introduction: Saving Desire?

F. LeRon Shults

This book has emerged out of several years of conversation among a group of scholars who share the conviction that something has gone wrong in the traditional Christian theological treatment of human desire. For the most part desire has been construed negatively, as a threatening force connected to the degrading and darkening experience of sin. We believe that desire can and ought to be understood also as a redemptive force connected to the enlivening and enlightening experience of grace. Our common passion, therefore, is *saving* desire — both rescuing the concept from its imprisonment within repressive, individualistic, and rationalistic categories as well as emphasizing the power of the phenomenon of desire for engendering human flourishing in relation to God.

Most people do not consider theology seductive. Its reputation in many western contexts is tied to Christianity's (apparent) obsession with regulation: desire ought to be restricted and repressed, closeted and controlled. The contributors to this book are passionate about doing theology, and they believe that the discipline has itself been seduced and seduced others into accepting a primarily negative view of desire. We find theological exploration itself powerfully and positively seductive — even erotic in senses to be explained below! Of course, experiences of seduction feel dangerous as well as delightful. Attending to desire — even in academic contexts — intensifies both our fear of vulnerability and our hope for intimacy. Theology is interested in the origin, condition, and goal of desiring, in the infinite ground of the human experience of being-interested. What could be more interesting than tending to that ultimate reality in which all things live and move and have their attraction?

The first conviction we all share, therefore, is that theology should learn to emphasize the *positivity* of desire. The salutary ordering of human life occurs through the appropriate intensification of desire, not by its repression or destruction. Desire has often been portrayed theologically in relation to lack, deficiency, loss, transgression, and guilt. We want to stress its potential relation to fullness, being, gift, creativity, and joy. These themes are articulated in a variety of ways in the following chapters. We pursue a theology of desire linked to the evocative power of beauty, the plenitude of life, and the constitution of subjectivity opened up by the arrival of the future. As we will see, there are many resources in the biblical tradition and in contemporary philosophical discourse for developing a positive construal of human desire within Christian theology. We believe that this also may have some impact for the understanding of Christian spirituality.

A second shared emphasis is on the *sociality* of desire. In other words, our interest is not simply in the individual will and the objects of its desire, but in the communal relations and practices that shape desiring itself. We all want to stress the importance of understanding desire in relation to broader structural and social concerns about justice in community. Saving desire — desire that saves — does not simply alter individual souls; it transforms the way we order our lives together. Here, too, the contributors engage this theme in different ways, emphasizing to various degrees the significance of traditional biblical themes such as law and wisdom, and the relevance of contemporary cultural issues such as capitalism and sexism. All of us, however, seek a theological understanding of desire that contributes to the redemption of concrete social relations in everyday life.

We also share an interest in emphasizing the *physicality* of saving desire. The traditional denigration of desire was connected to a dualism between body and soul; salvation was understood as the purification of the latter by its escape from the former. In various ways, the chapters that follow all celebrate the inherently embodied nature of desire. This celebration is motivated in part from engagement with late modern philosophical developments (especially feminism and postcolonialism) and scientific discoveries (especially in neuroscience and psychology). We are not saved *from* bodily experiences, but in and through them. This means that experiences of parental caregiving, going to the movies or shopping, washing the pots and pans, and even sexuality can be redemptive — transforming the concrete, embodied relations within which the human longing for the good life is originated, organized, and oriented.

Both the content and the order of the chapters reflect the outcome of our conversations about desire, and our multiple readings of each other's contributions. The three themes just outlined are evident in each chapter. The rationale for the flow of the essays is made clear as each author builds on earlier contributions and anticipates later ones. It is not possible in this context to explore human desire in all its depth, breadth, and pluriformity. Our goal here has been to offer an integrated set of essays that contribute to the growing trend among theologians to attend more carefully to the positivity, sociality, and physicality of desire. This approach places the work of theology firmly in the experiential realm of human life, and may in the long run have some impact on how Christian spiritualities are shaped and reshaped.

The dialogue among us has been mutually enriching, enhanced by the fact that we come from different Christian traditions, work in different theological disciplines, and live in different cultural contexts. Our collaboration has pushed us to reflect in new ways on the biblical tradition as well as on the challenges and opportunities posed by contemporary philosophy and science. What is saving desire? How are human desires related to the desire of God? Our contributions are intended to contribute toward satisfying answers to such questions, but even more to open up and intensify the insatiable desire for the infinite goodness of God.

Desire: Gift and Giving

Jan-Olav Henriksen

The Complexities of Desire

Desire is deeply rooted in human life. We run the risk of missing a lot in understanding the human condition if we do not contemplate desire and its place and role in our existence. Furthermore, we run the risk of losing sight of important *positive* theological insights and religious dimensions if we ignore or overlook what desire means for our existence. The basic approach in this chapter will be to develop an understanding of desire as that which helps us get an *incarnal experience* of (what we take to be) the good in human life. Desire is not only about our individual existence; it also shapes how we relate to others and how the world and others can present themselves to us. Hence, the struggle to satisfy desires does not take place only in order to realize or fulfill already-existing elements in human life. This *open quest* might imply that desire is what makes us open for something new and yet undetermined, which is nevertheless perceived (and thereby desired) as good. I will return to this point below when I develop the distinction between *opening and closing desires.*[1]

A central thesis in the following is that desire must be understood as both given and giving: It is given prior to subjectivity and reflection, but it is also something that gives us the opportunity to relate to ourselves and to the content of our lives in a way that strongly impacts our self-relation, our subjectivity. As subjectivity can be developed fully only by means of lan-

---

1. It must be said from the outset that this distinction is to be understood as *analytical,* and, moreover, should not be taken as identical with a moral assessment of "good" vs. "bad" desires. See below.

guage and reflection, it follows that desire and its appropriation into and by means of subjectivity calls for a nuanced and adequate understanding of its place in human life. As we shall see, this way of positioning desire presents theological reflection (which serves as a framework and a resource for such appropriation) with specific challenges.

According to French phenomenologist Maurice Merleau-Ponty, desire is not adequately understood if seen only as a primitive biological notion. Desire is neither the result of an involuntary biological impulse nor a phenomenon apparent for a lucid mind. Desire is the result of neither biology nor calculation, and hence humans cannot produce their own desire. I cannot and do not say that "I want to desire X" and by these words force desire to appear. Desire exists in another type of structure. Desire is a way of relating to the world, expressing a type of intentionality that conditions human existence[2] and the wills and wants that we articulate. Merleau-Ponty thus underscores the point I made above, when I referred to human existence as incarnal.

Desire is integrated in my embodied direction toward the world and toward myself, a moment in my being-in-the world. Desire emerges spontaneously in my experience of the world of/as the other and out of pre-thematic emotional being in the world. Desire is not primarily an element in consciousness, to be appropriated intellectually; rather, it exists in the world as the world is given with my body and its perception. This is the reason why we say that it is the other who stirs my desire. Hence, it is not only the case that I desire; desire is also what happens to me.

Desire as Individualizing

I want to suggest from the very outset that desire is the phenomenon that perhaps more than any other phenomenon relates us both to the world and to ourselves, and orients us, directs us, and *individualizes* us.[3] Desire is never generic but is always *somebody*'s desire. To become aware of the fact that our desire is our own is thus to become aware of ourselves in a new way. To be asked "What is your desire?" and thereby to be invited to state it

---

2. Cf. Maurice Merleau-Ponty, *Phenomenology of Perception,* trans. Colin Smith (New York: Routledge, 1962), Part I, Ch. 5 (pp. 178ff.).

3. Cf. In addition to Merleau-Ponty, passim, see also Jean-Luc Marion, *The Erotic Phenomenon* (Chicago: University of Chicago Press, 2007), p. 108.

(or them) is to be taken seriously as a person.[4] On the other hand, not to be asked for (to articulate) your desires is to be refused access to a world that could open you and others up to more than what is already present. Hence, desire has an important hermeneutical impact on the ability to interpret life and to get adequate access to the phenomena relevant for leading a good life. In some of the narratives in the Gospels, we see how this individualizing element plays an important role in the reshaping of people's lives.[5]

To take ourselves seriously and to take our desire seriously are thus two sides of the same coin. It is from this affirmation and recognition of desire that individualization emerges as a function of desire. Individualization may be seen as both a state of consciousness ("This is me/my desire!") and a way of expressing myself in a specific manner: "This is me saying/doing/longing for/grasping for and opening up toward . . ." Thus, in spite of its individualizing character, desire is nevertheless relational in its character, as it opens up the world and its significance to us.

Deeply embedded in the relational dimension of desire is the fact that desire ties us to the good. When we are alienated from our desires, not only are we alienated from ourselves but we also suffer from a problematic and distorted relationship with the world because we fail to understand how desire relates and connects us to the world. The lack of recognition of our desires in relating to the world leads, consequently, to a lack of understanding of what the world means to us, be it in fact or potentially. Hence, desire reveals the meaning of the world to us, as it discloses what it signifies to us. On the other hand, to recognize, affirm, and appreciate desires emerging from the relationship with the world makes us able to relate positively to the world and experience it as something we are deeply connected with.

In this sense, desire may open us up to the world in a way that overcomes the individualistic notion of humanity so prevalent in modernity.

---

4. Theologically and religiously, this is a point for the interpretation of Jesus' invitation to Bartimaeus in Mark 10 to state what he wants him to do. Most of this chapter in Mark can also be read and interpreted from the angle of desire (marriage, desire for the blessing of children or position, and how desire for wealth separates from the kingdom of God). For more on this, see my *Desire, Gift, and Recognition: Christology and Postmodern Philosophy* (Grand Rapids: Eerdmans, 2009), pp. 196ff.

5. However, as should be apparent already, desire is socially conditioned and shaped, and despite its ability to individualize it is not a phenomenon easily used for promoting an individualistic ideology.

But desire may also contribute to enforcing individualistic traits, given that desire always also allows us to fall back upon ourselves in a self-centered mode that relates the world more to us and our preconceptions of what it contains/entails than us to the world in a manner that makes us open for what we can mean to it and it can mean for us.[6] This has important consequences for understanding what happens in the repression and neglect of desire: such practice implies that those who subject desire to repression lose their world as a meaningful place — more or less.

The above presupposes several different elements that need to be elaborated and discussed further. I am posing a connection between desire and the (presumed) good that needs to be warranted further. While talking about *our* desire or how desire helps *us* already seems to indicate that there is a clear and transparent relation between desire and how and what we are as subjects relating to, having, or harboring desires for, that is surely not the case. Desire presents us with a lot of puzzles, some of which we need to clarify further in order to assess its theological importance.

The complexity of desire and its place in human life is often downplayed by religious and theological approaches that lead to oversimplification and distortion of its role. In the Norwegian context where I work, desire is often associated with either covetousness or sexual desire, both to a large extent judged negatively. Hence, to lecture on desire and try to develop a more positive and nuanced perception of its importance in human life, as I have done over the last years, always seems to present the audience with difficulties and worries. My experience in this regard has convinced me that the relation of religion to desire is one of the clearest instances where the place of desire in human life is dialectically constituted by its relation to the negative dimension of the law, that of prohibition (not only in the Pauline, but also in the Freudian and Lacanian sense), a point I will develop further below.[7] In other words, to provide theological reasons for the appreciation, recognition, and affirmation of desire (as I

---

6. This distinction is a variant of the above-mentioned distinction between closing vs. opening desires. Cf. again below.

7. The negative side of the "oedipalizing" function of law is treated in Shults's contribution in this volume. As will become clear, we do seek in the present volume to overcome a negative juxtaposition of law and desire. This is possible, however, only if we see both desire and law as gifts that relate us to the good (see both Yoder's and Svenungsson's chapters). From such an outset, it also becomes clear why desire and justice are internally related, and why it is only the law in a context shaped by distorted and closing desire that turns out to be problematic. For more on this theme, see below.

also will attempt to do here) immediately presents us with the challenge to break through some of the hermeneutical complications with which the theological tradition from Paul's "Do not covet" (Rom. 7:7) onward presents us.

In the following, I will develop a theologically relevant understanding of desire from three different approaches. First, I will point to how elements that constitute desire are firmly rooted in our incarnal mode of being, and what this means for understanding its basic and constitutive functions at a pre-subjective level. Second, I will look further into desire from a phenomenological point of view in order to make some basic theological claims. Third, I will look into desire as a phenomenon constituting the subject dialectically in the relationship between the immediately given and culture/reflexivity, in order to help us better understand the importance of desire for human growth and spiritual development.

Desire — Reflections on Its Incarnal Dimension

Desire is deeply rooted in human biological existence. In spite of this, and given our present level of evolution, it is probably not adequate to understand desire only as the drive toward satisfaction of biological needs — what we usually call appetite. To look into how desire works in humans as biological beings might nevertheless suggest to us some elements for a wider and deeper understanding of how desire works, and why it works the way it does. In the following I will elaborate the understanding of this incarnal dimension somewhat further, and thus develop a basis for understanding the initial points made by referring to Merleau-Ponty in the introduction above, which suggest that desire in human life is *not* to be understood as a biological drive only.

A basic function of desire is that it aims or directs us toward objects that satisfy our primary biological aims: to continue to live and to bring forth further life. Or, in short: to eat, breathe, and procreate. If such desires are not met, the result will (in the short or long run) be death or extinction. In this way, not only does desire *qua* appetite connect us with the reality of the desired object as life-providing, but the contemplation of the desired object, and in turn the attainment of it, almost always seem to involve an element of lust. This incarnal experience of the good in pleasure itself or the object desired implies that even the most basic gratification of desire is accompanied by a bodily response. In this way, desire, as it ex-

5

presses itself both in its orientation toward and contemplation of the object as well as in its gratification, is contributing positive and bodily experienced feedback to the one who harbors it. This feedback confirms that there is an internal relation between the desired object and the subject who desires, which introduces the desiring individual to the understanding of the object as something good and pleasurable for her.

Moreover, as we are to live for some time, desires cannot be gratified once and for all. In the interest of our continuous existence, human evolution has developed our basic desires as phenomena never finally satisfied: the drive for more water, more food, regular sex, or other objects secures that the basic aims of evolution are safeguarded over a long span of time. The most obvious example of how this lack of satisfaction of desire reoccurs is that the input of energy into metabolic processes needs to be repeated regularly. Hence, already on the evolutionary level, it is quite reasonable to make sure that desires cannot be fulfilled once and for all. The lack of final gratification or satisfaction keeps us going longer and directs us again and again toward what we biologically perceive or experience as good. In this way, the good (in the object of desire) can present itself repeatedly to the individual. In this sense, not only is desire for the good, but it is for the good that desire cannot be satisfied once and for all, as this makes us able to participate more fully and more continuously in the goodness of the world. If one wants to develop this point from the angle of natural theology, it means that God has given us the insatiable desire for the good in order to make it possible for us to enjoy the creation more fully and enduringly. We cannot finish our relation to the good but are "pushed back" toward it repeatedly.

As evolution goes on, this presentation of the good by means of the concrete desiring of an object turns into an ability to make representations of the perceived good. I understand the ability for representation here as the capacity to imagine and conceptualize the desired object, including how this can be done by language. The development of this ability increases during the evolutionary process, but it also contributes significantly to the transformation of desire and its functions when it is integrated in the social and cultural dimension of human life. This process leads to a development in which desire may shift position from being merely on the pre-subjective level of human life to also being something shaped by and developed further by the resources to which subjectivity has access by means of language and consciousness.

Desire and Subjectivity: Opening and Closing Desires

By placing my initial reflections on desire in the above perspective, I am thereby suggesting that desire is prior to the development of human subjectivity (the ability of human beings to make themselves the theme of imagination, reflection, and conceptualization by means of language). This pre-subjective element in desire is probably one of the features that make it so threatening, for example, within a religious framework aimed at socialization, control, and curbing of certain expressions of life: desire presents itself to us prior to our conscious choices, wants, and wishes. Desire can of course also present itself within and by these wishes, etc., but my point here is that there is a pre-subjective element in desire that makes it initially outside of our control. We have to relate to desire as something that is there prior to our understanding and interpreting it as desire for this or that. I make this point in order to suggest that theology, when relating to desire, relates to an element in human life that is deeply rooted in our existence. Desire is originally deeply rooted in the evolution-developed experience that desire is closely linked to goodness in the objects desired.

To understand and interpret desire theologically is thus not only to understand a basic feature in human life; it is also to understand and develop further how and why objects present themselves as good and desirable in and for human existence. Once humans develop subjectivity, desire becomes an element that conditions, influences, and transcends subjectivity. Thus, there is a double gift in the presence of desire. This notwithstanding, desire and subjectivity operate in a dialectical relationship with each other, not least because humans at the present stage of evolution are able to distance themselves from some of their desires, not only in order to control them, but also in order to refine them, transform them, neglect some of them, and intensify others.[8]

As it is not the purpose of this chapter to go into the evolutionary history of human biology, I simply want to suggest that the initial features of desire in human history present us with the ability to make a distinction between two different types of desires: first, we have the desires emerging out of biological (and psychological) need or lack, such as needs for safety, food, heat, sex, and response from others (i.e., appetite); second, we have the desires emerging out of more reflexive and conscious

---

8. Different ways of relating to desires in order to affirm, refine, and develop them are illustrated in several of the other chapters in this volume; cf., e.g., Farley and Yoder.

attitudes toward the self, as this becomes possible through the development of evolutionary history. These latter desires may be a result of identifying what we *want* more than what we *need,* and the wants here recognized may emerge out of socially conditioned situations and resources. They represent no immediate needs; rather, they are desires emerging out of human life as a socially and culturally constituted world. The mere presence of culture and communication with others allows us to become aware of such objects of desire, be it in terms of mimetic desire, the desire to understand and grasp what others say, or the desire for the other's desire in a sexual encounter.

The first type of desire is directly linked to how we are able to function and perform our "tasks" as biological beings, while the latter is far more complex but of course very much related to the former. Sometimes the lack of satisfaction of the first type of desire may to some degree damage the sound development of human life, but lack of satisfaction/gratification may also provide new and fruitful ways for exploring possibilities of human life. Perhaps the most obvious example of this is how ascetic practices serve, not to overcome or to suppress desires, but rather to focus on and intensify some desires on behalf of others.

We are now able to develop further the distinction suggested above between opening and closing desires. Opening desires are not only opening us up to and relating us to what may happen, or what may present itself, but they are also opening us up to another world than the one constituted by our already-present constitution. On the other hand, the closing desires are clearly defined, intentional, and aimed at getting a specific kind of gratification. Such desires close us off from anything other than what is already present in our quests, intentions, or expectations. The desire emerging out of the need for food, for example, can be satisfied only by food. This is not a desire that opens up the world to us; rather, it narrows the world and closes our attention with regard to our search for the gratifying element. The only openness in this is what kind of food might appear as an answer to the need behind the desire. Hence, closing desires are those most immediately related to our bodily and biological needs.[9] To harbor

---

9. This should not be read, however, as if the closing desires are only to be understood as biological. Desires to know can also be understood in this way, as when Hegel in his *Phenomenology of the Spirit* describes how the subject's desire to know itself implies that, in Judith Butler's words, it "wants to find within the confines of this self the entirety of the external world; indeed its desire is to discover the entire domain of alterity as a reflection of itself, not merely to incorporate the world but to externalize and enhance the borders of its very

or nurture opening desires requires that we participate in more than a merely biological world.

As indicated, the distinction between opening and closing desires may not be seen as a sharp, ontologically based distinction; rather, it is analytic. A type of desire that displays the *ambiguity* of desire as being both potentially opening and closing is sexual desire. Sexual desire can take both these forms, hence both opening us up to, and closing us off from, the world. Sexual desire can relate to the other in a way that sees her only as a means for gratification of immediate needs. The other is then fully determined by my intentions for her, and she is present as a mere object of my desire. Desire then appears as closing. However, sexual desire can also appear as a desire for the other's desire for me, and for my desire for being something for her. The situation then constituted by the desire is far more open, in a way that makes both of us appear as subjects. As such, the other and I can recognize each other as subjects of desire in a manner in which our desires may be part of a much wider and more open relationship, where the immediate sexual encounter and its display of sexual desire is part of a mutual enrichment and enhances our world.

A final example that expresses *opening* desires (and ways in which being open also opens us up to the world) is the following. In many types of artistic practice we find a desire for exploring artistically our hitherto unknown potential for expression. This potential is never fully in the control of the artist beforehand, but is linked to the ways in which she develops skills and uses her courage or what kind of still unknown paths of inquiry she embarks on. Creativity and curiosity are thus deeply connected to desire, and desire may express itself in both of these elements in a way that discloses more of the world to the artist, as well as to those enjoying her work. Hence, this is a desire that presupposes a certain element of reflexive consciousness, and it is more likely then to emerge in a nature/culture context of exploration. This example is thus one in which it becomes very clear how evolution has turned desire into a phenomenon that is partially also a product of, and framed by, culture.

This leads us back to the previous point of the individualizing function of desire and makes it possible to understand it more fully: desire, prior to reflection, nevertheless makes me able to recognize *me* in my desires. Not to recognize desire is accordingly to fail to recognize some of

---

self." Judith Butler, *Subjects of Desire: Hegelian Reflections in Twentieth-Century France* (New York: Columbia University Press, 1999), pp. xix-xx; cf. p. 49.

what we are and what we are relating to the world by. Although this may seem a description aimed at merely cognitive elements, I want to emphasize that, due to the evolutionary history of desire, all desire is in some way or another accompanied by, or even expressing itself as, a kind of bodily pleasure or lust. Hence, desire is our first and foremost way of experiencing ourselves as embodied, carnal beings. Furthermore, this experience of the body is a vital precondition for saying: "This is me," "These are my needs," "This is what I will do," or "This is what I long for."

By acting on desires, we become someone specific — both to ourselves and to others. Hence, if we do not relate to our desires in one way or another, we lose some of our chances for becoming a self for ourselves as well as for others. To become a self is a necessity in order to be something for others.[10] A theology that neglects desire's initial role in the constitution of selfhood and its counterparts in individuality and subjectivity robs individuals of chances for having a healthy and self-based relationship to others and makes them more vulnerable to exploitation or abuse. Because desire is so important, the lack of recognition, affirmation, and appreciation of desire might have fatal consequences.

A final word: against the backdrop of the previous description, there emerges in desire an element of *vulnerability*. Expressing an opening desire discloses us in a manner that makes us vulnerable. Desires may not be met — they may be disregarded, or not taken into consideration. This in turn may imply that the relation between the desiring subject and the good is not developed in the way desired. A certain relation is denied.[11] On the other hand, desire for an object or for another may also render the desired object vulnerable, as the object of desire is exposed to the powers of the desiring subject. A powerful desire that acquires the other may be seen as violent and as a threat to the object or person desired. Hence, both the subject and the object of desire emerge under certain conditions as vulnerable, and the distinction between opening and closing desires may prove a way to understand more of the dynamics implied here. For example, a closing desire may be more of a threat to the object than an opening one, while an

---

10. Hence, pathologies of self-sacrifice that express a total disregard of one's own desire here find a place. However, this is not to say that all self-sacrifice is the result of a neglect of desire; rather, it may at some point also be a way of expressing desire more fully. But when this is the case, the point is exactly that the person in question is then able to affirm fully that "This is me, and this is an expression of my desire!"

11. The psychological impact of this vulnerability cannot be developed here, but the effect of it is elaborated in modern psychology from Freud to Klein, Winnicott, and Kohut.

opening desire leaves much open to the other in terms of the development of gratification. However, in no way is this to be seen as a reason for "oedipalizing" desire by denying its presence; rather, it calls for a nuanced understanding of the relation between desire, the good, and the law.

Desire and the Law: Theological Considerations

Desire is often described as something that urges the subject, or the person, to grasp something, to occupy it for the subject's own sake — a phenomenon probably most clearly seen when desire is conflated with covetousness. Not only does this description suggest the *active, cognitive,* and simultaneously *relational* elements in desire (as there can be no desire without the object of desire), but it also suggests that desire is fundamentally related to agency, more specifically to the type of agency that (more or less consciously) strives for the occupation and appropriation of that object. As suggested tacitly above, I think this is a misleading description of what desire fundamentally is. Not only does this description take its point of departure in an active agent who has the possibility of agency and the ability to follow the agent's intentional desires, but thereby it also presupposes these conditions for agency without paying any attention to questions of gender or to political, economic, or other types of social status.[12] Such an understanding of the desiring subject also ignores how desire is fundamental (in the literal sense) to becoming an individual and a conscious and reflexive subject. Hence it ignores the pre-subjective level on which desire emerges and the role it plays in, and prior to, the constitution of human subjectivity. From this it follows that to understand desire primarily as the subject's intention to appropriate or to occupy the object of desire leaves out the dimension in which desire is something that both individuates the individual (makes me aware that this is my desire, one of my conditions for agency) and occupies or appropriates the individual.

In this sense, desire is not only prior to subjectivity or agency, but emerges from or within a state of *passivity* where the subject is occupied with desire before reaching out by the means of desire to occupy the other,

12. That this is a relevant point is most clearly seen in the way Deleuze develops his understanding of desire. Cf. Gilles Deleuze, *Nietzsche and Philosophy,* European Perspectives (New York: Columbia University Press, 1983); Gilles Deleuze, *Difference and Repetition* (New York: Columbia University Press, 1994); Gilles Deleuze and Félix Guattari, *Anti-Oedipus: Capitalism and Schizophrenia* (Minneapolis: University of Minnesota Press, 1983).

the object of desire.[13] Hence, I am made what I am because desire — as the other of consciousness or reflectivity — makes me become aware of who I am as a desiring subject. It is in the recognition and awareness of myself as a desiring subject that I become aware of myself as a self with potential for agency.

By being prior to subjectivity, *desire is also structurally prior to the law.* The law must, from a theological point of view, be seen as a gift that is given with the social dimension of human life. As such, the law emerges from the understanding of the good as this is shaped by the human under the conditions of the social and cultural world. Thus, the law develops a deeper and more basic understanding of the good than the one immediately present in desire. The first name of this dimension of the good is *justice.* Justice emerges when we, the subjects of human community, realize our common vision of (and thus our desire for) the good. From such a description, the law is not something that needs to repress or negate the desire for goodness; rather, it opens up to new dimensions of this desire. In this sense, the law also shapes new understandings of the desires that we harbor. It is only when desires are not rooted in what can also be integrated in the common vision for justice and the good that the law becomes manifest in expressions of conscious efforts to control and delimit desire. Hence, desire may also emerge in consciousness with and over against the law, a point made both in Paul and in Foucault.[14] One could even say that it is in the presence of, and in response to, desire that the law emerges.

However, when attention is given to law, focus also shifts toward *agency.* Agency implies control, choice, and deliberation. From a theological point of view, this is not without importance, as one of the basic features of sin is to take one's point of departure in one's own agency and in one's own ability to control the world. A subject that understands itself from agency (and thus from the law) will always perceive desire as the

13. Further on passivity, see Svenungsson's chapter in this volume.

14. For Paul on this, cf. Romans 7:8, on which the following quote from Foucault gives an interesting comment: "One should not think that desire is repressed, for the simple reason that the law is what constitutes desire and the lack on which it is predicated. Where there is desire, the power-relation is already present: an illusion, then, to denounce this relation for a repression exerted after the event; but vanity as well, to go questing after a desire that is beyond the reach of power." Michel Foucault, *History of Sexuality,* quoted in Judith Butler, *Subjects of Desire: Hegelian Reflections in Twentieth-Century France* (New York: Columbia University Press, 1999), p. 221.

other of consciousness, the other of law, the impetus on which to act or not. Hence, desire becomes subjected to the subject. In this process it inevitably also appears as a threat against agency, something that is potentially uncontrollable and a sign of a determining reality, something prior to agency. In this sense, neither desire nor the law is seen as a gift that, jointly, may enable the subject to realize the good given prior to the subject and independent of its agency.

It is this threat that makes desire so ambiguous in theological terms: not only because it suggests something potentially uncontrollable that transcends us but nevertheless influences us, but also because it reminds us that subjectivity is the product of something other than the conscious and acting human being, something that can be positively related to God, or can imply a disruption of the order that we attempt to establish in order to conform to what we take to be the will of God. The more emphasis is put on the law as posited over against agency, the more we attempt to avoid recognizing how our desire makes us vulnerable and dependent upon something given prior to our agency.

When, due to sin, we want to start with our own agency when relating to the world, desire is not only an indication of the good prior to agency, but also a message about the fact that agency is rooted in ambiguous elements prior to subjectivity. Hence, when we want to start with ourselves, with control, the initial passivity in which the good appears with and in desire confronts us with the limits of both agency and subjectivity. Desire then becomes a sign that the world is not constituted by us. Theologically speaking, this is a possible sign of transcendence, of the good desired, and (possibly) then of God. However, it is also a reminder that the law by which we understand and control desire is something that cannot allow desire to be totally suppressed, subjected, or controlled by us, because desire *is the condition for the individuated, desiring, and conscious* self.

The above analysis potentially sheds some light on how and why desire is so complex in its relation to religious subjectivity, but also says something about why it is so important to control and relate to desire from the point of view of this subjectivity. Religion is a way of ordering human life, and any kind of desire that is not in some way integrated within the order threatens to disrupt it. The law almost by necessity then becomes the other of desire. As indicated, this takes place in an ambiguous manner.

A positive religious employment of the law serves to transform, shape, and control desire, and thereby the law makes desire appear as something under control. This in turn may give rise to the illusion that desire can be fully controlled, that it is basically a controllable element. The sequel of this understanding is that the law can control everything and can be a means for establishing righteousness (that which is the result of the human desire for justice and the good). But when the law is consciously used in this way, not only is the pre-subjective element of desire already mentioned ignored, but also the presumed good that desire relates to *prior* to the law is ignored. The "presence" of this good[15] signifies that goods given as gifts are apparent in creation and are not constituted by human agency, although human agency in different forms always attempts to appropriate them as elements that are related to an economy of achievement, merit, and exchange, thereby integrating them into an economy of occupying and controlling (closing) desire.[16]

God and Desire

One consequence of the above is that, when human agency is understood as the initial means by which we can access the goods given by God and as a result of God's agency, God's gifting activity becomes secondary. A notion of righteousness that leaves out or ignores the fundamental role of desire for the non-economic and opening gift in human life is doomed to make human agency the central element in human life, and the desire to control that expresses itself in the law (as a closing desire) is a feature of human subjectivity that erodes subjectivity's own foundation in life and goodness (desired) as gift. This is one version of why the human attempt to become righteous by obeying the law is bound to fail. It ignores how desire is related to gift, and God's gifting of the good, as the initial condition that makes the good present in desire.

I want to develop these insights further by developing how faith and the law can be seen in this light, as representing open/opening or closed/closing (controlling) desires, respectively.

God (as gifting) cannot be understood as something that humans relate to in analogy with basic, biological needs. Biology of course contrib-

15. The term "presence" here needs further elaboration, not least because desire in a sense is desire for something not fully at hand, something that implies a negation with regard to the desiring subject. Cf. further on this below.

16. Various negative features in controlling and closing desire are described in more detail in different contexts in other chapters in this volume, e.g., those of Rita N. Brock and Ola Sigurdson.

utes to making us open to something transcending us,[17] but what stirs the thematically expressed desire for God first and foremost is language in which God is presented as incarnated and internal to experiences of the good — the Word of God, to put it theologically. Hence, John's explication of incarnation makes perfect sense here — also to the senses! Only the word "God" — with all its implications for justice, community, restoration, and hope — can stir the desire for God. Given this situation, the desire for God is principally and fundamentally defined as something that cannot be fully reduced to lack or need, although it may also be rooted in experiences of such kind. Rather, God adds a surplus to the concrete, carnal experience of goodness. Consequently, faith as desire for God has to be understood as an opening desire, a desire in which we accept that this desire can never be fully satisfied, a point made already by Gregory of Nyssa.[18] An opening desire, in which we put ourselves in the hands of the other, implies trust, a vital element in faith. Hence, the way from opening desire to trust and faith proves to be a very short one.

To be more concrete, when we believe in God, we desire to be in relationship with God, because we think that there is something in this relationship that is important — and good! — for us, that surpasses what is immediately present. However, for theological reasons as well as those mentioned above, we cannot and should not talk about this desire as resulting exclusively from either lack or need. Countering modern critics of religion, we can thus say that God is more than we need, because the relationship with God relates us to something that might be indicated as a *surplus* compared to the kind of reality that we can constitute for and by ourselves and that can be defined solely by our needs. Hence, God transcends both our needs and our potential for agency, but without necessarily ne-

---

17. This is a basic point developed theologically in the anthropology of W. Pannenberg. Cf. Wolfhart Pannenberg, *What Is Man? Contemporary Anthropology in Theological Perspective* (Philadelphia: Fortress Press, 1970); Wolfhart Pannenberg, *Anthropology in Theological Perspective* (Philadelphia: Westminster Press, 1985); Wolfhart Pannenberg, ed., *Sind Wir von Natur aus Religiös?* (Düsseldorf: Patmos, 1986).

18. In Gregory, faith is closely linked to the process of learning, through which the believer enters into an eternal progress of searching and never ceasing to ascend to God. The believer is the one who has her desire awakened by God's love, so that the believing desire is stirred by God's desire for her. Whenever her desire is fulfilled, it produces further desire for the transcendent, for God. Cf. on this M. S. Laird, *Gregory of Nyssa and the Grasp of Faith: Union, Knowledge, and Divine Presence,* Oxford Early Christian Studies (Oxford and New York: Oxford University Press, 2004), p. 97. Cf. Wendy Farley's contribution to this volume for the systematic points.

gating them. To define God's importance to us exclusively in terms of how God fulfills our needs is to make God a smaller god. That would be to define God on the basis of our world and then to close up the relation to God and the desire for God in a way that is exactly what we need to avoid if we are to hold open a conceptual space in which God can be God and hence not determined by us and the preconceptions contained in our desire of what God can mean to us.

To define the belief in God based on a conception of lack would be to make the mistake of saying that we believe in God because we lack something that God can give us, something of which we already have a clear understanding. But belief in God results from God addressing us by the goods and the gifts offered us in creation (including the gift of desire). God gives us what we need, surely, and also something of what we lack, long before we believe in God. But God's function as gifting is never restricted to what is defined by our lack; God transcends it in principle.

Hence, desire based solely on our conception of needs and lacks is an ill-fitting desire if we try to understand what kind of desire is involved in true faith as an expression of opening desire. Note that this is also a normative statement that we can develop over against popular critiques of religion which claim that belief emerges only because of people's needs for comfort, anxiety reduction, their will to power, or their need to escape a boring everyday life. We have to be aware of the valuable insights of such — functionally based — critiques of religion if we are to make a useful definition of the desire involved in true religious and Christian faith.

Desire Transcending Lack and Need

Desire transcending lack and need — but still deeply rooted in our own lives — is what is implied in faith. Recently, several thinkers have contributed to such a wider understanding of desire. Faith as indicated by desire points beyond that which is immediately present, be it in our understanding of ourselves, our needs, or what we want or strive for — and how we can concretely perceive all of this. Again, this might be seen in correlation to our understanding of the necessity, in developing a theological conception, of starting with God and God's gifts, not with something in the world: this desire is for more than what is in our awareness of the present world; it is an openness to something new, something else, something that represents a surplus compared to what is presently given.

This surplus might also be called *the impossible,* i.e., that which does not seem possible when seen from the present conditions of life. This dream for the impossible is what constitutes Jacques Derrida's and John Caputo's approach to postmodern theological thought. They want to overcome or pass through the constraints and conditions imposed by modernity, and to think that which cannot be thought as possible within a modern framework, and which for that very reason is what we desire most. The desire for something that is not the same, that is not a repetition, a continuation of what now maintains us in our given identities is what is expressed in such desire: "The incoming of the same, on the other hand, would simply further confirm the present, already familiar horizon, would be more of the dreary, pedestrian, humdrum sameness of the possible."[19] The alternative to this sameness is an eschatological reality that we relate to through *eschatological desire,* which may be interpreted as Caputo's words for what I have above called the opening desire.

The theological point in understanding faith as an expression of opening or eschatological desire is that we need to recognize, affirm, and appreciate how faith as desire opens up to the uncontrollable — and that this uncontrollable dimension is exactly what makes it necessary to understand faith as trust and confidence in the open, undetermined, and uncontrollable (even impossible, in the Derridean sense) eschatological dimension of life that desire/faith relates us to. In and by means of desire we have already an internally constituted relation to this dimension of life, although it is present as something still outstanding, yet not present, or present also by means of its absence.

Derrida's notion of the impossible is helpful here because it is a means by which to explore that which cannot be understood in traditional metaphysical terms. To think otherness, or to think infinity, is always "to be at risk of exposing it to the reincorporation by metaphysics, unless we proceed by the way of the aporias" of the impossible. "An aporia cannot be

---

19. John D. Caputo and Michael J. Scanlon, *God, the Gift, and Postmodernism,* Indiana Series in the Philosophy of Religion (Bloomington: Indiana University Press, 1999), p. 3. The most serious effects of this type of desire we see in the crippling of desire and its flourishing by its abuse: how closing desire closes the other's desire in abuse or in economic exploitation. To recognize the other's right to an open and opening desire is necessary in order to safeguard the other's chance for development. It is also mostly a prerequisite for allowing the other to concentrate her desires on those of justice, beauty, and goodness in a way that allows for furthering community and a sharing of goods and pleasures with others, instead of shutting them out because of a desire wounded, hurt, and vulnerable.

solved through recourse to reason but only re-solved through recourse to a kind of faith," says R. Horner about Derrida's position. This aporia interrupts control-oriented metaphysics and suggests that there is something beyond or prior to it.[20] This interruption cannot be deduced by our systems of understanding, rationality, and interpretation. The impossible means, says J. Caputo,

> something whose possibility we did not and could not foresee, something that eye has not seen, nor ear heard, that has never entered into the mind of human beings (I Cor. 2:9). So I am plainly advising us to revisit the idea of the impossible and to see our way clear to thinking the possibility of the impossible, of *the* impossible, of the possible as the "im-possible," and to think of God as the "becoming possible of the impossible," as Derrida also says.[21]

This understanding of desire/faith as relating us in an incarnal way to the impossible also has profound consequences for the understanding of the identity of the believer. To believe and to desire is also to strive for identity, as identity is not something given, but something that is constructed on the basis of the experiences, relations, and givens of human life. Hence, it is something we desire all our lives. To become a mature or balanced human being is thus paradoxically also a question about to what extent I am able to realize the fundamental flaw in my own conception of myself as a self whose needs can be met once they have been brought to light. Faith allows for development of this maturity, and the lack of maturity is something that closes desire and makes faith a means for control. The law is then used to close the desire of faith and to establish the illusion of the possibility for achieving my own righteousness. True faith, on the other hand, implies understanding myself in the light of a desire impossible to gratify. Maturity implies living without full gratification or satisfaction, and with the insight that nothing, i.e., no *thing*, can satisfy my soul's desire and its needs. On this, Rowan Williams writes:

> Instead, I come to see that I cannot fail to be involved in my incompletion; and that *no thing* completes me. My "health" is in the thinking or

20. Robyn Horner, *Jean-Luc Marion: A Theo-Logical Introduction* (Burlington, VT: Ashgate, 2005), p. 45. More concretely, such interruption is manifested in the saturated phenomena of gift, forgiveness, hospitality, etc.

21. John D. Caputo, *On Religion: Thinking in Action* (London and New York: Routledge, 2001), p. 10.

sensing of how I am not at one with myself, existing as I do in time (change) and language (exchange). Were it otherwise, the self would not be something that could be thought of at all. It would disappear in the fulfillment of its supposed desire; it would be identical with itself; it would have gone beyond language and reflection. To nurture such a picture while living in a vulnerable and mobile body is a recipe for the most damaging inner dislocations and the gravest dysfunction in relating to a material world in which other perspectives are presented, "spoken for."[22]

In the framework that Williams relates to, we can see how the construction of the given or created desire is most fruitful when it does not imply an instant gratification of full unity with the desired object — in this case my own final self. But we can also say that the same is true when we speak of God as the reality toward which desire/faith is directed. Thus, the existence and maintenance of desire keeps me on the track, allows for further development, further promotion of reflexivity about what I can and should be. That my identity as a human being and as *imago Dei* is still something to be fully realized, still in the future, is thus not to be considered negatively as a flaw, but to be considered positively as something that makes it possible for us to be liberated from our own instantly self-seeking selves.[23] Self-seeking is exactly what closes desire and consequently, then, also closes and narrows the world that desire relates to.

Paradoxically, though, when we seek ourselves in a not-yet-fulfilled destiny, the realization that this cannot be wholly appropriated or fulfilled at the present safeguards the possibility of living here and now, while recognizing the vulnerability of both others and ourselves. We are not perfect, and to realize this is to be confronted with the vulnerability that is given with the fact that we are dependent upon others and live exposed to the power of others. Writes Williams:

> The self becomes adult and truthful in being faced with the incurable character of its desire: the world is such that no thing will bestow on the self a rounded and finished identity. Thus there is in reality no self — and no possibility of recognizing what one is as a self — without the

22. Rowan Williams, *Lost Icons: Reflections on Cultural Bereavement* (Harrisburg, PA: Morehouse, 2000), pp. 151-52.

23. Cf. the reference to Gregory of Nyssa, above, and to the importance of not understanding faith or God as a response exclusively to ontological lack.

presence of the other. *But* that other must precisely *be* other — not the fulfillment of what I think I want, the answer to my lack.[24]

Thus, through the opening desire expressed in faith, we acquire a fuller identity by realizing or being confronted with what that identity is — and what it cannot yet be. This acknowledgment of being unfulfilled paradoxically helps us relate to what is not yet present in our own life, in a manner that both decenters and contributes to the stabilization of our identity. In the description above, Williams also offers a possibility for spelling out the positive function that God as the Other can have in the development of human identity: God is the stability that we cannot have in ourselves, and the relation to God by means of desire/faith offers us the possibility to grasp ourselves as an unfinished and problematic project, and to live with the impact of that insight. To see God here as the Other underlines how every attempt to make God a function of our own gratification of desires not only implies the attempt to overcome God's otherness and, thus, to make God less than God; it also implies that, when we do so, we lose our self, our soul,[25] a point that corresponds well with how a closing desire also narrows our world and our potential.

The Presence of the Infinite in Desire

The presence of God in desire (as the one who nevertheless cannot be acquired by the subject and brought under the subject's control) also testifies to the way in which believers recognize both their own finitude and God as the infinite Other. The desire of a finite being is always an indication of the fact that, as finite, we are never fully realized, never fully rounded-up and independent. Here is a difference between God's desire for us and our desire for anything, including God: we realize in and through desire a chance to experience our finitude and to dwell in and enjoy this finitude as a condition for relating to something that is not us, and that might eventually lead us to a fuller life.[26] God does not need us; God's desire for us is be-

24. Williams, *Lost Icons*, p. 153.
25. This is a point that, as indicated above, I think is important to argue against recent and former forms of critique of religion.
26. This is what Wendy Farley so well describes as the eternal flame of desire. Cf. Wendy Farley, *The Wounding and Healing of Desire: Weaving Heaven and Earth* (Louisville: Westminster/John Knox, 2005). Cf. also her contribution in this volume.

cause God desires the good for us by desiring that we participate in the community and in the goodness, beauty, and justice of which God is the source. However, it is nevertheless God's desire for us that is the background of the incarnation, in which God's desire for us becomes embodied: Jesus' proclamation of God stirs up the desire that God's love desires in us. God desires our desire for God, and the incarnation is the fullest expression of how this comes to the fore, appears, in the world.[27]

Recognizing that justice is still to come, not yet achieved — a desire unfulfilled — we understand the law as a means for directing desire toward the good that conditions justice. The law thus is a means for desire, not a means against it.[28] The law is thus not primarily the prohibition of specific types of desire, but a way of addressing the temptation of human agency to totalize itself (cf. above). The law has the ability to make present what we take to be God's will, by ordering the world from the point of view of desire for control. In this way, the law as an expression of desire serves, as I have already indicated, in an ambiguous manner: it may serve as a means for establishing the subject in the center of the world, or it may serve as a means for justice and the good. The tension and possible conflict between opening and closing desire, between faith as an open way of relating to God and the law and as a controlling way of relating to God (one that shapes the image of God in the controlling desire of the subject), thus comes to the fore in how we relate to and understands our own desire as a relation to a specific conception of God. God is either the Good to be desired over all things — the infinite Good — or a God to be desired as the means for control over one's own life (and thus as a God to be controlled by desire for control). A constitutionally control-oriented desire is based on what we already are. That desire aims at control and is basically not open to anything new or different, to the Other. In this way, control-oriented and closing desire is an expression of lack of trust in God; it is trust in oneself instead. It strives to remain in control of the given world, a trait that paradoxically expresses lack of trust in the world!

In such a world, relationships with those who are different, those who are the real others, might prove disturbing to such control. In the controversies between Jesus and the Pharisees, as the New Testament records them, this desire is expressed in the need to marginalize those who do not conform with the given rules of conduct or fit the religiously and socially

27. Further explorations of God's desire compared to human desire in relation to goodness and justice can be found in Jayne Svenungsson's chapter in this volume.

28. This is developed further in Yoder's chapter in this volume.

accepted patterns. Jesus confronts and contradicts such desire. Thereby he opens up for new community and for other, open forms of desire. Instead of closing the world to those who are different or appear unacceptable, he opens them up to a new world, by taking their desire for salvation (i.e., new life, freedom, community) as an opportunity to change their world. He lets the word "God" enter their world(s) in a new way that reorients their perception of themselves and of him. Hence, we become able to see a difference between the desire to control and master reality and the desire to enjoy, participate, and communicate. The first emerges out of concern, worry, and insecurity, the other out of trust and gratitude.

I think the above analysis leads to two important insights concerning how to understand desire within the context of fundamental theology. First, to understand desire only from the point of view of the negative and restricting functions of the law implies a reduction in which one loses sight of how both desire and the law open us to the gift of God/goodness that is prior to our entire agency. Second, as the above analysis inscribes desire and the desiring/believing subject into an ambiguous context, this points to how desire both destabilizes the subject and decenters the subject in a way that makes it necessary to educate desires as well as the attitude one has toward them. As long as God is present in our desire, God is not under our control or subjected to our controlling desire; rather, God is still to come, still under way.

The need for educating the desires thus points to a manner of relating to them that transcends mere moral cultivation for the sake of the other, which is often predominant in the contemporary Christian discourse on desire. Moreover, these insights provide no reason to claim that all desires should be fulfilled or all wants satisfied. The gratification of desire is never a mere natural thing but is interwoven with our conceptions of importance, what we hold to be acceptable, how we relate with others, and how we perceive ourselves in general. Hence, for all desires that emerge out of our relations with the world and with cultural conceptions (including the conception of God), there is no *natural* way for these desires to be understood or to be gratified.

Desire and Personal Growth

To understand desire presupposes that one is already an understanding, conscious subject. Probably no one has developed a more reflexive understanding of desire and its importance for the development of human existence than Hegel. In his *Phenomenology of Spirit,* desire appears in different contexts as a vital factor in the development of the human mind or consciousness. In this context, it is the task of interpreting some of the elements in Hegel within the framework of a constructive theology that concerns us. In the following I will try to pursue this task by appropriating constructively some of the observations made by Judith Butler in her important study on the reception of this theme in Hegel by contemporary French philosophy.[29]

Butler develops an understanding of desire similar to the one I have sketched above, in which its presence is prior to acknowledgment of lack or need. We can see how one way of approaching desire sees it as potentially serving the pursuit of knowledge relevant to our development as human beings. This approach to desire implies that it already contains a kind of tacit knowledge, or that it can be "cultivated to be a single-minded motivating force for knowledge." Butler suggests that this reading of Hegel implies that there is "no necessarily irrational desire, no affective moment that must be renounced for its intrinsic arbitrariness. Over and against a naturalistic understanding of desires as brute and random facts of psychic existence, this model of desire vindicates particular affects as potential bearers of truth, rife with philosophical significance."[30]

What this approach immediately implies, of course, is the call for a specific hermeneutics of desire, a call that, in my opinion, also testifies to a significant lack in contemporary theology. As Butler says,

> [T]he task becomes that of developing the appropriate hermeneutics of self-reflection to uncover their implicit meaning. The ideal of an internal integration of reason and desire not only poses an alternative to a naturalistic or positivistic understanding of desire, but promises to expand the very notion of rationality beyond its traditional confines. If desires are essentially philosophical, then we reason in our most spontaneous of yearnings. Reason is no longer restricted to reflective rationality, but characterizes our immediate and impulsive selves. In other words, the immediacy of desire proves to be always already mediated, and we are always much more intelligent in the moment of desire than we immediately know ourselves to be.[31]

29. Butler, *Subjects of Desire.*
30. Butler, *Subjects of Desire,* p. 2.
31. Butler, *Subjects of Desire,* p. 2. A concrete development of a similar model is to be

I think a basic framework for the interpretation of desire, which she is here pointing toward, may be suggested in the above reflections on the different expressions of desire as opening or closing, and as linked to the good. The good and the reasonable appear here as connected. This hermeneutic framework is also in line with the correction I have suggested above, which tries to overcome the limiting elements that seem to approach desire in a way that simply makes it "the other" of the subjectivity of the rational subject. Instead, this framework suggests that relating to and appropriating the reason in desire is a way of expanding the scope of one's own rationality and subjectivity.

However, such a framing also calls for a correction of the place that desire has in Hegel's own understanding of desire, as something that makes the subject simply able to rediscover or constitute its own metaphysical place. Instead of accepting this description, one should ask if it is not more in line with recent understandings of subjectivity to see desire as that which really points to the necessary "homelessness" and to the unfulfilled character of subjectivity that I developed by means of Williams above. This would then not only suggest a post-metaphysical conception of desire, but also open it up to a more theologically relevant interpretation, as this would enhance the importance of seeing desire, which contributes to the constitution of the subject, as something that is in turn not constituted by the self. The relational self then emerges out of processes external to it, by the very means of desire as relational. Hence, desire as relational allows the self to become a (relational) self. I take it as a tacit presupposition in this argument that these external elements, albeit related to the self, are those which are first and foremost of relevance to a theological interpretation of the forces and processes that make the self a desiring self. This is also an approach that is in accordance with, but need not be reduced to, naturalistic processes, especially when we understand desires as something emerging out of more than bodily experienced lack/need.[32]

A post-metaphysical approach to desire that allows for understanding the subject's principal "homelessness" is of theological importance for sev-

---

found in Rita Nakashima Brock, *Journeys by Heart: A Christology of Erotic Power* (New York: Crossroad, 1988), p. 19, who develops a similar strategy concerning anger and its implications for liberation. For a comparison of similar moral/spiritual/philosophical strategies to mere therapeutic and immediate approaches to desire, cf. Charles Taylor, *A Secular Age* (Cambridge, MA: Belknap Press of Harvard University Press, 2007), pp. 618ff.

32. The necessity for expanding the understanding of desire in this direction appears clearly in Cristina Grenholm's chapter in this volume.

eral reasons. First, it allows for recognizing the unfulfilled desire as a constituent in human life that cannot be overcome, but that nevertheless relates the subject to a reality where its own finitude is affirmed and appreciated as part of what it is to be a human. Second, it also implies that desire is not primarily constituted by its relation to law, or by the implicitly controlling character of a metaphysic and a law where its function is clearly delineated. Desire is — for positive theological reasons — that which *disrupts* subjectivity, that which transcends what is conceived as right in the struggle for justice and righteousness, that which creates fissures and disturbances in our complacencies.

To affirm that this is a necessary and welcome function of desire is imperative in order to make transparent how a consumer society in which desire is constantly advertised as something that is possible to gratify can be met with rejection and critique.[33] It is imperative for directing and orienting us toward a justice that is higher than the simple, one-to-one justice of a legal system or a society based on merit, a desire that basically must be understood as closing.

If desire does not open up to the metaphysical place of the subject or is marked by some form of moral intentionality, one possibility is to see the result of this in how the subject may then be threatened by internal fragmentation, nihilism, and metaphysical dislocation. As Butler points out, contemporary interpreters of Hegel's notion of desire have developed an understanding that sees it as increasingly signifying the impossibility of a coherent subject over against harmony models of the relationship between reason and desire. One main reason for this is that desire is always also an instantiation of the other in consciousness, in a way that enables the subject to grow, develop, and reflect.[34] The otherness of desire thus suggests

33. Cf. Wendy Farley's comments on the relationship between desire and consumerism in her chapter in this volume. William Irvine argues that to be pleased with what you already have is the basic remedy for not being possessed with your desires. I agree. But Irvine's book seems to underrate the type of desire that I reflect on here, a desire that can function both as critical and as a means for not making the reality of God fully overlap with the present state of affairs. Cf. William Braxton Irvine, *On Desire: Why We Want What We Want* (Oxford and New York: Oxford University Press, 2006).

34. Cf. Butler, *Subjects of Desire*, p. 33: "we learn that human desire is distinguished from animal desire in virtue of its reflexivity, its tacit philosophical project, and its rhetorical possibilities. At this point, however, we are equipped only with the insights that Force and Explanation have provided us; we understand *movement* as the play of Forces, and Explanation as the necessary *alterity* of consciousness itself. Predictably enough, the experience of desire initially appears as a synthesis of movement and alterity."

that reason is not alone in constituting the subject, but it also suggests that the subject of desire has a project with itself in order to develop a subjectivity that comprises both reason and desire.

The theologically fruitful result of this development (and a source of growing insight into the Hegelian project) is that reason, and the self-conscious subject, can no longer be seen as the principle that establishes human identity. Human identity is due to forces external to the subject, forces that operate within and beyond (as well as behind) desire, but are never to be overtaken or fully integrated in rationality.[35]

As becomes visible in the above understanding of desire, Butler's observations concur with those who attempt to develop an alternative to the Freudian understanding of desire that has dominated much of the psychology of religion for many years. Another author who has argued for a revision of that framework is Sebastian Moore. In *Jesus the Liberator of Desire* he sees desire's meaning as linked to the mystery of human life. As he says, "The desire for a full life stretches out to the infinite source of life in which we must become lost as, desiring to know life's meaning, we are lost in an answer that is mystery."[36]

Moore's approach allows us to see how the kind of desire might have important consequences for the way we understand its gratification. In what I have called "opening" desire, there is no final gratification. Moore adds an important element to this analysis, however, when he stresses that when this desire is satisfied, it *increases:* "This increase of desire with fulfillment, of course, is only intelligible once we understand desire as a trustful relationship. One can always be more trustful, more connected, which means more desirous."[37]

Moore elaborates his understanding of desire farther than we can follow here, but there is one more point to make, which is linked to the question of how one recognizes oneself and others in new ways when it comes to desire. This approach is linked to what we said above about the individualizing function of desire, but it also underscores more strongly the social

---

35. In Wolfhart Pannenberg's theological anthropology, this testifies not only to the hubris of a philosophy of mind, but also, more positively, to how the divine providence guides the processes that establish human identity in a manner that is still open to the future and never self-enclosed. Cf. Pannenberg, *Anthropology in Theological Perspective* (Philadelphia: Westminster Press, 1985).

36. Sebastian Moore, *Jesus the Liberator of Desire* (New York: Crossroad, 1989), p. 7.

37. Moore, *Jesus the Liberator of Desire*, p. 11. This is another place in which the present discourse on desire seems to be anticipated by Gregory of Nyssa.

dimension of the effects of desire in *recognition,* an issue I will deal with later. Moore uses an illustrative example about falling in love to make his point:

> One of the puzzles of falling in love is that desire is not only fastening on a new object (this I understand) but finding a new subject (but who am I?). Intrinsic to the excitement of "you" is a new "me." . . . "Who am I?" and "What do I want?" — these questions exist in a dialectic that is in the nature of growing selfhood. It can be most frustrating. Thus the growth of a person is the progressive liberation of desire. It is the process whereby desire finds ever more deeply its subject, whereby desire comes to be in one who can say, ever more deeply and wholly, "I want."[38]

As Moore here points to how desire is both relational and individualizing, he also implicitly suggests that all desire presupposes an undetermined I, or ego. This ego becomes disclosed and grows, becomes individualized and differentiated, articulated for itself and others, by how it relates with, in, and by desire. The increasing liberation of desire is thus a liberation of the self by which the self becomes aware of itself — realizes or discovers the contents of its soul, so to say.

> This process comes from the first cry of infant desire to the final liberation of desire in union with God. . . . Desire is fully liberated when a person comes to the deepest self, where identity is at one with the God in whom we "live and move and have our being."[39]

In a certain sense this means that the trusting relationship with God that is expressed in desire is not aimed at becoming satisfied or getting something for which I can feel pleased. As indicated earlier, that would imply an understanding of the relationship with God based on lack or need. It is more a question of finding one's own identity in the relationship with God: "The desire whereby I am drawn to another is partly constitutive of who I am. To be drawn to another is to become more myself."[40]

The strength of Moore's conception is how he relates desire to growth, relatedness, and the overcoming of the egotistic self. Hence, desire does

---

38. Moore, *Jesus the Liberator of Desire,* p. 17.
39. Moore, *Jesus the Liberator of Desire,* p. 17.
40. Moore, *Jesus the Liberator of Desire,* p. 18.

not reside in, or is not only situated in, the lustful and self-seeking ego, but expresses itself in the very ways in which I relate to the world and thus individualize myself. Moreover, this calls for an understanding of desire that allows me to *enjoy* my own desire: the enjoyment of desire is present not only in its fulfillment but also in the striving relationship with that which I desire. To enjoy my desire and to enjoy the other's desire for me is to exist in a trusting relation in which I can grow. That is what happens when I can see myself as desired by God and relate to God in my own desiring faith.

Summing this up, we can see that the "Other of desire" is the "place-holder" for God. By harboring desire, we get an incarnal experience of what it means to have the image of God as our destiny. God as the Other is related to the subject and to self-consciousness in a manner that cannot in principle be understood as the result of the subject's own activity. This, Butler points out, is the case already in Hegel:

> To say, then, that the Other appears is not to claim that the initial self-consciousness discovers a phenomenon that previously had no ontological status; rather, it is only now that the Other becomes explicit in virtue of its centrality to the initial self-consciousness' pursuit of an identity that encompasses the world. The Other becomes the general object of desire.[41]

The overcoming of this as a metaphysical description of self-consciousness is possible only if one also ascribes to the Other a desire that enables human freedom and subjectivity. That is what happens when God incarnates in the world. It is when we become able to speak of God's desire for human desire for God that we also can see God (incarnated) as one who liberates human desire in a manner that creates human freedom. In Hegel's understanding of recognition, this plays out in a manner that underscores how the mutual and relational element in desire enables the closed desire of humans to become open and free. Butler summarizes it thus, analyzing the dialectic of slave and bondsman:

> Recognition, once achieved, affirms the ambiguity of self-consciousness as both ecstatic and self-determining. The process of recognition reveals that the self-consciousness that is self-estranged and unrecognizable to itself is still the author of its own experience: "There is nothing in it of which it is itself not the origin." When the Other is viewed as the same as

41. Butler, *Subjects of Desire*, p. 47.

the subject, and this subject understands his own act of recognition as having brought the Other into explicitness, then the self is also revealed as the author of the Other. As it becomes clear that the same truths hold true of the Other's relationship to the self, the Other is also viewed as the author of the subject. Desire here loses its character as a purely consumptive activity, and becomes characterized by the ambiguity of an exchange in which two self-consciousnesses affirm their respective autonomy (independence) and alienation (otherness).[42]

In the struggle for recognition by the other, desire manifests itself as the desire for the other's *open* desire. Moreover, the ambiguity of desire is disclosed in a manner in which I am unavoidably referred to the other in order to become myself, in a manner in which I am not estranged from the content of my own desire. Here a deeper form of autonomy can be gained, because this is not a mere self-affirmation but a question of being given back myself and my desire as recognized by the other in a way that enriches me because it is now affirmed in the other's recognition. More than anything, I think this is one important reason why we need to speak of God in personal terms, and in a manner that does not make God appear as outwardly related to or coercing human development and growth.

As a sequel to God's desire for humans we can also see God's desire to become human. This is a desire to become carnal, material, in order to be loved, to be saving. God materializes in the incarnation. Moreover, the desire for the other's desire is constitutive for the recognition of the other as other, and part of how the other (human) makes God incarnate (and thereby also manifests a new identity, expressed in God's desire for incarnation). The incarnation both presents (makes present) and re-presents God. God's presence is still a surplus of his re-presentation in Christ. God is fully present there, but also more than what is present there.[43] As such,

---

42. Butler, *Subjects of Desire,* pp. 50-51.

43. Cf. Robyn Horner, *Rethinking God as Gift: Marion, Derrida, and the Limits of Phenomenology,* Perspectives in Continental Philosophy, 19 (New York: Fordham University Press, 2001), p. 244, saying that "God cannot be seen, not only because nothing finite can bear his glory without perishing, but above all because a God that could be conceptually comprehended would no longer bear the title 'God.'" Naming God does not result in a theology of presence, but one of absence, a phrase Marion immediately qualifies: "By theology of absence . . . we mean not the non-presence of God, but the fact that the name that God is given, the name which gives God, which is given as God . . . serves to shield God from presence . . . and offers him precisely as an exception to presence." Horner cites Marion from Caputo and Scanlon, *God, the Gift, and Postmodernism,* p. 37.

Jan-Olav Henriksen

God is then the most fitting "object" of our desire: never to be fully integrated into the human project, but nevertheless enabling the human to transcend the given and long even more for the one who gives us the opportunity to grow and become more than we are. Hence, desire as desire for life is oriented toward *God as the source of life*. When God allows for desire to happen, God as the source of goodness and justice is present. Hence, to relate to desire is in a profound sense to relate to the reality of God, as this reality is present — exactly — in our desire.

The Passion of the Christ:
On the Social Production of Desire

Ola Sigurdson

According to Friedrich Nietzsche in *Beyond Good and Evil*, "Christianity gave Eros poison to drink: — he did not die from it, but degenerated into a vice."[1] It is not unfair to claim that the Christian tradition historically has taken an ambivalent position in regard to desire, and still remains ambivalent. Even if the Christian church, in the past, has held a view on human sexuality as something peripheral, at best, the same church at the same time spoke about the true fulfillment of erotic desire in the love of God. The position of the contemporary church, however, seems to be almost the reverse; while it often goes out of its way to announce that human sexuality is something good, it is now *eros* that is regarded with suspicion or even is secularized and so understood as of no theological concern.

Compare, for instance, how the Swedish Lutheran theologian Anders Nygren in his influential book *Agape and Eros: The Christian Idea of Love* makes a categorical distinction between *agape* and *eros*, and pronounces only *agape* as a genuinely theological form of love; compare, further, how Karl Barth, although trying to integrate *eros* in theology, still views it with some suspicion in the same sentence where he acknowledges its integration when speaking of human sexuality: "God the Lord and sexual *eros*, well known in Israel especially as a dangerous daemon, are brought into close relationship."[2] One reason for the modern suspicion of *eros* as a way

1. Friedrich Nietzsche, *Beyond Good and Evil: Prelude to a Philosophy of the Future*, Cambridge Texts in the History of Philosophy, ed. Rolf-Peter Horstmann and Judith Norman (Cambridge: Cambridge University Press, 2003), § 168.

2. Anders Nygren, *Agape and Eros: The Christian Idea of Love*, trans. Philip S. Watson (Chicago: University of Chicago Press, 1982); Karl Barth, *Church Dogmatics* III/2: *The Doctrine of Creation* (Edinburgh: T. & T. Clark, 1982), p. 314.

of conceiving of the relationship between God and human beings is that erotic love nowadays more often than not has come to be associated with sexuality, so that as a consequence it seems theologically imprudent to speak of the divine relationship as a matter of erotic love, as this would imply a sexualization of the divine-human relation.

Through the emergence of a *scientia sexualis* from the seventeenth century onward, the development of medical science, and not least the prevalent sexualization of western society in the twentieth century, *eros* and sexuality have come to be identified in a way that probably would have been unrecognizable for most ancient philosophers and theologians.[3] Among other things, this is an effect of the secularization of sexuality, meaning that the conceptual relationship between sexual acts and religion has been dissolved. Moral authority on all matters concerning sexual acts was transferred from the "doctors of the soul" to the "doctors of the body" as medical science established the new *scientia sexualis*.[4] When human sexuality begins to be acknowledged as something good by Christian theology, it is, ironically, often a sexuality that has been domesticated by medical science as well as popular culture. The "dangerous daemon" of *eros* does not seem so very dangerous anymore, at least not from the point of view of the early twenty-first century, when human sexuality is thoroughly secularized, domesticated, and commodified. When any conceivable variety of sexuality is instantly available on the Internet, and when strong sexuality is used in advertising and televised at all hours of the day, our situation begins to look like the scene from Monty Python's *The Meaning of Life,* when the zealous teacher tries to teach his pupils about sexuality by performing intercourse with his wife on the school desk, but miserably fails to catch their attention. Sex does not seem that interesting anymore.

It seems to me that if we wish to advance a theology of desire for our times, we have to escape from the impasse between a sublimated or domesticated sexuality on the one hand and a suspicion of desire as such on the other. One reason for the interest in desire in contemporary theology is probably the return to premodern theology as a source of inspiration, as this theology, no matter how weak or limited its understanding of sexuality might have been, still emphasized the continuity between human and

---

3. Cf. Michel Foucault, *History of Sexuality: An Introduction,* vol. 1 (Harmondsworth: Penguin/Pelican, 1981).

4. Cf. Thomas W. Laqueur, *Solitary Sex: A Cultural History of Masturbation* (New York: Zone Books, 2003), p. 186.

divine love. We might, from a contemporary perspective, have all sorts of critical objections against premodern theology, but still wish to become aware of the limitations of our own intellectual horizon through a comparison with the historical horizon. Another reason for the interest in desire is, arguably, that theology shares some misgivings about modern instrumental reason with recent theory such as critical theory, deconstruction, or psychoanalysis. A common denominator between many of these theoretical movements, despite their very strong disagreements, is that desire is not incidental to human thought or action but a prominent feature of human existence as such. Take away desire and you take away what makes us into what we are.

But for any theology of desire that wishes to be true to its theme, it is imperative to recognize that an investigation of desire in the Christian tradition cannot be content with regarding desire as a discursive concept. Desire has to do with human action as well as human thought, and so it is important to focus not only on normative statements about the role of desire in theology but also on the life-world practices in which desire is produced. It might not be too bold to presume that Christian desire is produced even in spite of a theology that is quiet or negative on the topic. The relationship between human beings and God has always, at least in popular spirituality, been understood as an erotic relationship, though not necessarily in sexual terms. Consider, just as an example, what Richard Rambuss writes about English religious poetry in the fifteenth century:

> Articulating a devotion that is profoundly attuned to the Christian doctrine of the Incarnation, of God becoming flesh — becoming man — these religious works exhibit surprisingly little inclination to efface the corporeal. Rather, they proffer a spirituality that paradoxically bespeaks embodiment, doing so in ways that often enhance or extend the expressive possibilities of bodies and desires.[5]

Through devotion to Christ, thanks to the doctrine of incarnation, a very nuanced spirituality was developed that did not shy away from expressing this relationship in explicitly erotic terms, and examples of this through the ages, including our own, could be multiplied. In general terms I would claim that any human practice embodies a certain form of desire, and so the theme of desire for theology would need to consist not only of doc-

---

5. Richard Rambuss, *Closet Devotions* (Durham/London: Duke University Press, 1998), p. 2.

trinal questions but also of an investigation into how desire has been embodied socially in and in between different practices — and further, of an enquiry as to how doctrine and practice inform or come into conflict with one another.

This task is, of course, immense. My aim in this chapter must, accordingly, be more modest.[6] I shall therefore limit myself to, first, a discussion of desire in Augustine's theology of love and especially how he regards the social production of Christian desire. Despite the fact that both historical and contemporary theology have been quite ambivalent concerning the role desire should play in Christian existence, the church has always, as a social institution that consists of several transformative practices, implicitly or explicitly embodied a certain therapy of desire. Second, as the theme of desire in theology is best pursued when it is sought after not only in a certain discourse about desire but also in the practices implied by such a discourse, we need to look at contemporary experiences of the production of Christian desire to pursue a theology of desire today. In contemporary postsecular society, however, no church can any longer claim to occupy any hegemonic social embodiment, and so it becomes important to see how Christian desire is produced in between different social practices, such as for example the church and the cinema. A concrete example of this will be the topic for my third section, a discussion of the production of Christian desire in Mel Gibson's movie *The Passion of the Christ.* Finally, I will conclude with some short comprehensive remarks.

The Production of Desire in Augustine's Theology of Love

Desire might be a permanent feature of human existence, but what to desire — the object of desire — is not something that is naturally given to us but something that is acquired through repeated actions. How we learn what to desire, then, is — unsurprisingly — a disputed question among philosophers and theologians. While the German philosopher G. W. F. Hegel suggests that our desire is a desire for recognition by the other, a desire for the other's desire, the French philosopher René Girard proposes

6. Some further explorations along these lines could be found, however, in my article "How to Speak of the Body? Embodiment between Phenomenology and Theology," *Studia Theologica: Nordic Journal of Theology* 62, no. 1 (2008): 25-43, and also in my book *Himmelska kroppar: Inkarnation, blick, kroppslighet,* Logos/Pathos 6 (Göteborg: Glänta, 2006).

that our desire is a desire *according to* the other's desire, that is, a mimetic desire in which our desire is constituted by the other's desire; we learn what to desire through the other's desire.[7] My desire is, in other words, not just a biologically given instinct inherent in my individual existence as a member of the species *Homo sapiens sapiens,* but socially constituted by a triangular relationship between my own desire, the object of my desire, and the desire of the other. I would not know what to desire if some significant other had not desired something before me. In this way, desire is mimetically constituted, according to Girard. In what follows, I shall take Girard's notion of mimetic desire as a starting point for my outline of Christian desire as a social production. No doubt other theoretical paths may be pursued in this matter, and so I claim nothing more here than that Girard's theory of mimetic desire is illuminating in regard to my question.

The question, then, is how a particular Christian desire is produced. Given the socially constituted character of our desire as mimetic, the answer is likely to be in terms of institutions rather than mere individuals, although institutions would hardly exist without individuals, and we need to understand institutions not as autonomous agents (or as conglomerates of autonomous agents) but rather as made up by a network of hierarchical and reciprocal relationships driven by mimetic desire. This means, among other things, that any institution is a dynamic, complex, and even conflicting network of practices. For the sake of the clarity of the argument I shall nevertheless proceed, for most of the time, to speak of relevant institutions such as the church as if they were discrete entities, but occasionally noting that this is really a reduction of a more complex social reality.

There are several ways of making the social production of Christian desire more explicit with the help of premodern sources. In a later chapter in this volume, Christine Roy Yoder puts forward an interpretation similar to mine, but one dealing with a biblical text, Proverbs 1–9.[8] My own example of a classic reflection on how Christian desire is produced will be Augustine's theology of love, interpreted in terms of the triangular relationship suggested by Girard. Augustine famously suggested in *De doctrina Christiana* (c. 397-426) that there is an important distinction between two kinds of love, i.e., between *uti* and *frui,* or between the use of things and

---

7. René Girard, *Things Hidden Since the Foundation of the World* (London: Athlone Press, 1987).

8. See pp. 148-63 below.

the enjoyment of things.[9] Let us take our cue from this distinction and see what kind of understanding of desire this implies, if it is interpreted in light of Augustine's other writings on love.

I shall start with the first node in this triangular relation, my own desire. What is it? To enjoy something, according to Augustine's distinction above, means to love it for its own sake, but to use something means using it to achieve what is worth loving for its own sake.[10] This distinction that characterizes my own desire becomes a normative distinction between proper and improper kinds of love. A problem arises when I enjoy those things that are supposed to be used, since then I do not achieve what is worth loving for its own sake. Augustine exemplifies this with a journey toward our homeland *(patria)*, the only place where we can live contentedly. Longing for our homeland makes us want to go home, and to do that we must travel by land or sea. But if we become fascinated by the journey itself and what we learn on our way home, we might become strangers to our own homeland. Augustine explains his parable himself:

> So in this mortal life we are like travelers away from our Lord: if we wish to return to the homeland where we can be happy we must use this world, not enjoy it, in order to discern "the invisible attributes of God, which are understood through what has been made" or, in other words, to ascertain what is eternal and spiritual from corporeal and temporal things.[11]

This particular Augustinian distinction has often been interpreted as a devaluation of earthly existence, as a peculiar kind of Christian nihilism, scorned by Nietzsche, among others. Although this interpretation of Augustine is not entirely implausible, at least according to some of his modern commentators, in my own view there are some indications that this is not exactly what Augustine intends. In *The City of God,* for instance, Augustine has a long panegyric on the beauty of the created world that strongly suggests that Augustine was able to appreciate the relative worth of creation as such.[12] Instead of interpreting him as a Christian nihilist, it

9. Augustine, *De doctrina christiana,* edited with an introduction, translation, and notes by R. H. Green, Oxford Early Christian Texts (Oxford: Clarendon Press, 1995), 1.7-10.

10. Augustine, *De doctrina christiana,* 1.8.

11. Augustine, *De doctrina christiana,* 1.9. Augustine quotes Romans 1:20.

12. Augustine, *The City of God against the Pagans,* ed. R. W. Dyson, Cambridge Texts in the History of Political Thought (Cambridge: Cambridge University Press, 1998), 22.24.

would make sense to understand Augustine's distinction between *uti* and *frui* as making a theological point that has to do with how to avoid idolatry rather than the worth of creation as such. If the love of God is the true calling of human beings, putting something that will not bear the sheer weight of that calling as a substitute for God means getting entangled and eventually losing one's way in the world. The problem is not that what is created is finite and therefore of lesser value but, rather, that what is finite takes on infinite pretensions.

Human desire for money, power, and sex has a tendency, because of human frailty and sinfulness, to become a substitute for the love of God; but as human beings we are created for the love of God, and so our desire becomes disordered when we love created things instead of God. Disordered desire means that we are no longer masters of ourselves, but the things we desire become our masters. But when our desire is ordered by the love of God, we are free to love what is created (perhaps even including our own selves?) according to its own intrinsic worth. The love of God becomes a contrast to the love of creation only when the love of creation takes precedence over the love of God.

True human freedom is accomplished through the love of God, since this love liberates us from the tyranny of things to the true use of things (which has nothing to do with an instrumentalistic attitude toward creation). Thus, any ascetic renunciation of created things is just a relative renunciation since creation is God's good creation, which God sustains and upholds, and through which God is revealed. The fundamental question with regard to my own desire is, thus, not how I shall get rid of desire but how I shall achieve a desire that is truly my own desire and so does not keep me captive (in a way not entirely dissimilar to modern practices of psychoanalytical therapy). This, I would suggest, is the point of the distinction between *uti* and *frui*.

But how, then, does Augustine conceive of the production of desire in terms of the object of desire, the second node in the triangular relationship? What are the practices through which Christian desire is transformed from idolatry *(cupiditas)* to the love of God *(caritas)?* Here it is imperative to remind oneself that Augustine's theology shared some but not all ideas with his contemporary philosophers. For them as well as for Augustine, philosophy or Christian doctrine is not a speculation on "what there is" above or before any consideration of the existential predicament of human beings. Philosophy is for them, with Pierre Hadot's appropriate phrase, "a way of life" that is supposed to teach its practitioners how to live.[13] Philosophy (or theology) is not even "about" how to live, but is in itself a practice, a way of life. The very modern distinction between "life" and "thought" or "practice" and "theory" does not apply to Augustine and his contemporaries. Theirs is not an anthropology that detaches will from reason or desire; as James Wetzel writes, apropos Augustine: "There is no faculty of the will, distinct from desire, which we use to determine our actions."[14] To will something is not independent of being attracted to something.[15]

This is the way we are created; as human beings, our will is not, as for instance Immanuel Kant would later claim, ideally independent of desire but, rather, is realized as a free will through the liberation of our true desire. We do not choose our objects of desire in any voluntaristic sense, and this is not only because of sin, but because it is in our human nature to be defined by what attracts us. In a certain sense, Augustine would agree, as would most of his contemporaries, with what Aristotle writes in book 1 of the *Nicomachean Ethics,* that "the good has rightly been declared to be that at which all things aim," except that Augustine would be more pessimistic about human beings really of and by themselves aiming at the right thing.[16] Christian desire is produced through transformative practices by which we as human beings learn to love what is truly worth loving and so, through these transformative practices, become emancipated from idolatry.

Augustine's best-known work, *Confessions,* could accordingly be read, as suggested by Margaret R. Miles, as "a narrative deconstruction of what is ordinarily thought of as pleasurable, and a reconstruction of 'true' pleasure."[17] This deconstruction is not primarily an effort of the will of an individual, but has to do with the attractiveness of the true object of desire, God. Nothing could be achieved without God's initiative. This is a trait in Augustine's theology that distinguishes him from his contemporary non-Christian philosophers, as this would mean that a human being is funda-

13. Pierre Hadot, *Philosophy as a Way of Life: Spiritual Exercises from Socrates to Foucault,* ed. Arnold I. Davidson (Oxford: Blackwell, 1995).

14. James Wetzel, *Augustine and the Limits of Virtue* (Cambridge: Cambridge University Press, 1992), p. 8.

15. Augustine, *Confessions,* trans. Henry Chadwick, Oxford World's Classics (Oxford and New York: Oxford University Press, 2008), 8.8-10.

16. Aristotle, *Nicomachean Ethics,* vol. 2 of *The Complete Works of Aristotle,* Revised Oxford Translation, ed. Jonathan Barnes (Princeton: Princeton University Press, 1991), 1729.

17. Margaret R. Miles, *Desire and Delight: A New Reading of Augustine's* Confessions (New York: Crossroad, 1992), p. 20.

mentally passive in a certain sense that I will come to below. But this initiative still calls for the response of the human being, a response given by Augustine in book 10 of *Confessions* in explicitly erotic terms:

> You called and cried out loud and shattered my deafness. You were radiant and resplendent, you put to flight my blindness. You were fragrant, and I drew in my breath and now pant after you. I tasted you, and I feel hunger and thirst for you. You touched me, and I am set on fire to attain the peace which is yours.[18]

Augustine is the lover burning for the love of God through the initiative of God's calling, to which he was created in the first place. When it comes to the question of the second node in the triangular relationship, then, the object of desire, this object is God. That it is God who is the true object of desire means that any initiative for the true transformation of desire must come from God. The goal of the ascesis of the spiritual life is not *enkrateia* or self-control, understood as complete autonomy or apathy on behalf of the spiritual person, as this would amount to an isolation not only from other human beings but even from God.

To be a truly spiritual person means to be the kind of human being that is open to being drawn toward God, and this takes place with and through desire. To be drawn by God means that we are liberated *by* our desires rather than *from* our desires. Or, to put it in another way, ascesis does not really mean the extinction of our desire but rather the cultivation of our desire. The problem with our desire is that it is alienated, not that it is desire. The liberation of desire is a consequence of finding the true object of desire — according to Augustine, God — but this object is found only through letting it find us. The first node of the triangular relationship, my own desire, is thus not independent of the second node, as this second node is the practical presupposition for the right ordering of my own desire.

Thus far, it might sound as if desire is produced in the relationship between the human being and God, understood as a private commerce between two autonomous subjects. Once again, we have to remind ourselves that Augustine was a premodern philosopher and theologian. His was not, I would claim, an understanding of human beings as atomistic individuals (or of God as an autonomous subject). Even if Augustine is sometimes in-

---

18. Augustine, *Confessions*, 10.38. For more on desire and a theology of beauty, see Wendy Farley's chapter "Beguiled by Beauty: Reformation of Desire for Faith and Theology" in this volume.

terpreted as a kind of proto-Cartesian, as for instance in Charles Taylor's magisterial *Sources of the Self* (to take a more nuanced example), I think this misses the mark.[19] As I have already stated, and unlike Descartes' self, the Augustinian subject is constituted by a radical exteriority, the call of God, that could never coincide with human interiority without denying the qualitative difference between creation and Creator, which would amount to idolatry. The relationship between the lover and the beloved, although joined together by love, would cease to be a relation if this difference were to be denied. Moreover, it has been argued, again in my opinion persuasively, that the Augustinian subject is a liturgical self.[20]

This means, among other things, that the self according to Augustine is constituted socially. The human relationship toward God is not, despite its being initiated by God, something that goes on or is even initiated somehow beside or independent of the created world with all its social institutions. Augustine's theology is a theology both of the incarnation and of the Trinity, which means that God's call is mediated and also reciprocal. As Michael Hanby puts it, "Selfhood is doxological. It is only through delight in Christ, a gift of the mutual delight between the Father and the Son, that 'I' can finally be myself."[21] And the created institution for this doxological event is what Augustine calls the church.[22] Participation in eternity is mediated through temporality, and so the meaning of eternity is hardly a farewell to temporality but rather the redemption of temporality.

"You'll Never Walk Alone," the famous song by Rodgers and Hammerstein and now also the motto of Liverpool FC, is as true of Augustine's conception of the self as it is of football. The third node of Girard's triangular relationship of desire, the other's desire, is an integrated part of Augustine's theology of love, and perhaps also the most important part for understanding the Christian production of desire. Learning to love in the right way is made possible by the initiative of God but is mediated through concrete social practices that make up what we call the church. This mediation does not mean any compromise with the graciousness of God's gift but instead becomes the way to learn how to participate in God's love more fully.

19. Charles Taylor, *Sources of the Self: The Making of the Modern Identity* (Cambridge: Cambridge University Press, 1989), pp. 127-42.

20. As by, for instance, Michael Hanby, *Augustine and Modernity* (London and New York: Routledge, 2003).

21. Hanby, *Augustine and Modernity,* p. 91.

22. Augustine, *Confessions,* 13.

According to Augustine, you become what you love, and so it is of importance where your desires are schooled or what company you keep. In *The City of God* Augustine distinguishes between two cities, one ruled by the love of self *(amor sui)*, which also takes expression in a lust for power *(libido dominandi)*, and the other ruled by the love of God *(amor Dei)*.[23] Although Augustine also is keen to emphasize that the actual church is a *corpus permixtum* where one cannot make any final distinction between the city of God and the city of men, it is still important to recognize that Augustine means what he says when he uses the word "city" here; different cities are defined by different social practices, each with their own *telos*. And these different practices consist of people, and so the practice of the church is designed (ideally; we know that this is not always the case) to further our growth in love by ordering our desires.

To understand in more detail what this means, I would suggest that such a practice (or such practices, since they are many although with the same goal) could be understood as a version of what Martha C. Nussbaum calls a "therapy of desire." Her main examples of such antique therapies are drawn from Aristotle and Hellenistic philosophical movements such as Epicureanism, Skepticism, and Stoicism, but together with Augustine they would all "insist that human flourishing cannot be achieved unless desire and thought, as they are usually constructed within society, are considerably transformed."[24] A "therapy of desire," then, is a practice for the transformation of these desires according to the *telos* of human flourishing. Augustine would agree, I think, but he would also insist that the Christian church has a quite different version of human flourishing than most of the pagan Hellenistic philosophers, including an emphasis on the initiative of God and a corollary emphasis on human vulnerability.[25]

A "therapy of desire" is a way of schooling our desires so as to transform them toward their true *telos*, human flourishing, which in Augustine's version would mean loving God. To learn to love God, Augustine is dependent not only upon the call from God but also upon spiritual leaders who have gone before him and friends who will go with him in his search

23. Augustine, *The City of God*, 1.14, 28.

24. Martha C. Nussbaum, *The Therapy of Desire: Theory and Practice in Hellenistic Thought* (Princeton: Princeton University Press, 1994), p. 11.

25. Nussbaum, *The Therapy of Desire*, pp. 18-19. But see also her article, "Augustine and Dante on the Ascent of Love," in *The Augustinian Tradition*, ed. Gareth B. Matthews (Berkeley/Los Angeles/London: University of California Press, 1999), pp. 61-90, where Nussbaum acknowledges an Augustinian therapy of desire.

for God — but also upon more or less institutionalized rites in the church. In this sense Augustine's desire is also a mimetic desire, since it is based upon the *imitatio Christi,* mediated through the concrete persons and institutions that he would find in his time. If his *Confessions* can be read as "a narrative deconstruction of what is ordinarily thought of as pleasurable, and a reconstruction of 'true' pleasure," according to Miles, it is important to understand that this "reconstruction of 'true pleasure'" takes place in, through, and with a community — a city. And so *Confessions* should also be read as the story of a search for the kind of community that would produce and sustain the kind of virtues needed to love God truly and that could be listened to in matters spiritual.

The third node in Augustine's triangular relationship, the other's desire, is made explicit in *Confessions* and his other writings as the mediation of God's active love in human practices with the intention of facilitating the transformation of desire in the individual believer's life. There is consequently hardly any notion in Augustine's theology of a "natural" or a "given" desire, meaning a desire that is given in any straightforward sense in and of itself, but all desires are socially mediated. Thus it matters what kind of practices you participate in, as these might be an embodiment of or at least on their way toward either the love of self or the love of God.

A final objection against my interpretation of Augustine's theology of love should be noted, one that concerns the distinction between love of God and love of self. Is it not the case that Augustine really does not offer any place for a proper kind of self-love? Does he not pose the relation between love of self and love of God as an either/or, as a separation rather than a distinction between *amor sui* and *amor Dei?* Moreover, we should not forget the (in)famous passage in *Confessions* book 1 where Augustine retells the story of his own infancy and childhood as a kind of prelude to sin in the full sense of the word, and not only claims that he was "conceived in iniquity" but also claims that he showed all the symptoms of a jealous mind.[26] So, if even the infant's hunger for love and nourishment could be interpreted as selfish and potentially even sinful (at a more conscious age), is there really any place for an appropriate love of self in Augustine? I would say yes; in his general argument about love Augustine — at least implicitly — allows for a kind of love of self, which at the same time could be appropriately lodged within a love of God. The distinction

26. Augustine, *Confessions,* 1.9.

between *amor sui* and *amor Dei* is really a distinction, and *amor Dei* includes rather than excludes a proper love of self.

But the point of my argument is to claim neither that Augustine is perfectly consistent nor that every aspect of his theology of love is commendable for a contemporary theology of desire. To be sure, there are aspects of Augustine's theology that we would want to question today, and it certainly might be true that there are parts of the effective history of his legacy that are part of the problem rather than part of the solution. However, as my aim is not the ambitious one of giving a full account of Augustine's theology of love but the more modest one of presenting a usable model of how Christian desire is produced from a premodern tradition, I shall leave this objection for now and move on to the discussion of contemporary experiences of the production of desire.

The Production of Desire: Contemporary Experiences

Augustine's theology of love could, I would suggest, be used as a model for understanding how desire is produced even in our day, although many of the institutions important for the production of desire today were not invented at that time. If you were to ask which institutions matter most in the life of an average person in contemporary western society, very few would probably answer that the church does. And even if some of us still go to church each and every Sunday, it would hardly do to claim that this means the church and the practices it consists of have a hegemonic position in the formation of our desires. As soon as we start to reflect on what produces our desire today, we become, I suppose, very aware of the mixed variety of practices in which meaning and desire are produced in modern society — a trait of modern society being the functional differentiation of spheres such as economy, politics, religion, and science.[27]

The church today is very evidently a *corpus permixtum* in which we seldom are aware of where to draw the line between the city of God and the city of men. In general terms, Augustine is still relevant in that his theology of love is a version of the triangular relationship between my desire, the object of desire, and the other's desire, which could help us make sense of the social production of desire and which also has a principle for dis-

---

27. Cf. José Casanova, *Public Religions in the Modern World* (Chicago and London: University of Chicago Press, 1994), pp. 20-25.

cerning between different ways of loving, i.e., the distinction between *amor sui* and *amor Dei,* which could be helpful for a theology of desire even today. "A theology of desire," as Wendy Farley writes in a later chapter in this volume, "provides an antidote to the formation of desire by consumer society preoccupied with individual satisfactions" — and this is also the aim of the present section and chapter.[28]

To understand how Christian desire is produced at present, we need to look a bit closer at the contemporary conditions of this production. Without claiming that this dimension is exhaustive, I would suggest that it would still be a good idea to start with the so-called turn from a "textual" to a "visual" culture in the West, in which the written or printed word no longer has a hegemonic status when it comes to the production of meaning.[29] Pictures, and indeed "moving pictures," have an immense impact on the cultural sensibility of the entire planet, in that they constitute a culturally dominant form of mediation of the stories that make sense of our lives. One aspect of this is formulated by the Norwegian journalist and film critic Anne Hoff in a book with the very apt title *Mitt liv som film* (*My Life as a Film;* compare the Swedish director Lasse Hallström's film *My Life as a Dog* from 1985):

> Movies are one of the most important cultural expressions in our time. [The movie] offers a profound insight into the longings, ideas and ideals of our society. The moving pictures constitute our common frame of reference, and have a unique influence on how we dream, live and think. So has the storytelling of movies taken over a lot of the functions of classical myth, which consisted in providing us with a common ground for understanding and interpreting existence.[30]

Regardless of which sector of society one tries to understand, it is hardly possible to underestimate the importance of film and other visual media for the understanding and interpretation of politics, religion, family life, and so on. To take just one short example: How could it be possible to picture what "true love" is all about, without being influenced by the movies? The claim is not that you by necessity are determined by the movies in your conception of "true love"; but even if you wish to distance yourself

---

28. Wendy Farley, "Beguiled by Beauty," p. 129 below.

29. Cf. Nicholas Mirzoeff, *An Introduction to Visual Culture* (London and New York: Routledge, 1999).

30. Anne Hoff, "Mitt liv som film," in *Mitt liv som film,* ed. Anne Hoff (Oslo: Tiden Norsk forlag, 2002), p. 9.

from the cultural clichés, this is then done with a reference to the prevailing cultural standards. And this is not lost on film directors such as, for instance, Baz Luhrman, whose *Moulin Rouge* (2001) is in a certain sense a postmodern meta-commentary on all these clichés about love in the movies, while still continuing in their tradition.

The thesis is not just that people *use* movies when they try to think of the purpose of individual human life as such, but also that movies — to a large extent — *provide* the categories, the narratives, or the raw material with the help of which we construe purpose or meaning in our lives.[31] Movies are a source for understanding and constructing the meaning of my life, and their cultural influence goes so far, I would claim, that it is more to the point to say that I am the co-author of my life rather than its sole author. This is one of the reasons why film and religion are such important fields of study today. Historically, the church or other religious institutions provided the stories, rites, and contexts for the meaning of life, but in the semi-secularized, fragmented society of today, this function is more or less taken over by media. According to J. R. R. Tolkien — you might know him as the author who wrote the books that the film trilogy *The Lord of the Rings* is based on — narratives are a way of creating community with other human beings, and so to ask for the origin of narratives is at the same time to ask for the origin of language and consciousness.[32] And so we could perhaps rephrase the question from the Lutheran large catechism, "What does it mean to have a god?" in a more contemporary fashion: "Who writes the manuscript for my life?"

But as I discuss desire here, we should not forget another aspect of the cultural importance of movies, namely, that Luhrman's *Moulin Rouge* (for example) has the power to influence our values and ways of life because of its very seductive visuality. As a cascade of colors and form, sometimes it does not really tell anything at all but just shows pictures that overwhelm our field of vision. The story of the film makes way for the sheer visuality, which appeals directly to our affects without any detour through our intellect. Moving pictures are accordingly not just about the story they tell but also about how they tell it, what kind of appeal they make to our senses. They are in many ways very much like the church, an institution for trans-

---

31. Cf. Tomas Axelson's thesis *Film och mening. En receptionsstudie om spelfilm, filmpublik och existentiella frågor* (Uppsala: Acta Universitatis Uppsaliensis, 2008).

32. J. R. R. Tolkien, "On Fairy-Stories," in *On Fairy-Stories* (London: HarperCollins, 1990), pp. 115-88.

forming our desire not only through telling a certain story about how to live a good life but also through being aesthetically pleasing to the beholder. This, of course, raises the entire question of cinematic idolatry, but I have to leave that for now. Suffice it to say that this, in itself, calls for something like an Augustinian discernment of different kinds of love.

As long as we are concerned about some version of the proper transformation of our desire — not necessarily the Christian one — questions of the ubiquity of alienated desire are bound to come up. Theologian David Jaspers of Glasgow University, for instance, would claim that the "danger of Hollywood cinema lies in its deliberate and commercial habit of absorbing all vision into its own, offering the viewer a commodity which can be consumed without fear of significant change or disturbance."[33] Popular movies cultivate voyeuristic tendencies among their audience. This calls for a sustained theological reflection on moving pictures as a medium.

Movies, in short, are an institution for the production of desire in ways similar to the church.[34] On the one hand, film gathers together people in the dark, influencing their audiences through stories and pictures that mimetically attract their fantasies and desires. On the other hand, the church could be likened to a movie theater, as it, like the moving pictures, dramatizes in word and action a story — the story about Christ — about what is the exemplary life. This assertion is not falsified by the existence of DVDs and other ways for the digital distribution of moving pictures for consumption in the privacy of your own home. Even if we need to distinguish television's more "private prayer" from the more "public liturgy" of cineplexes, private prayer and public liturgy have always coexisted, even if the form of their relationship has varied over time. Of course, *how* you use movies as an individual varies with age, gender, and class, but even if you practice cinematic ascesis, the message and imagery of mainstream movies exert an influence on society as a whole. When the first part of *The Lord of the Rings* had its premiere in 2001, my eldest son, who then was three years old, quite soon knew the general story by heart. Not, of course, because he had seen the movie, but because of the various "tie-ins" — advertisements, collector cards, foods, toys, etc. Have you seen the film? No, but I've eaten the cereal.

33. David Jaspers, "On Systematizing the Unsystematic: A Response," in *Explorations in Theology and Film: Movies and Meaning,* ed. Clive Marsh and Gaye Ortiz (Oxford and Malden, MA: Blackwell, 1997), p. 244.

34. For a particularly interesting discussion of the relationship between film and church in the context of a production of desire, see Gerard Loughlin, *Alien Sex: The Body and Desire in Cinema and Theology* (Oxford: Blackwell, 2004).

If moving pictures have an enormous influence on how desire is produced today, this has consequences also for the Christian production of desire. Let me mention two aspects of this. The first has to do with the more general point that any story — at least of any interest — embodies certain ways of enacting your life, and thus implies a particular production of desire. When I use the concept of story here, it is shorthand for some very different phenomena; even if it makes sense to speak of the same story being told through several media, it is the same story in a very limited sense. It makes a difference for your reception of, say, *The Lord of the Rings,* if you read it or see it as a film in a movie complex. In a visual age such as ours, visual enactments of stories have a very powerful cultural impact on how to conceive of human existence, both through what they tell about what is desirable and through their seductive aesthetic appearance. One may have all sorts of misgivings about that; my point here is only that moving pictures tell a story about human existence that involves its audience through visual, audible, and narrative means and so, effectively, in itself becomes a "therapy of desire." This story is always reinforced by a certain kind of structure — the cineplex, for instance, or the family television — which also embodies a certain ritual.

Some of the most popular movies convey highly conventional and conservative conceptions of race, class, and gender, having as their primary aim economic profit.[35] Some Hollywood movies succeed, even despite themselves, in conveying a more unconventional therapy, becoming, as it were, parody and prophecy at the same time. The general point is still the same, however: that any telling of a story, be it in words, dance, rites, pictures, or moving pictures, embodies certain ways of enacting a life, and by implication a particular production of desire. The view that visual media, or any media, could be used for didactic purposes without interfering with their message is not very plausible.

The second aspect could perhaps be illustrated by asking how the central story of the Christian church is disseminated today. According to historian Gary R. Edgerton, "television is the principal means by which most people learn about history today."[36] In the same spirit, I would claim that visual media such as television and cinema are the principal means by

---

35. Margaret R. Miles, *Seeing Is Believing: Religion and Values in the Movies* (Boston: Beacon Press, 1996).

36. Gary R. Edgerton, "Introduction: Television as Historian — A Different Kind of History Altogether," in *Television Histories: Shaping Collective Memory in the Media Age,* ed. Gary R. Edgerton and Peter C. Rollins (Lexington: University Press of Kentucky, 2001), p. 1.

which most people learn about religion today, including the stories of the Bible. In particular, the question about the identity of Christ negotiates between images of Christ in popular culture and images of Christ in the Christian church — given that, for now, a neat distinction between popular culture and church is hardly possible. (As I have already hinted, neither the church nor popular culture is in reality a discrete entity but consists of complex and conflicting practices and narratives.)

Even if, in a hypothetical example, the church wished to tell a different story about Christ than those you would encounter in popular culture, it has to do this against the background of these different versions of the story. Given that the Christian church in contemporary society has no cultural hegemony (this is true at least in Europe) even in matters that concern its own stories, it has no choice but to attempt retelling the versions of the story disseminated in popular culture and so unavoidably influencing its members' thoughts and practices. A reflection on the production of Christian desire today (and this is probably true in any culture) must recognize that any reenactment of its central story is contextual and so takes place against the background of its own cultural horizon — and also, that the interpretation of this central story is disputed even from within itself, as we shall see.

The Passion of the Christ

Let us then look a little closer at one (in)famous example of a movie that presumably will influence how many people think about Christ and that implicitly will influence how Christian desire is produced today: Mel Gibson's *The Passion of the Christ* (2004). The reason for choosing this film is that it may illuminate how Christian desire is produced today. Given the somewhat surprising marketing of the movie by established churches, and given the number of people who went to see it or have seen it on DVD, it is probably not a very daring hypothesis that this particular movie has had and will have a major influence on the representation of Christ in contemporary cultural consciousness. In most European nations at least, biblical literacy is not very high, not even among regular churchgoers, and this means that the "information" most people receive about Christ, for example, will be influenced by the cultural clichés of the day.

The Passion of the Christ is probably not the only source of popular "information" about Christ, but it is nevertheless bound to be — as the first commercially successful Jesus-movie ever! — an important influence. This is cause for concern for Christian churches, I would presume, as they realize that they can no longer claim any hegemonic position for defining the representation of Christ or of any other biblical story for that matter. The difference between now and the era of Christendom, when the church in Europe had hegemonic status in religious matters, is not that the reception of Christ in popular religion is now conditioned by a cultural consciousness and earlier it was not; this has in a certain sense always been the case. The difference is, rather, that the official church is one competitor among many, even for the representation of Christ, and perhaps not one of the most publicly powerful.

When it was released, *The Passion of the Christ* was accompanied by claims that it would reproduce the passion of Christ with historical or at least biblical accuracy.[37] The actors spoke Aramaic and Latin, but this in itself is no sign of historical accuracy. Rather, to most of the audience, this only suggested a semblance of historical accuracy, since very few understood the languages spoken. It is also often pointed out that *The Passion* was influenced by extracanonical sources — for example, the visions of a nineteenth-century Roman Catholic nun, Anne Catherine Emmerich, usually not cited for establishing historical accuracy of the Gospel narratives. Furthermore, and more interesting for my purposes here, there are indications that the actor who played the role of Christ, James Caviezel, was replaced by a robot during some of the scenes from the crucifixion to add to the realism of the movie; what counts as realism according to the filmic conventions in movies of this genre is not necessarily what really happens when someone is crucified.[38] Be that as it may, what is important here is the producer's wish to give a semblance of historical or biblical accuracy, but according to the filmic conventions of realism. This becomes a way of underlining the importance of what the movie would want to convey to its audience.

Even more interesting for my theme here is the extremely violent character of the movie. The movie is about two hours long, and according to my estimate about half of it consists in explicitly violent scenes. As any movie is polysemic, this violence meant that the movie had its audience

---

37. On this question, see Arnfríður Guðmundsdóttir, "More Pain, More Gain! On Mel Gibson's film about *The Passion of the Christ*," in *Recent Releases: The Bible in Contemporary Cinema* (Sheffield: Sheffield Phoenix Press, 2008).

38. See Anders Johansson, "Mel Gibson's Robot," in *Nonfiction* (Göteborg: Glänta, 2008), pp. 105-9.

not only among those interested in Christ, but also among those who could not care less about him but would not say no to a good splatter movie. In the context of the movie's depiction of violence we could ask the central question: Why did Christ have to suffer? Of course the movie's answer is much the same as the answer of the Christian tradition: Christ had to suffer for our sins to redeem a rebellious humanity. A quotation from the book of Isaiah (53:5) opens the movie: "He was wounded for our transgressions, crushed for our iniquities; by his wounds we are healed" — but with the line "the chastisement of our peace was on him" curiously left out as if to concentrate on the torture, not the healing.[39]

Given the extremely violent depiction of Christ's sufferings in *The Passion* — remember that the account of the passion of Christ in the Gospels hardly dwells upon the actual torture — the question becomes acute: Who needs all this blood? One answer could be the devil who lurks in the fringes of the movie, but he does not really qualify, since it is never explained what good it would do him to see Christ suffer. He even actively tries to persuade Christ to defect from his impending bloodbath, so the actual suffering does not seem to be a ransom paid to the devil. But is it God who needs to see his only begotten Son suffer? This is not an implausible hypothesis, as this has been the position of some interpretations of the so-called "satisfaction" theory of atonement — as will be clear from the next chapter in this volume, by Rita Nakashima Brock.[40] But if this is the case, the depiction in *The Passion* becomes problematic to the extreme.

In the scene where Christ is whipped in front of a Roman officer, he sinks to his knees, overcome by the pain inflicted on him. All his skin is stripped from his back, which is one big wound, a simmering *tableaux* of pain. "*Satis*," cries the officer, "enough." But what happens then is that Christ stands up once again to let the whipping continue, as if taking the saying "no pain, no gain" literally in a quantitative sense. A certain amount of whipping seems to be necessary, then, to atone for the sins of humanity: not one hour but rather two. So the question of the movie seems to be not *why* Christ suffered but *how much* Christ suffered. This is very much in line with the Hollywood dramaturgy of the movie.

We could compare it to, for instance, Gibson's own epic movie *Braveheart* (1995), where the director himself also plays the principal part as

---

39. Johansson, "Mel Gibson's Robot," pp. 103-4.

40. Brock's chapter is an extended discussion and critique of sadomasochistic renderings of atonement theologies.

the thirteenth-century Scottish freedom fighter William Wallace. *Braveheart* has many similarities to *The Passion of the Christ,* one of them being the final scenes when Wallace is being tortured by the English conquerors but refuses to give in and instead dies with the word "freedom" on his lips. Seeing *Braveheart* as a parallel to *The Passion* alerts us to the fact that even if *The Passion* had been more authentic, authentic in a more biblical sense, it still would have been a contextualized interpretation of the story of the passion, screening its story with the help of a particular aesthetic and dramaturgy from the beginning of the twenty-first century. Since there is no such thing as an innocent rendering of any narrative whatsoever, any particular movie with Christ as the central character is inevitably a theological, political, and cultural statement.[41] This is not in itself a critique of Gibson's *The Passion,* since this recontextualizing of a biblical story is needed to make it intelligible and existentially relevant for us today — the same things happen every Sunday in church. What becomes problematic is the kind of desire produced through the movie's violent aesthetics.

One could argue that the narratives of passion in the Gospels are the central stories for the Christian church. The way they are interpreted becomes the paradigm for the understanding of what it means to follow Christ, and so for the production of Christian desire through the other's desire. As movies, or other media, are hardly just containers for narratives but structure the way the content is mediated, the extremely violent character of *The Passion* communicates a certain sadomasochistic version of the story. Sadomasochism is unfortunately not a new way of interpreting the gospel message, as it can be found in versions of the doctrine of the atonement in which there is a need for sacrifice and so sacrifice in itself becomes pleasing to God. In the sadomasochistic version of the passion, God becomes human primarily to die.[42] The focus on the torture and death of Christ in *The Passion* becomes a valuation of pain in and of itself as the way to God, and so a desire is produced that cannot account for a pleasure without pain, which becomes immoral. The atonement is conditioned upon the ability of Christ to endure pain, and so attachment to pain becomes what constitutes the follower of Christ.

---

41. Cf. Tomas Axelson and Ola Sigurdson, "Om frälsaren, filmstjärnan, och samtidsmänniskan: Jesus på vita duken," in *Film och religion: Livsåskådning på vita duken* (Örebro: Cordia, 2005), pp. 119-49.

42. This is the central claim of Rita Nakashima Brock's critique of atonement theologies in the next chapter. But cf. also S. Mark Heim, *Saved from Sacrifice: A Theology of the Cross* (Grand Rapids and Cambridge: Eerdmans, 2006), pp. 297-302.

The result of this aesthetically dazzling account of violence and torture, which is also in accordance with a certain Hollywood dramaturgy, is that desire is produced for the way of pain that is exemplified by Christ. Our point of identification with the movie is not as someone who takes the position of Christ, but rather as someone who receives the gain of Christ's pain. This gain, then, creates a new debt of gratitude from the follower of Christ, a debt that it is possible to pay only through more pain. Rather than being the sacrifice to end all sacrifices, Christ's sacrifice on the cross, according to *The Passion,* produces a desire that never will be able to escape from the vicious circle of debt and repayment. At the very end of *The Passion,* the risen Christ does indeed show up, but his resurrection is remarkably unrelated to the rest of the movie, as if it was just an incident, not very important for the central content of the film where Christ's sufferings are shown in slow motion.

In terms of the triangular relationship, *The Passion* becomes a significant mediator of the other's desire in that it is a popular, aesthetically explicit, and culturally important retelling of the story about Christ's passion. It models a transformation of desire in terms of a sadomasochistic version of my own desire, engendered by an object of desire — God — with an apparent need for the blood of an innocent victim. Thus, according to the triangular relationship, *The Passion* teaches me not only what to desire but also how to desire it, i.e., what kind of desire is appropriate for me in relation to what is to be desired. As Christ has suffered on my behalf, not only in a qualitative but also in a quantitative sense, I become emotionally attached to him as he compensates for my sins. This is a desire that always is haunted by the feeling of a lack of gratitude on my behalf as the recipient of the atonement, a lack that breeds, as one of its expressions, compensatory dreams of revenge and resentment. In the quantitative logic of the movie, the more Christ suffers, the bigger my sins must be, and so I could discover my true gratitude only through the immensity of my sins. No pain, no gain, also on behalf of my own desire. The charge that *The Passion* was anti-Semitic has a ground in the structure of desire that it communicates, where our persistent lack of gratitude as recipients of atonement results in a search for those who bear the original guilt for the passion, more than the way it pictures Jews as characters in the movie.

My point is not that this is the standard version of a Christian theology of atonement or of desire, nor that this is the only way that the Gospels are rendered for Christians in today's world. Rather, what I have tried to illustrate with the help of Gibson's movie is, first, the way desire is produced through the stories by which we make sense of our lives and the institutions through which these stories are mediated; and, second, the way desire (my own desire as well as the object of desire) is produced structurally and institutionally not only or primarily through what is said about desire but through the way desire is staged as a relation between the different agents in a story and how this story is related to its audience (the other's desire). To the first point I would like to add that, as previously stated, the notion of Christ prevalent in the Christian church is more likely to be something that is the result of a negotiation between the contemporary cultural horizon and the preaching and liturgy of the church.

But what matters in this contemporary cultural horizon is not only the notion of Christ found in *The Passion* and other portraits of Christ, but also the form of desire that is produced in popular culture as a whole. Even if Mel Gibson had not made *The Passion of the Christ,* the structure of desire implied by, for instance, *Braveheart* would be as problematic for the Christian church as *The Passion.* If desire is never natural or neutral, there is always the distinction between the city of men and the city of God to account for. With regard to the second point I would like to emphasize the importance, for the theme of desire, of a phenomenological investigation of the position of subjectivity implicit in any practice.[43] Whether we are watching a movie, praying, sleeping, talking to a friend over the phone, or walking to our job, these activities imply a certain position in regard to God, our fellow human beings, the nonhuman creation, and ourselves. That some of them might seem more relevant for the theme of desire may be true, but nevertheless no activity or practice is theologically neutral as long as we are talking about the comportment of human beings in the world.

Conclusion

In this chapter I have argued that any viable theology of desire needs to explore the way in which different practices embody certain structures of desire and also to study the explicit discourses of love. It will then be clear how desire always is in the process of being transformed in some direction.

---

43. See further my article "Prayer, Subjectivity, and Politics," in *Phenomenology and Religion: New Frontiers,* Södertörn Philosophical Studies 8, ed. Jonna Bornemark and Hans Ruin (Stockholm, 2010), pp. 267-89.

Given that it lies in the interest of theology that this process should take the direction toward a productive form of desire, a love that is generous rather than greedy, some version of a normative distinction, such as the one we found in Augustine or elsewhere, is needed for the practical discernment of different versions of desire. As practices of the Christian church hardly have a hegemonic status in contemporary society now (if they ever had it), such a discernment needs to be aware of how desire is produced not only in but also in between different practices, for instance when they mediate the meaning of Christ, as exemplified in Gibson's Hollywood rendering of the story of the passion.

The example of *The Passion* also shows the need for a critical discernment even when it comes to recognizably Christian themes or practices; they carry, of themselves, no guarantee of a successful or constructive therapy of desire. If we as human beings are creatures of desire, and if desire is a prominent feature of human existence, it is perhaps not by chance that we might be enriched by the historical experience of premodern theology as well as contemporary theory in our search for a theology of desire. The production of Christian desire — the formation of a particular spirituality of desire — takes place in liturgical as well as nonliturgical spaces, and there remains a lot to discover about this innermost trait of human existence. Wendy Farley will discuss in her chapter the transformation of desire through such everyday practices as prayer, mindfulness, and compassion, so there is no need for me to repeat it in advance here. Suffice it to say that, as desire is not a given but a gift, there is always reason for hope. Even in the grim circumstances of late capitalism, as in history before our times, a more genuine desire has always made it through, perhaps through a practice of "making do" with whatever cultural resources are available, but perhaps also due to the fact that our bodily comportment and our social practices always exceed our theory.

Paradise and Desire:
Deconstructing the Eros of Suffering

Rita Nakashima Brock

The tortured, dead body of Jesus has haunted the western imagination like no other image. It stirs pious embraces of its wounds, compels devotion to his suffering, and elicits desire to bond with his pain and humiliation, a piety exemplified in Mel Gibson's film *The Passion of the Christ.* This was not always so.

Though now ubiquitous in western art, images of the dead Jesus did not exist as objects of church worship during the first millennium of European Christianity. Instead, ritual spaces were adorned with images of rescue from danger, the resurrected saints, and happy life on earth, accompanied by the risen, living Christ. In early images, we find life on earth in a lush garden fed by four rivers. Golden cloud-strewn or sapphire, star-studded skies hover over green meadows dotted with flowers and trees. Human souls often appear as lovely doves, serene deer, and snowy sheep.[1]

---

1. Most explanations for the absence of crucifixion images are theological or political. For a variety of explanations, see Diane Apostolos-Cappadona, *Dictionary of Christian Art* (New York: Continuum Press, 1995); John Lowden, *Early Christian and Byzantine Art* (New York: Phaidon Press, 1997); Peter and Linda Murray, *The Oxford Companion to Christian Art and Architecture* (New York: Oxford University Press, 1996); and Gertrud Schiller, *Iconography of Christian Art,* vol. 1: *Christ's Incarnation, Childhood, Baptism, Temptation, Transfiguration, Works and Miracles,* trans. Janet Seligman (London: Lund Humphries, 1971) and *Iconography of Christian Art,* vol. 2: *The Passion of Jesus Christ,* trans. Janet Seligman (London: Lund Humphries, 1972).
Images of Jesus standing alive on a platform in front of a cross began to appear in

---

This essay is based on research done for *Saving Paradise: How Christianity Traded Love of This World for Crucifixion and Empire,* by Rita Nakashima Brock and Rebecca Ann Parker (Boston: Beacon Press, 2008) and elaborates material found, especially, in chapter 11.

The trajectory by which crucifixion took center stage has often been attributed to the Constantinian creation of an imperial church, but this does not explain why the crucifixion is absent for another six hundred years. The crucifixion appeared in Europe's churches only beginning in the tenth century. The emergence of atonement theology in the eleventh century correlates to this new iconography of the dead Christ. Crucifixion gradually escalated in gore and horror over several centuries, as torture and capital punishment became public spectacles.[2] Once he dies, that is virtually all Jesus does. Mel Gibson's film, which distorts the Gospels' subdued and understated depiction of the crucifixion, reflects this escalation.

Atonement theology marks a major rethinking of christology, soteriology, and theological anthropology. The new medieval focus on atonement eroticized violence and produced an otherworldly form of Christianity that came to dominate western Europe. This focus drew a sharp cleft between heaven and earth that separated sacred and profane. This split turned a spatial, vertical cosmology of constant interaction between heavens above and earth below on its side, creating an eschatological arrow of time that constructed the present as a historical process that would yield a reunion of humanity with God in a distant future.

This essay describes the process by which premodern Christian theology moved from a this-worldly Christianity, with a therapy of desire that shaped it toward an expansive love of creation and of human life in a sanctified community, toward a narrow obsession with an ever-delayed salvation that worshiped death and sanctified suffering and violence. This later

---

small, minor relief sculptures in the fifth century and are called "crucifixion" images, but they are Christus Victor representations, in which he has defeated death. He was not depicted as dying on a cross until the first subdued images of the tenth century, in which his eyes are closed and his body slumped. Such images slowly evolved into large church images for devotion and worship over several centuries. Robin Margaret Jensen, *Understanding Early Christian Art* (New York: Routledge, 2000), suggests that the crucifixion is not absent, but is present in disguised forms, such as the intersected *chi* and *rho* symbols and images of Abraham attempting to sacrifice Isaac. However, narrative sequences of Jesus' passion, e.g., the sixth-century St. Apollinare Nuovo in Ravenna, Italy, characteristically skip any image of Golgotha or crucifixion; and the book of Hebrews as well as images of Abraham and Isaac frame the story as rescue from death.

2. Mitchell B. Merback in *The Thief, the Cross and the Wheel: Pain and Spectacle of Punishment in Medieval and Renaissance Europe* (Chicago: University of Chicago Press, 1998) discusses crucifixion images in relation to the social context of Europe in the medieval period, especially the development of torture and capital punishment as public spectacles that reenacted the passion story.

faith disciplined desire toward individual salvation, a wish to suffer and die like Christ, and hope for the destruction of this world as the culmination of a divine plan for salvation.

Desire for the Resurrection

Paul believed that death had no power over Jesus Christ, and that, like him, Christians lived for the *doxa* or beauty of God.[3] In his meditation on the cross, he asserts:

> Christ rose from the dead, and he will never die again. Death no longer has any power over him. He died once to defeat sin, and now he lives for the *(doxa)* glory of God. So you should consider yourselves dead to sin and able to live for the glory of God through Jesus Christ. (Rom. 6:9-11)

Jesus Christ had said to the thief in Luke 23:43, "*today* you shall be with me in paradise." This emphasis on *today* echoes Luke 4:21, when Jesus began a discourse on the meaning of Isaiah 61 by saying, "*today*, this scripture is fulfilled in your hearing." The Isaiah text uses images of oaks, "the planting of the Lord," and a garden to describe the salvation that comes with justice and righteousness. This framework of *today* meant, many early Christians believed, that Jesus had shown with his life and ministry how life in paradise should be lived and that he had reopened the garden with his resurrection. Baptism was its portal. Christians died to sin at baptism and lived eternally thereafter together in the paradise on earth.

Desire grounded salvation — the desire to enter and remain in paradise as a good citizen in its midst. Union with Christ came through the Spirit, and the newly baptized were proclaimed brides of Christ, just as Isaiah 61:10 said the bride of God adorned herself with a robe of righteousness. The liturgies often quoted liberally from the Song of Songs, which was the story of humanity as God's beloved and God as humanity's beloved. The sanctified church incarnated the same Spirit of power, wisdom, and love that Jesus Christ showed in his life and ministry, doing divine deeds in his name. Love, *eros*, for life in the sanctified church was its great power.[4]

---

3. *Doxa* can be translated as "beauty," "splendor," "glory," or "shining presence."

4. For texts of early baptismal liturgies, see Thomas Finn, *From Death to Rebirth: Ritual and Conversion in Antiquity* (New York: Paulist Press, 1997), and E. C. Whitaker and Maxwell E. Johnson, *Documents of the Baptismal Liturgy* (Collegeville, MN: Liturgical Press, 2003).

Many early theologians, beginning with Irenaeus, said the church was paradise in this world. They described it, not as an idealized, perfect utopia, but as a garden with the serpent in it. Hence, paradise was the blessed place where humanity struggled with Satan and learned to become wise about how to love each other and do the divine deeds that fostered justice, mercy, healing, wisdom, and peace. Among many fourth-century theologians, Ambrose of Milan and Ephrem of Syria had wide influence in articulating paradise both as a real material place on earth and as a journey in the Spirit toward human divinization. The desire to grow wise and to develop moral virtue bound Christians to what they loved: God, creation, and paradise.[5]

The incarnate, risen Christ, eternally present in the church, hosted every Eucharist in paradise as a feast of abundant life. The meaning of the feast was captured in the Gospel stories of the feeding of the multitude with loaves and fish. The great feast trained desire, *eros,* toward greater appreciation for divine creation and its blessings, perception of the Spirit in them, and a moral relationship to life in this world. It encouraged acute attunement to present experience as a way to love the world and its blessings and beauties, love that was the source of an ethical commitment to maintain life in paradise.[6]

The Holy Spirit was called down in the *epiclesis* prayer of the Eucharist to consecrate the whole community, which was lifted up to commune with Christ and with the great cloud of witnesses who had departed from this life. Thus blessed, the entire community feasted together, past and present. This eucharistic movement of descent and ascent reflected an incarnational christology in which the Spirit descended into human flesh so that

---

5. Jean Delumeau, *History of Paradise: The Garden of Eden in Myth and Tradition* (New York: Continuum Press, 1995), ch. 1, surveys these early church traditions and asserts that the most common understanding of paradise, established most clearly by Ambrose and Ephrem, said it was both a material place on earth and a spiritual journey toward God.

6. In the time of Julius Caesar, one-fourth of the population received a bread dole, designed to suppress urban riots of the poor. Bruce W. Winter, *Seek the Welfare of the City: Christians as Benefactors and Citizens* (Grand Rapids: Eerdmans, 1994), pp. 168-77, discusses the Roman practice of feasts to the citizenry and Christian responses. Schiller, *Iconography of Christian Art,* vol. 2, p. 34, notes how these interpretations predominate in the art. For examples of early Eucharist prayers and liturgies, see Lucien Deiss, *Springtime of the Liturgy: Liturgical Texts of the First Four Centuries,* trans. Matthew J. O'Connell (Collegeville, MN: Liturgical Press, 1967); R. C. D. Jasper and G. J. Cuming, eds., *Prayers of the Eucharist: Early and Reformed* (Collegeville, MN: Liturgical Press, 1980); and J. H. Srawley, *The Early History of the Liturgy,* 2nd ed. (Cambridge: Cambridge University Press, 1949).

humanity could be lifted up to divinity. Augustine told his newly baptized catechumens to imagine, at their first Eucharist, their own newly resurrected and glorified bodies on the Eucharist table. To eat and drink was to taste and see freedom and new life.[7]

Excommunication from the Eucharist and penance were a "therapy of desire," a system for reshaping perverse and harmful desire and restoring it to life in paradise. The post-Constantine church sought to maintain a longstanding tension between the moral demands of Christian life and the obligations of Roman political and military service. If Christians shed human blood, even in self-defense or in service to a just war, most bishops required them to confess before the community and to undergo penance as medicine for a sick soul, which, if left untreated, could affect the entire community. To sin again in any other grievous way revealed failed therapy and resulted in permanent excommunication from the community of paradise.[8]

A christology of glory through incarnation and resurrection was joined with a theological anthropology that understood the power of the Holy Spirit in human flesh as a transformative power, grounded in the power of love of this life, especially in the power of beauty to evoke love for this world. The soteriology of paradise as the church in this world was delivered at baptism. The responsibility of the sanctified community was to maintain this gift of grace in their journey toward wisdom, Sophia, revealed by Jesus Christ. The cultivation of moral virtue and works of justice and love were a response of gratitude to grace already given, not a works-righteousness to achieve grace. Christians shared the blessings of paradise, this "Medicine of Life," and sought to live according to its values and virtues. They were to safeguard the gifts of the Spirit and to hold them fast against all threats and all odds, even, if necessary, against threats of torture and death.

Death, what the second-century Bishop Irenaeus called "a necessary mercy," was the thin curtain through which the departed passed, but through which Satan could not pass. The beloved departed had earned a blessed rest in a new neighborhood of paradise where they no longer struggled against evil. Prayers and blessings flowed back and forth through the curtain of death, and the departed visited in visions and dreams.

7. Augustine, *Sermon 227*, quoted in Margaret Miles, *Carnal Knowing: Female Nakedness and Religious Meaning in the West* (Boston: Beacon Press, 1989), p. 41.

8. Rita Nakashima Brock and Rebecca Ann Parker, *Saving Paradise: How Christianity Traded Love of This World for Crucifixion and Empire* (Boston: Beacon Press, 2008), pp. 181-87.

Churches put images of them on their walls, just as they did of the risen Christ, to convey their presence in worship.

Lamentation and Desire

The passion narratives, focused on Jesus' death and comprising nearly a third of the Gospel material, also offer a therapy of desire. The way the four Gospels tell the story of Jesus' torture, dying exclamations, and death are important clues to how they shape desire. They tell about Jesus' betrayal, trial, torture, execution, and burial in a cave. They expose how his male disciples abandoned him while women stayed with him to the end. They place words about prayer, thirst, love, forgiveness, paradise, and despair on his dying lips.[9]

These details defy the Roman strategy of crucifixion, its most horrifying and humiliating form of punishment. It was designed to destroy both bodies and identities and to make love of the crucified too dangerous to sustain. The empire used it to discourage people from joining dissident movements, escaping slavery or military service, or conducting magical arts. In the slave rebellion of Spartacus that was defeated in 71 BCE, six thousand crucified bodies rotted along the Apian Way from Capua to Rome. Roman soldiers erected crosses in public places, often at the site of the crime, to terrorize subject peoples. Victims were tortured, and then they died in slow agony, sometimes over days. A quick death was a mercy. Rotting bodies were left to be eaten as carrion; broken or scattered fragments were usually all that remained of a person's identity. There was no burial, no lasting memorial.

Crucifixion required no trial and was more akin to lynching than to formal execution. Seneca was one of the few ancient writers to discuss its brutal uses and methods, and he spared no words in describing its humiliations and horrors. Crucifixion was used against the underclasses and slaves and was regarded as so shameful that even families of victims would not speak of it. It functioned to fragment communities, tearing the fabric of even the strongest bonds of connection and commitment.

9. This interpretation of the passion stories as lamentation is based on the work of Kathleen Corey in her unpublished work "Gender and Jesus: History and Lament in the Gospel Tradition," which John Dominic Crossan cites in *The Birth of Christianity: Discovering What Happened in the Years Immediately Following the Execution of Jesus* (San Francisco: HarperSanFrancisco, 1998).

In speaking explicitly about Jesus' crucifixion, the Gospels used words of lament from the Psalms and Prophets. In doing so, they tied his death to earlier imperial carnage visited upon his people. In their descriptions of Jesus' corpse, they said he had no broken bones, was removed intact, and was properly buried by members of his community. Though properly buried, the grave could not hold him. He could not be found there. These details said Rome was impotent to trap Jesus in death or erase him from memory.

The authors of the passion narratives constructed an innovative strategy to resist public torture and execution. They created a literature of disclosure and wove the killing of Jesus into the fabric of a long history of violence against those who spoke for justice. In placing the opening of Psalm 22 on Jesus' lips, they evoked the bitter lament of grief and struggle that runs through the whole psalm:

> My God, my God, why have you forsaken me?
> Why are you so far from helping me, from the words of my
>   groaning? . . .
>   a company of evildoers encircles me.
> They stare and gloat over me . . .
>   and for my clothing they cast lots. (Ps. 22:1-2, 14-18)

The passion narratives broke silence about the shame and fear that crucifixion instilled. To lament was to claim powers that crucifixion was designed to destroy: dignity, courage, passion, love, and memory. Crucifixion sought to kill desire for the one who had been crucified; lamentation unleashed remembrance of his life. While providing details of the community's last meal together, the struggle in the garden, the arrest, the betrayals, and the trials, the passion narratives move quickly to his death. Out of respect, perhaps, for the victim of torture and execution, the narratives minimize the horror, refuse to tell the details, and describe a dignified death and a loving burial.

The purpose of such writing is assuredly not to valorize victims, to reveal "true love" as submission and self-sacrifice, or to say that God requires the passive acceptance of violence. Such interpretations mistakenly answer the abusive use of power with an abnegation of power. The story of Jesus' crucifixion, in marked contrast, asserted that the answer to abusive power is the courageous and decisive employment of the powers of life and the desire for justice.

The passion narratives would not exist without the agency of women.

From ancient times, women have tended the bodies of the dead, and they have carried the public role of grieving. "Call for the mourning women to come . . . let them raise a dirge over us, so that our eyes may run down with tears," Jeremiah cried (Jer. 9:17-18). As professional mourners, women also composed the words of lamentation. The long history of women's lament-poetry expressed sorrow, outrage, and resistance to the killing of desire.

Rooted in such age-old practices of keening, the women who mourned Jesus preserved his memory and held fast to the power of desire. The passion narratives reflect women's roles in public lamentation and their construction of literatures of lament. In the particular details and ele-giac emotional quality of the stories, we find witnesses who hold to life against all odds and every power arrayed against them. In her study of women's poetry of lamentation, Constantina-Nadia Seremetakis con-cludes that lament is "a prelude to the staging of women's reentry (as indi-viduals and as a collectivity) into the social order on their own terms."[10] It is, in other words, an assertion of life-giving power in the face of unjust structures that suppress, exclude, violate, and control life.

The Gospels placed before Jesus' movement the choice to speak against the silencing powers of violence and state terrorism. Just as Jesus, in John's Gospel, stood before Pilate and said, "You have no power over me," the pas-sion narratives defied the power of crucifixion to silence those who fol-lowed Jesus and to erase all that he taught them. Speaking about his cruci-fixion has abiding importance. Whenever violence is used to instill fear, to fragment human community, and to shame and suppress those who desire justice, the Gospels compel us to break silence and reclaim such desire.

The Gospels said life is found in surviving the worst a community can imagine, in lamenting the consequences of difficult choices, in holding fast to the power of God, and in affirming the core goodness of this world, blessed by the continual resurrection of divine justice and abundant life. In the fourth century in Jerusalem, the church recited the passion stories of lamentation once a year on the Friday before Easter, but they told stories of incarnation and resurrection every week at the Eucharist and lit a light ev-ery evening in churches to signify the presence of the risen Christ. Remem-bering the sorrows injustice and violence inflicted, the early Christians filled their churches with images of the life that lamentation allowed to break free, the life of paradise on earth.

In early Christianity, the assurance of paradise in this world was an

---

10. See Corey, cited in Crossan, *The Birth of Christianity,* p. 528.

inebriating grace, a life-giving recipe drawn from many ancient sources: Genesis, the Song of Songs, the Psalms, the Prophets, and the many stories of those who remained faithful under imperial persecutions. Christians drank the elixir at the Eucharist, where they communed daily with the risen Christ in paradise. They believed the spiritual journey was toward wisdom, Sophia. Sophia's fruits were courage to struggle for truth, works of love, a desire for justice, care for the sick and the poor, an appreciation of beauty, the discernment of the Spirit in the community, and love of this world as good, as blessed, and as beloved by God.

They did not believe that suffering was sanctifying; they sought to alleviate it by taking care of each other. They depicted and valued Jesus' work as healer, miracle worker, and teacher. They believed that all violence, even shedding pagan blood, was a mortal sin and harmed their community. In the courage of martyrs, they saw models of steadfast faith that benefited them spiritually, even from beyond the grave. Joy and wonder seeped into a world afflicted with violence and sorrow. Life, granted through baptism, encompassed death and overcame its finality.

Desire for the Dead Christ

Dramatic changes in western Europe began in the fifth century, when northern tribes penetrated the Roman frontiers, sacked Rome, and destabilized life in Mediterranean Europe. With the collapse of the Roman Empire in Europe, the loss of North Africa and southern Spain to Islam, and the Eastern Emperor's failure to protect the western church, the social stability supporting European churches disintegrated. Cycles of violence engulfed both churches and monasteries. The church leaders most preoccupied with these conflicts attempted to justify the use of violence to protect church property and people.[11]

The Carolingian empire in the eighth century reestablished social stability. Charlemagne, whom the pope crowned as Emperor of the Roman Empire of the West, inflicted his "Latin" Christianity on all the people he conquered. He dissolved the ethical injunction against violence. His 797 Law Code for the Saxon territories instituted a death penalty on resisters.

---

11. Thomaš Mastnak, *Crusading Peace: Christendom, the Muslim World, and Western Political Order* (Berkeley: University of California Press, 2002), traces the church's slow devolution into violence in this period that culminated in the crusades.

Charlemagne used the cross in imitation of the legend of Constantine, as a symbol that inspired his battle victories against enemies of the empire. Charlemagne, however, added his own twist to that use. His imperial cross waged war on the enemies of God, a symbol, not just of the empire's victories over military enemies, but also over the forces of evil, unmediated by the ethical injunctions of the church against unjust wars and shedding human blood.

Carolingian missionaries to Saxon lands preached vividly the suffering of Jesus on the cross to show what Saxon sins had done to him. As innocent victim, Jesus' corpse replaced the real victims of the Carolingian sword who were transformed into the sinful murderers of Christ. The Saxons were to regard their suffering at the hands of their Christian conquerors as divine punishment for their sins. Augustine's idea of original sin became the prevailing view of human nature. Jesus' death eternally revealed that sin. Through this network of ideological control united with the sword, Charlemagne attempted to impose loyalty to his empire.[12]

In the wake of this preaching, a debate erupted in the 830s between the Saxon and Carolingian theologians about the meaning of the Eucharist. The Carolingian theologian Paschasius Radbertus offered a new interpretation: the Saxon Eucharist no longer contained the risen Lord whose power of spirit filled all who took the bread and cup. Instead, their Eucharist contained the crucified blood and flesh of the Lord. In proposing that the eucharistic elements were the literal body and blood of the crucified Christ, Paschasius reinterpreted the Eucharist as an encounter with Christ the Judge. Unrepentant Saxon sinners dared not approach the Eucharist without having performed sufficient penance, or they would eat and drink damnation.

The ninth-century Archbishop Hincmar went further in sanctifying violence, suggesting that the Mass reenacted Christ's crucifixion. He proclaimed, "Declare him killed and offer him to be sacrificed in his mystery."[13] He said that by eating the flesh and drinking the blood of the crucifixion, repentant Christians obtained the benefit of Christ's sacrificial death on the cross, which redeemed the sins of humanity.

12. The theological changes in Christianity during the Carolingian period are analyzed in Celia Martin Chazelle, *The Crucified God in the Carolingian Era: Theology and Art of Christ's Passion* (New York: Cambridge University Press, 2001), and Rachel Fulton, *From Judgment to Passion: Devotion to Christ and the Virgin Mary, 800-1200* (New York: Columbia University Press, 2002).

13. Hincmar, quoted in Chazelle, *The Crucified God*, pp. 218-19.

Theologians in Saxony and elsewhere reasserted the traditional resurrection-based theology of the Eucharist. They were denounced, stripped of their priestly offices, flogged, and imprisoned. Their texts were burned. The ensuing conflict about the Eucharist would not be fully resolved — in Paschasius's favor — until the middle of the eleventh century under Pope Gregory VII. Believing otherwise was declared heresy.

Now, instead of having defeated the power of death and living eternally in divine beauty and glory, Jesus Christ's power was in dying. His death judged humanity's violence against God, not against other human beings. Every Christian was a crucifier of Christ the victim, judged by the blood of the cross. At every Eucharist, the eternal and feared presence of the crucified Christ accused communicants of killing him. Life everlasting in paradise on earth receded into the afterlife, eventually disappearing into the ever-delayed hope of a post-apocalyptic new world.

The Atonement and the Eros of Violence

With the momentum of these theological shifts, Pope Urban II could promise in 1095, when he launched the first crusade, that all who "took the cross" could count their duty as penance for sin. The pope promised that, if the crusaders died, all their financial debts would be forgiven and they would immediately enter paradise. Killing or being killed in God's name became a holy act and the fastest route to salvation. Genocide became the fulfillment of divine justice against all enemies deemed "evil."

Three years later, Anselm of Canterbury reinforced the pope's ideas by underscoring Jesus' death as payment of the debt of sin. In *Why God Became Man,* Anselm constructed a coldly rational theology to support the crucifixion-centered Mass and holy war, setting salvation in feudal terms of debt, retribution, and justice. Anselm said the sole reason for the incarnation was for Christ to die to restore God's honor. He failed even to mention the resurrection. He taught a spiritual piety, not of desire, but of intense terror of hell.

Peter Abelard, younger than Anselm by twenty years, opposed the crusades and criticized Anselm:

Indeed, how cruel and perverse it seems that [God] should require the blood of the innocent as the price of anything, or that it should in any way please Him that an innocent person should be slain — still less that

God should hold the death of His Son in such acceptance that by it He should be reconciled with the whole world.[14]

Theologians of the twelfth century were especially interested in Augustine's idea of the love that transforms faith, but unlike Augustine's sense of love as taking pleasure or joy in God as beauty, Abelard's contemporaries were obsessed with suffering, self-sacrificing love. Augustine's doctrine of original sin was favored especially by Abelard's most vehement foe, the popular and influential Bernard of Clairvaux, who preached the second crusade. Bernard had Abelard condemned for heresy twice, the second time in 1139, just a few years before Abelard died.[15]

Abelard rejected the idea of original sin because we cannot be held guilty for something inherent in our nature. Though humanity did not bear the guilt for Adam, human beings suffered the consequences for his sin. Those innocent of sin could suffer the consequences of the sin of others. Blame for sin, however, lay in intention. Abelard asserted that the intentions of the actor determined the morality of acts. Abelard hung everything on consent, not on behavior. His emphasis on intent, or the consent of the acting agent, is considered a major innovation in ethics. Actions derived their moral value from intent, which only God could judge truly. Actual behavior did not have to occur for sin to be present — consent was the key, though not exclusive, element in sin.

Many in Abelard's time believed that internal urges themselves were sinful. Abelard accepted desire as a neutral capacity of the soul, and he did

---

14. *Epist. Ad Romanos* II, 835D-836A.

15. Abelard's writing is difficult to evaluate. His work was not well preserved, and he never taught long in a single place. He had a tendency to leave books unfinished, and his work is more episodic than systematic. The earlier part of his career was focused on philosophical questions of logic and dialectic. For analyses of his theology, see Daniel F. Blackwell, *Non-Ontological Constructs: The Effects of Abelard's Logical and Ethical Theories on His Theology — A Study in Meaning and Verification* (New York: Peter Lang, 1988); George P. Fedotov, *Peter Abelard: The Personality, Self-Consciousness, and Thought of a Martyr of "Enlightenment"* (Vaduz, Liechtenstein: Büchervertriebsanstalt, 1988); Leif Grane, *Peter Abelard: Philosophy and Christianity in the Middle Ages* (London: Allen & Unwin, 1970); John Marenbon, *The Philosophy of Peter Abelard* (New York: Cambridge University Press, 1997); J. Ramsay McCallum, *Abelard's Christian Theology* (Merrick, NY: Richwood, 1976); Richard E. Weingart, *The Logic of Divine Love: A Critical Analysis of the Soteriology of Peter Abelard* (Oxford: Clarendon Press, 1970); and Paul L. Williams, *The Moral Philosophy of Peter Abelard* (Lanham, MD: University Press of America, 1980), who develops his thinking in a variety of ways, from Enlightenment categories to orthodox ones.

not believe that any particular act was either inherently good or evil. He neither disparaged desire nor denied the ambiguity of what people desired. Behavior could be morally evaluated only when a moral agent consented to evil, in other words, intended evil, not because people had desires or personal weaknesses, which everyone had.

Abelard based his understanding of atonement on divine grace, which was the boundless love of God for sinful humans. He contrasted this divine generosity with the Anselmian lack or need in God that required a ransom or substitution. For Abelard the atonement revealed the objective, already-completed aspect of divine love. God, omnipotent, omniscient, and good, created the best of all possible worlds; the Fall created the need for the atonement, which created a deeper love for God than would have been possible without it.

Abelard's most important move in explicating his theory of the atonement was to reject Anselm's notions of rational jurisprudence and replace them with the pieties of personal relationship. He said incarnation was most exemplified in the crucifixion. God gave the ultimate sacrifice of his own Son to reach out in selfless love to sinners, not to restore his own honor. Through his suffering, Christ proved the extent of this love. As supreme moral exemplar, Christ was patient in suffering, steadfast in prayer, perfect in obedience, and selfless in sacrificing for others. This sacrifice indicted all sinners and asked them to recognize their sinfulness. To consent to follow Christ's example effected the inner transformation of the human soul, the animating principle that provided human beings with a new incentive to accept the cup of salvation and walk in righteousness by a change of heart.

Abelard asserted that only love, *dilectio,* of God could guide the will to do good because God was the highest good. Estrangement from God came from self-love, which caused humans to fail in their filial responsibility to love God selflessly. Hence, love must be motivated without regard for self. Salvation lay in the turn of heart toward love of God, without fear of punishment or hope of reward. Selfless love of God meant to desire what God required for God alone, absent all self-interest and inconstancy.

In imitating Christ, Christians followed the moral example of the crucified Christ, submitting to crucifixion to demonstrate love. Selfless love for God in response to grace was, therefore, the ultimate basis for Christian ethics. All other love flowed from this selfless love for God. The neighbor was loved through love of God, for the sake of God. Actual people injured by sin played no necessary part in the process of repentance, and restitu-

tion for those sinned against was not required for absolution. The efficacy
of absolution came from an internal change of heart, not the outward action of the church and its representatives.

Abelard's theory of the atonement presents different and greater dangers than that of Anselm. Anselm framed the death of Jesus in objective jurisprudence terms and made redemption a one-time occurrence. The
event only needed to be accepted as true to be efficacious. Abelard used the
framework of feudal filial piety, setting crucifixion in terms of family relationships; his atonement is based in love for the crucified victim and a desire to fuse with and to be like him. The depth of divine love for sinners
was revealed in the extremity of Christ's suffering — the more hardened
and recalcitrant the sinner, the greater must be the emphasis on suffering
to effect a change of heart and a desire to change. Anselm's driver toward
salvation was fear. For Abelard it is desire for self-annihilation.

By reducing sin, love, and absolution to individual consent and identification with Christ, the supreme victim, Abelard turned knowledge of sin
inward into the soul's experience of guilt, contrition, and repentance. The
fullest desire is the desire to suffer and to die for love. The ideal of selfless
love begs the question of what remains as love when there is no self to consent to love. It also begs the moral question of who or what holds unrepentant perpetrators of violence accountable for their sin.

Abelard defines love as powerless passivity. His selfless love was a form
of passive acceptance, of willingness to suffer, to endure the sin of others.
As he notes: "*Love has its origin in goodness. . . . Goodness, in fact, is not
power* or wisdom, and *to be good is not to be wise or powerful.*"[16] Abelard
grounded love in Jerome's and Augustine's Trinity, describing the Spirit as
the bond between Father and Son. As many have noted, this version of the
Trinity made the Spirit a very weak third party, more a bond than a full
third person.

As with Anselm's theory, Abelard's atonement had no role for the resurrection, no escape from perpetual dying for God. Because his Holy
Spirit was an internal transaction between Father and Son, the community
was not a category in Abelard's theology. He lacked a robust sense of ongoing incarnation in this life. Abelard provided no means for individual accountability to community as a place where God dwelt and encountered
persons. The individual's relationship to God and to him- or herself determined innocence of sin or guilt — an individual subjectivism at its most

16. McCallum, *Abelard's Christian Theology,* pp. 46, 88. Italics added.

narrow, a form of self-scrutiny without grounding in anything beyond its own turning on itself.

Abelard's atonement confuses violence and love. This confusion is psychologically accurate. Recent work in trauma studies, especially on the psychological effects of repeated, inescapable violence, shows that violence can destroy healthy distinctions between selves. Perpetrators of violence see their victims as extensions of their own needs, rather than as distinct selves, what psychologists call narcissism. Abelard's critique of self-interest can be applied to the dangers of this sort of narcissism, a critique he raises against his own predatory behavior toward his student, lover, and wife Heloise. However, narcissism is not overcome by witnessing violence, which is what he suggests in his theory of the atonement. In creating a narcissistic structure for salvation and moral responsibility, Abelard provided no way for Christians to participate in each other's journeys toward greater moral virtue and nearness to God, in the community of saints, filled with the Holy Spirit.

Abelard sought both to use and to deny desire. His redemptive relationship is the bonding of the contrite perpetrator and loving victim. The more the perpetrator could imagine Christ's suffering, the stronger was the sinner's emotional trigger, or desire, to bond with the victim. He noted that the crucifixion was necessary because, without it, human beings would not love God as profoundly as they could in gratitude for Christ's suffering. With this theology, Abelard romanticized suffering, violence, and death and intertwined them with desire as a necessary condition for redemption. He eroticized them into sadomasochism, as if the only conceivable response to witnessing violence was guilt, gratitude, and love, as opposed to outrage, revulsion, and resistance. He made witnessing extreme suffering ethically necessary to evoke compassion, repentance, a change of heart, and a loss of self for the sake of union with the victim — self-annihilation or, in other words, the end of subjective desire.

Abelard's chief opponent and nemesis, Bernard of Clairvaux, had a more active understanding of love and desire and more successfully joined love and crucifixion to eros as an ongoing love of violence. He became the most sought-out preacher and religious advisor of his time. In sixty-seven sermons on the Song of Songs, Bernard led his monks to follow the path to mystical, erotic union with God, casting the feminine soul as the seeker of God.[17]

17. For discussions of popular love poetry in the twelfth century, which shaped the context for Bernard's interpretation of the Song of Songs, see Michael Routledge, "Songs," in

Bernard called sufferings sweet, and he eroticized torture. He described God's beloved as wounded and disfigured and used her black color in the Song of Songs to mark her as humiliated. The bride's black skin was a sign of her deep pain and therefore her deep love, like the blows Christ endured on the cross. Torture and abuse marked the Bride of Christ, who gloried in the cross of affliction because it united her to Jesus, in mystical, erotic union. Bernard prayed that he would suffer similarly: "Sufferings are their joy equally with their hope. . . . Let me be not merely weak, then, but entirely resourceless, utterly helpless, that I may enjoy the support of the power of the Lord of Hosts!"[18]

For Bernard, who preached the second, disastrous crusade, war forged a new form of love: ecstatic union with Christ's sufferings in life and death. Many have noticed the homoerotic dimensions of Bernard's interest in eros, but love between same-sex people had long been appreciated by Christians, especially in the environments of monastery and convents. Few, however, have discussed how Bernard eroticized violence and pain. The heterodox union of love and war was Bernard's own contribution to atonement theology by which he thwarted Eros's creating of harmony out of chaos. Thus, Bernard's uniting of monks and warriors into a holy army transformed the inebriating grace of paradise into a toxic elixir of violence, suffering piety, and necrophilia.

Conclusion

Abelard and Bernard were harbingers of change in western Europe that would long shape the modern world's understanding of desire and love. Abelard's narcissistic ideal of self-sacrificing love as the highest Christian moral achievement encouraged victims to acquiesce to violence in forgiv-

---

The Oxford Illustrated History of the Crusades, ed. Jonathan Riley-Smith (Oxford: Oxford University Press, 1995), pp. 91-111, and David Nichols, The Evolution of the Medieval World: Society, Government and Thought in Europe, 312-1500 (New York: Longman, 1992), pp. 329-34. See also Caroline Walker Bynum, The Resurrection of the Body in Western Christianity, 200-1336 (New York: Columbia University Press, 1995), and Caroline Walker Bynum and Paul Freedman, eds., Last Things: Death and the Apocalypse in the Middle Ages (Philadelphia: University of Pennsylvania Press, 2000).

18. Bernard, Commentary on the Song of Songs, Sermon 25.8, in The Works of Bernard of Clairvaux: Songs of Songs II, trans Killian Walsh (Kalamazoo, MI: Cistercian Publications, 1981), p. 56.

ing, impotent, selfless love. Bernard's faith, loving and yearning, pastoral and kind, had a Janus-face of hatred for infidels and even other Christians, like the Cathars, who opposed the crusades. He sanctified killing for God as a form of love, and he exalted self-abasement as true erotic love, as ecstatic desire.

Christianity moved increasingly toward love that was submissive, broken-hearted, and perpetually unrequited, always longing for final fulfillment. The church in western Europe was once in love with the risen Christ who joined his bride in the earthly garden of delight and helped her tend it. However, beginning in the ninth century, she began to doubt her lover and took a violent Lord into her bed, lay with him, blessed him, and finally, took him into the Christian family by marrying him.

Erotically enthralled by her seductive abuser, the church spawned devotional pieties of fear, sorrow, torture, and death, whose progeny journeyed into the world determined to destroy their own shadows and neighbors. To solidify this unholy union, the church sacrificed her former love by killing him repeatedly and partaking of his mutilated body. She told herself that conquest, genocide, and the colonization of Jerusalem were God's will, a holy pilgrimage that would someday, if she sacrificed and suffered enough, deliver salvation, end the violence, and restore her to her first love. This delusional pattern would later carry conquistadors and pilgrims to the Americas and leave Jerusalem as one of the most contested cities on the planet. To assuage her broken heart and bleeding body, the church told herself that such a marriage was good and pleasing to God. She hung, suspended in eschatological terror and hope, longing elusively for release, relief, and love's fulfillment. They did not come.

The longing for paradise on earth has been a hunger since it was displaced by crucifixion. The hunger is felt in the nostalgia of utopias, in poetic longings, in idealizations of wilderness, and in the romantic movements of the eighteenth and nineteenth centuries. This-worldly forms of Christianity began to participate in democratic movements. Christians began to look again at the New Testament kingdom of God traditions and their vision of justice on earth as it is in heaven. Supernatural promises of an afterlife were displaced by calls to create justice and peace in this life. These forms of post-Enlightenment, modern Christianity have at least unlocked again and, perhaps, opened a crack in the portals of paradise that the atonement had closed.

Love for the living, incarnate, and risen Christ is a different piety and moral sensibility than love for the suffering, dying Christ. Faithfulness to the risen Christ means commitment to the body of Christ, sustained by works of love. The early church did not expect individual conscience and personal feelings to bear the entire burden of sin and repentance. Moral responsibility involved an interactive, relational process of self-scrutiny and accountability to the community of the Spirit, which used the rituals of baptism and Eucharist to train desire for right love and right works.

Love for beauty; care for the material life that gives pleasure and joy; appreciation for the numinous world, revealed by the Spirit in life; and embrace of the eros that empowers human beings as social creatures to seek others — these are spiritual powers that deliver salvation. They are elusive, fleeting, and stubbornly persistent. They ground the struggle for justice and the journey to God in a response to the gift of life in this world and a desire to see it flourish. They encourage a responsibility for the common good motivated, not out of violence, guilt, and selflessness, but out of gratitude, generosity, and joy. They enable us to see that the atonement theology that haunts the western imagination should be unimaginable in paradise, which is our salvation in this life and any other lives to come.

Another Christianity is possible. It begins when we understand that paradise is already present. Paradise is not withheld, closed, or removed from us. Realizing this requires us to let go of the notion that paradise is life without struggle, life free from wrestling with legacies of injustice and current forces of evil. Assuredly, we are in a world in which the struggle continues. However, it is also true that we already live on holy ground, in the presence of God, with bodies and souls sanctified by the Spirit's anointing, surrounded by the communion of saints. Our spiritual challenge is to live facing into this reality: histories of harm are all around us, current forces of evil operate within and among us, and everywhere, the bushes are on fire, the risen Christ is with us on the road, the Spirit rises in the wind, the rivers of paradise circle the earth, and the fountain of wisdom springs up from the earth we walk on, from this holy ground.

We reenter this world as sacred space when we love life fiercely, and, in the name of love, protect the goodness of our intricate web of life in all its manifold forms. We recommit ourselves to this world as holy ground when we remember the fullness of life that is possible through our communities, our life-affirming rituals, and our love of beauty, of truth, of goodness. Thus immersed in the flow of desiring, we find ourselves more responsive to and responsible for life in this world. We give thanks for gifts of love that have been ours all along, an ever-widening circle of beauty, the Spirit in life, the heart of our deepest desires, our most saving desires.

De-Oedipalizing Theology:
Desire, Difference, and Deleuze

F. LeRon Shults

> *Castration, incest, fantasy:* the stuff of psychoanalysis in late modern capitalist societies.

> *Lack, guilt, idealization:* the stuff of traditional Christian interpretations of human desire.

The tragic journey of the figure of Oedipus — from Sophocles to Freud and beyond — has more to do with theology than one might initially think. Both the classical interpretation of the Genesis myth as a "Fall" and the orthodox model of the oedipal conflict articulate their understanding of human desire with privative, punitive, and palliative categories: anxiety, prohibition, and displacement from a desexualized familial paradise. The primarily negative image of the role of desire in traditional theological anthropology and psychoanalysis has contributed to the religious colonization and social repression of human desire that characterizes so much of contemporary western culture.

This chapter is a call for saving desire through *de-oedipalizing* theology. On the one hand, this means looking for ways to liberate theology from its reliance on the notion of human desire as the culpable concupiscence of individual souls. On the other hand, it means producing theology in a way that has a de-oedipalizing effect, making a difference in the world as a liberating force in society. Might the refiguring of theological desire itself engender the transformation of concrete, embodied social structures and help us overcome our dependence on frigid and flaccid intellectual abstractions that reinforce repression and oppression?

One relatively untapped resource for this reconstructive theological task is the work of Gilles Deleuze, who understands desire *positively* in relation to production, joy, and immanence, rather than *negatively* defined in relation to lack, guilt, and transcendence. The concept "Oedipus" is used by Deleuze to indicate a wide range of forces (sexual and social) that constrain and organize desire by tying it to insufficiency, law, and idealization. He blames this "triple curse" on "the priest" (understood broadly as the social inscription of these repressive forces, whether executed by theologians, psychoanalysts, or other figures). Deleuze's *oeuvre* celebrates and aims to facilitate "other" forces, those that liberate, deterritorialize, and draw lines of flight. To what extent can we appropriate Deleuze as we seek opportunities for saving theology from its negative modeling of human desire? Can he help us escape from "Oedipus"? Do we really want him to?

1. Dealing with Deleuze

Approaching Deleuze as a potential resource for Christian theology is both promising and perilous; his work creates both opportunities for and challenges to the task of saving desire. A prima facie reading of Deleuze's corpus could lead one to think he is not worth dealing with at all. His complex and idiosyncratic terminology can be off-putting and confusing for newcomers, and his detailed treatment of philosophical thinkers and movements throughout history often makes for difficult reading. In addition to the formal difficulty in entering his conceptual world, some readers might find some of Deleuze's material claims and imaginative ideas curious or even offensive. The primary audience for the current book is Christian theologians who are (or might become) concerned with saving desire. Although few (if any) of us will follow Deleuze all the way, I think most (if not all) of us need to follow him farther than we might initially like. So let me begin with a few words of introduction intended to encourage us not to give up too quickly; the theoretical and practical payoff of engaging Deleuze may be well worth the effort.

Some theologians might view with suspicion the fact that Deleuze takes Oedipus so seriously, fearing that this is a return to outdated and problematic debates surrounding classical Freudian psychoanalysis and its role in reinforcing patriarchy and promoting sexist interpretations of human desire. Such a quick dismissal would be unfortunate, because a careful reading of Deleuze shows that his *anti*-oedipal efforts can support many of the concerns of feminist (and liberationist) theologians. As we will see, Deleuze's engagement with Oedipus challenges orthodox psycho-analysis theory and practice at its philosophical core. Far from accepting the Freudian imposition of the same masculine (phallocentric) pattern on the development of all "normal" subjects, for Deleuze all movement, all becoming, begins with and passes through "becoming-woman."[1] This may feel alien to us, but it is certainly not a return to the problematic Freudian anthropology from which twentieth-century feminism struggled to liberate us.

In this chapter I hope to show how Deleuze may be a resource for de-oedipalizing theology in a way that is complementary to the insights of many of the other contributors. In the previous chapter, Rita Brock observed the extent to which most western atonement theory in the last millennium has been dominated by the imagery of legal payments and punishments between a divine Father and Son. The payoff (for human beings) in these kinds of theories was no longer an experience of paradise that heals us now in this world (as in the early church) but an otherworldly paradise that can be experienced only after our own suffering. As Christina Grenholm and Wendy Farley will show in the next two chapters, much Christian theology has ignored or repressed the experience of mothering and the importance of everyday practices in the formation of desire. We may not accept all of Deleuze's philosophy, but his resistance to male-dominated construals of law and idealization and his attention to the joyful practice of productive desire suggest that he may be an ally in our attempts at saving desire.

A second objection could be that Deleuze's approach appears to be simply one more version of nihilism, which provides us with no criteria for moral judgment or any hope for relating to the Good. Such a concern is understandable since his philosophical heroes include Lucretius, Hume, Spinoza, and Nietzsche — all of whom are typically seen as inimical to and destructive of traditional theology and moral philosophy. Part of our goal in this book is to contribute to the theological discussion of the formation of desire in right relation to God. The last two chapters in this volume, by Christine Yoder on erotic desire and divine wisdom and by Jayne Svenungsson on the importance of pathos and justice (human and divine), are particularly focused on this crucial aspect of theological dis-

1. Cf. Gilles Deleuze and Félix Guattari, *A Thousand Plateaus*, trans. B. Massumi (New York: Continuum, 1987 [French, 1980]), p. 306.

course on desire. A hurried reader of Deleuze will not have difficulty finding comments that suggest that he wants us to abandon our repressive shackles and let our desires run wild, without any heed to criteriological questions about justice or love. If this were the whole story, Deleuze would indeed be simply an enemy of Christian theology. In fact, Deleuze is concerned about struggling against destructive forms of "justice" (e.g., totalitarianism, fascism) and against destructive expressions of "love" (e.g., addiction, paranoia). The more serious challenge is the way in which Deleuze deals with the notions of the responsible subject and the social construction of desire. As Jan-Olav Henriksen argued in the first chapter, desiring preconditions subjectivity. The experience of desiring can be opening or closing, that is, orienting a "subject" toward the ongoing reception of new life as gift or toward a satiating grasping of a particular object. As Ola Sigurdson observed in the second chapter, the formation of (open or closed) desire — in relation to the self, others, and God — is socially produced. Sigurdson pointed to the special role of movies in the production of desire; in another venue it would be helpful to explore the extent to which Deleuze's massive philosophical treatment of the cinema[2] could provide a resource for ecclesiological analysis of this phenomenon. For our purposes here, however, the focus will be on acknowledging some of the ways in which the church itself has produced negative desire and negated the desiring-production of its "subjects," and on exploring new possibilities for redeeming desire.

A third possible objection to dealing with Deleuze might arise in relation to his rejection of transcendence and his metaphysical valorizing of the plane of immanence. This might initially appear to be another naïve philosophical version of materialism, which has little (if anything) to offer a theological project that is serious about engaging the infinite as in some sense "Creator" (much less "Redeemer"). However, this dismissal would also be unfortunate. Deleuze's work is just beginning to be engaged and appropriated theologically, albeit critically and cautiously,[3] with special at-

---

2. Deleuze, *Cinema I — The Movement Image*, trans. H. Tomlinson and B. Habberjam (New York: Continuum, 1986 [French, 1983]), and *Cinema II — The Time Image*, trans. H. Tomlinson and R. Galeta (New York: Continuum, 1989 [French, 1985]).

3. For example, Peter Hallward, *Out of This World: Deleuze and the Philosophy of Creation* (London: Verso, 2006); Jacob Holsinger Sherman, "No Werewolves in Theology? Transcendence, Immanence and Becoming-Divine in Deleuze," *Modern Theology* 25, no. 1 (January 2009): 1-20. Cf. the briefer treatment of Deleuze in Charles Winquist, *Desiring Theology* (Chicago: University of Chicago Press, 1995).

tention to his "mysticism." Explaining the sense in which this champion of "immanence" could possibly be a resource for mystical theology would take much more space that I have in this chapter. However, in what follows I hope to hint at some ways in which Deleuzian categories might alter the way in which we conceptualize our engagement with what has traditionally been called "transcendence." In fact, as I will argue in the final section, he might even help us develop further some of the most significant late modern trajectories in Christian theology related to Infinity, Trinity, and Futurity.

At the very least, Deleuze is relevant for the purposes of this volume because he has contributed so significantly to turn-of-the-millennium reflection on three of the major themes that run throughout this book: otherness, embodiment, and community. First, Deleuze was one of the key players in the late modern shift toward privileging difference over sameness in philosophy, preferring alterity over identity as a generative category for understanding and articulating human experience.[4] Other chapters in this book critically engage other authors who participated in the shift, such as Jacques Derrida (Jan-Olav Henriksen's phenomenology of gift and giving) and Emmanuel Levinas (Jayne Svenungsson's theology of pathos and emotion). We could also point to other late modern philosophers whose analyses of desire pay special attention to the human experience of limitation of, by, and with finite others and the infinite Other (e.g., Jean-Luc Marion, Paul Ricoeur). However, few scholars push the turn to alterity as far as Deleuze.

As we will see below, his emphasis on difference and repetition (rather than sameness and representation) is at the core of his attempt at a "reversal" of Platonism, which in turn provides the context for his critical analysis of Oedipus and his constructive proposal for understanding the genitality of thought and the productivity of desire. Deleuze argues that the metaphysics of sameness and identity and the dominant western negative attitude toward desire are inextricably intertwined. This suggests that saving desire in practice will require loosing theology from the bonds of Platonic theory. While Deleuze's philosophy of difference does indeed threaten the foundational assumptions upon which so much western Christian theology has been built, it also provides an opportunity for re-

---

4. For a brief historical account, cf. F. LeRon Shults, "The Philosophical Turn to Alterity," in *Christology and Ethics*, ed. F. L. Shults and B. Waters (Grand Rapids: Eerdmans, 2010).

trieving and refiguring marginalized theological voices in the tradition that celebrate the transforming power of desire, in joyful relation to concrete, empirical others.

This brings us to the two other themes in this book that also play a central role in Deleuze's thought in general and his understanding of desire in particular: sexuality and sociality. Paying philosophical attention to otherness somewhat naturally leads to an emphasis on embodiment and community. Most of our interesting experiences of alterity are socially mediated encounters with bodies — others' and our own. Other chapters in the present book explore and expand theological discourse on the erotic or gendered politics of desire (Cristina Grenholm on the role of mothers and Christine Yoder on the proverbial woman of wisdom) as well as its economic and cultural dimensions (Rita Nakashima Brock on the embrace of worldly paradise and Ola Sigurdsson on the social production of desire) or both (Wendy Farley on consumer culture and the retrieval of the mystical tradition's erotic embrace of the divine).

After centuries of sexual repression, we can understand why Deleuze's references to bodily orifices and genitalia, or his critique of patriarchal forms of family organization, would make many Christians nervous. After centuries of the dominance of Platonic metaphysical dualism and the hermeneutical category of sameness (identity), we can understand why many theologians might feel worried by his stress on the univocity of being and the creative power of difference (alterity). After centuries of pervasive individualism, we can understand why Deleuze's critique of the social formation of the "subject" and its desires, not to mention his celebration of the forces of deterritorialization, would threaten classical models of theological anthropology and ecclesiology. Many will worry that Deleuze goes too far, that his vision of desire is *too* positive. Is the metaphysical, epistemic, and ethical cost for ransoming desire from Plato too high? Are we willing to pay this philosophical price for saving desire?

However, we should not miss the opportunity here. Deleuze's radically new set of conceptual resources may shock us out of our habit of discussing desire primarily in terms of the prohibited bodily desires of individuals, and open us up for fresh insights into — and for redemptive practices of — the joyful production of desire that transgresses and heals social boundaries. Perhaps an engagement with different thought forms, such as the Stoic-inspired concepts of singularities, events, and multiplicities, will be required in order to produce a positive theology of desire. This will be a difficult pill to swallow for those who *identify* the Christian tradition with formulations that are saturated by Platonic categories. We should take such concerns seriously. As we explore this new conceptual space, however, it will also be important to attend to the ways in which our own forms of social embodiment are shaped by fear as well as desire. If for no other reason, it is worth staying engaged with Deleuze (at least for a while) because he will force us to think about the extent to which our understanding of desire has been shaped not only by lack, but also by particular socially embedded constructions of law and idealization.

2. Becoming-Oedipal?

How did we — or do we — become oedipalized in the first place? What exactly does Deleuze mean by "Oedipus"? On the one hand, he means the Freudian appropriation of the literary figure of Oedipus, the tragic mythological hero in Sophocles' story who fulfills — precisely by trying to avoid — a prophecy that he would kill his father and marry his mother, to refer within psychoanalytic theory to the family dynamics that shape the subjectivity of every child. On the other hand, his critique of this theory involves an exploration of the ways in which broader social dynamics also inscribe and repress and evoke desire all at the same time. As we will see below, for Deleuze "Oedipus" stands for all the forces that establish or reinforce the threefold "priestly curse" on desire, including not only family triangulation and the capitalist socius but also the whole philosophical realm of Platonic representation dominated by the category of sameness.

The figure of Oedipus pops up at key points throughout Deleuze's theoretical magnum opus *Difference and Repetition*[5] and dominates several of the chapters in *The Logic of Sense*.[6] Attention to the sexual and social dynamics that organize thinking and language is even more prominent in Deleuze's collaboration with (anti)psychoanalyst Félix Guattari in *Anti-Oedipus* and *A Thousand Plateaus*.[7] These two volumes together form their broader project titled *Capitalism and Schizophrenia*. The significance of

5. G. Deleuze, *Difference and Repetition*, trans. Paul Patton (New York: Columbia University Press, 1994 [French, 1968]); cf. especially pp. 87-89, 92-93, and 195.

6. G. Deleuze, *The Logic of Sense*, trans. Mark Lester (New York: Continuum, 2004 [French, 1969]); cf. especially the 27th through 32nd "series" of this book.

7. G. Deleuze and F. Guattari, *Anti-Oedipus*, trans. R. Hurley, M. Seem, and H. R. Lane (New York: Continuum, 1983 [French, 1972]), and *A Thousand Plateaus*, trans. B. Massumi (New York: Continuum, 1987 [French, 1980]).

these terms for their understanding of desire will become clear in our exploration of these dynamics below (§§4-5).

From a psychoanalytic perspective, the oedipal task arises in the "genital" phase of development, during which the child is supposed to resolve the earlier issues that arose related to the oral and anal phases. Early Freudian theory was formulated with a primary focus on boys: competition with the father evokes fear (castration anxiety), and the longing to connect with the mother evokes guilt (incest prohibition).[8] The "resolution" of the oedipal conflict, according to classical psychoanalysis, is "assuming one's sex," which means resignation in either case: the boy's renunciation of male protest against other males and the girl's renunciation of the desire for a penis. The intentional self emerges and solidifies as the child integrates what has gone on subconsciously in the anal and oral phases, now consciously defining the self in relation to and distinction from mommy-daddy. The underlying chaotic urges of the unconscious are converted into desexualized energy, through which one can regulate oneself in relation to the "images" of the father and the mother, "represented" in consciousness.

Deleuze and Guattari are critical of this theory at several levels, but they also recognize the sense in which it points to a real (repressive) phenomenon. There is a kind of triangulation and colonization of desire within the family, powerfully at work in the very formation of the subject. The emergence of intentionality is shaped by the child's increased recognition of the sexual distinction between the father and the mother (or other adults), which exerts pressure on the child to adapt to his or her sexual role in a particular society. Becoming-oedipal involves moving from the unregulated systems of mouth-anus or aliment-excrement, in which "bodies burst and cause other bodies to burst," into a new "genitally" organized system in which we "think" and use language to manage our relations with others, and fit into society according to a prescribed sexual "identity."

The psychoanalytic solution is the engendering of an individual subject who resolves the fear of castration that elicits a desire to kill the father, and the guilt associated with the prohibition of sex with the mother, a subject who comes-to-be through the internalizing of socially constructed idealized images that are always displaced into a fantasized future. In a

---

8. Like many later psychoanalysts, such as Lacan, Klein, and others, Deleuze and Guattari are critical of Freud's use of the idea of penis-envy and challenge his way of relying on the concept of "phallus." However, they do acknowledge the sense in which the genital "zone" is at play in the binding together of the other partial zones (orality, anality).

sense oedipalization does "help" us deal with the anguish and culpability surrounding our felt incapacity to control our desires. The process of becoming a conscious "thinking" self involves the regulation of desire so that an intentional subject emerges — defined by anxiety and lack, on the one hand, and fear of punishment, on the other. The oedipal self appears within and is organized by its orientation toward an idealized healed family. Even if we reject the Freudian theory in its details, there is an important intuition behind it; although most of us do not want to kill our fathers or sleep with our mothers, all of us are (more or less) anxious about our *power* over others and the possibility of our *intimacy* with others.

Deleuze and Guattari also point out that the oedipal regulation of desire within the triangulation of the idealized family creates a double bind. "Oedipus creates both *the differentiations that it orders and the undifferentiated with which it threatens us.* . . . Oedipus says to us: either you will internalize the differential functions that rule over the exclusive disjunctions, and thereby 'resolve' Oedipus, or you will fall into the neurotic night of imaginary identification."[9] On the one hand, oedipalization inserts desire into familial triangulation, setting the task of following the lines of differentiation between daddy-mommy-me. But at the same time it prohibits desire from being satiated within this triangulation. Despite his pious intentions, the mythical hero Oedipus is, according to Deleuze, ultimately and inevitably destructive. The story *always* ends tragically (for each of us) because the conditions that structure the task of becoming-subject are both created and blocked by the regulation and repression of all the depths of desire that emerge from the chaotic unconscious.

3. The Oedipalization of Christian Theology

What does any of this have to do with theology? In *A Thousand Plateaus* Deleuze and Guattari suggest that "every time desire is betrayed, cursed, uprooted from its field of immanence, a priest is behind it." The priestly betrayal or cursing of desire is threefold: the negative law, the extrinsic rule, and the transcendental ideal.[10] The figure of Oedipus lurks in the background: lack, guilt, and idealization. It is no accident that these curses and betrayals of desire are attributed to the figure of "the priest." In *Anti-*

9. Deleuze and Guattari, *Anti-Oedipus*, p. 87.
10. Deleuze and Guattari, *A Thousand Plateaus*, p. 171.

Oedipus, Deleuze and Guattari had listed the three errors concerning desire as lack, law, and signifier. These notions inevitably drag "their *theological* cortege behind — insufficiency of being, guilt, signification."[11] Following Nietzsche (and Freud on this point) Deleuze lays much of the blame for the repression of desire in the lap of ecclesiastics. The other social force that is a favored target for blame in relation to the cursing of desire is psychoanalysis, which he believes is too easily prone to inscribe these three negative features of desire: the negative law of lack, the external rule of pleasure, and the transcendent ideal of fantasy.

Nevertheless, Deleuze views religion as the basic force that represses the will to power.[12] In *The Logic of Sense,* to which we will return below, Deleuze links the "religious man" to anguish and culpability, attacking the mythology of theological phantasm that presupposes an ideal capacity for infinite pleasure (and pain). Deleuze does not engage *Christian* theology in any detail, and when he does it is often through stereotypes. Rather than quickly taking a defensive stance against the Deleuzian challenge, in this context I try to listen carefully to his critique and acknowledge those places where there is some basis in fact to such stereotypes. We should admit that there is some correlation between oedipalization, the "priestly" cursing of desire, and Christian theology.

The three negative features of desire were dyed into the fabric of some streams of the western theological tradition that followed Augustine's interpretation of the Genesis myth as a "Fall" — as the shameful loss of paradise. For Augustine desire is — quite literally — a sexually transmitted disease. Because of the first parents' transgressing of a divine prohibition human desire is now deficient and damaged. Diseased inordinate concupiscence and the guilt associated with it are passed on to each new individual soul through sexual procreation. Desire is the problem. The solution is God's provision of the just penalty for violation of the divine law for (some of) Adam and Eve's offspring. This material linking of "fallen" human desire to damaged human sexuality has clearly registered its effect on the Christian understanding of salvation as a future ideal. Those who believe the right things and accept their lack and guilt, repressing their earthly desires, may receive idealized, spiritual pleasures in heaven.

Many late modern theologians have attempted to overcome what

11. Deleuze and Guattari, *Anti-Oedipus,* p. 121; italics added.
12. Cf. Deleuze, *Nietzsche and Philosophy,* trans. H. Tomlinson (New York: Columbia University Press, 2006 [French, 1962]), p. 185.

Deleuze calls the first curse — construing desire as *lack* — by engaging and contributing to the discourse among philosophers who construe desire in relation to notions of excess, gratuity, gift, and the arrival of eschatological fullness (e.g., Jean-Luc Marion, Richard Kearney, John Caputo). However, the effect of the second and third curses on the idea and experience of desire have not been as carefully examined in Christian theology. This is unfortunate because, if Deleuze is right, lack, guilt, and idealization all work together. This suggests that the task of saving desire in and for and through theology will require more theoretical attention to and practical experimentation with overcoming traditional ways of regulating desire vis-à-vis law and fantasy.

It will be exceptionally difficult to overcome the oedipalization of Christian theology. The vision of heaven as the recapitulation of a lost desexualized familial paradise, an idealistic (spiritual) celestial reward for repressing our terrestrial (bodily) desires, is deeply embedded in much of the tradition. "The Father" and "the Son" are dominant in most articulations of the economy of salvation, and their relation to the Holy Spirit (and Mother Church) is somewhat ambiguous. The ecclesiastical structure that prevailed throughout most of western church history is characterized by a hierarchy of priests (fathers) under a pope (the Holy Father). The concept of grace has often been dialectically tied to particular conceptions of law. Reconstructing such formulations will be difficult indeed, but this is the task that faces every generation, and a task we must accept if we hope to save desire in and for Christian theology.

The challenge is not only conceptual; de-oedipalizing theology will open up all kinds of practical possibilities that could threaten the dissolution of our cherished political, cultural, and ecclesial forms of life. Theology has traditionally been more comfortable interpreting (working in an abstract world of ideas) than experimenting (playing with changes in the concrete world). Why are we surprised that so much Christian theology is abstract rather than concrete, essentially theoretical rather than pragmatically liberating and transformative? Most theologians in the last few centuries have privileged ideas over appetites, thought over conatus, Descartes over Spinoza.[13] Deleuze prefers the voluntarists over the intellectualists; Scotus and Ockham are the only theologians he cites positively (albeit briefly). As we will see, he invites us to break out of the "ideal" Platonic

---

13. For Deleuze's treatment of the latter, cf. his *Spinoza: Practical Philosophy*, trans. R. Hurley (San Francisco: City Lights Books, 1988 [French, 1970]).

realm of representation within which the West has been imprisoned for over two millennia.

I think it is important to acknowledge that Christian theology has sometimes played a role in casting the "triple curse" on desire, and has itself been triangulated within the repressive oedipal web. The remainder of this essay explores resources in the philosophy of Deleuze that might facilitate the liberation of theological desire. For Deleuze, desire is not defined in relation to insufficiency, prohibition, or transcendent ideals; it is *being* itself, a "clamor of being" between desiring machines and the social. For the authors of *Anti-Oedipus*, "There is only desire and the social, and nothing else."[14] Below we will see that Deleuze's philosophy also has a special place for "nonexistent entities," which provides an opportunity for engagement on explicitly theological grounds. Before exploring this philosophy in more detail (§§6-7), we need to outline (§§4-5) his new way of conceptualizing desire.

4. Anti-Oedipus: Desiring-Production

In *Anti-Oedipus*, Deleuze and Guattari attempt to reverse all three of the curses of "the priest." First, for them, desire has nothing to do with *lack*. It has to do with *production*, and "desiring-production" is at work everywhere; "it breathes, it heats, it eats. It shits and fucks. What a mistake to have ever said *the* id. Everywhere *it* is machines — real ones, not figurative ones: machines driving other machines, machines being driven by other machines, with all the necessary couplings and connections."[15] The classical model of desire presupposes that we must choose between acquisition and production. Once the decision is made on the side of the former, desire becomes an idealistic conception, an idea of a need for something that is *lacked,* which creates longing. For Deleuze, desire "does not lack anything; it does not lack its object." On the contrary, it is rather "the *subject* that is missing in desire, or desire that lacks a fixed subject; there is no fixed subject unless there is repression" (*AO* 28).

In other words, lack appears with Oedipus; only when desire is repressed in the oedipal triangle does a subject emerge who experiences lack,

14. Deleuze and Guattari, *Anti-Oedipus,* p. 31.
15. Deleuze and Guattari, *Anti-Oedipus,* p. 1. Hereafter, this book will be cited in the text as *AO.*

prohibition, and idealization. Defining desire in terms of need and acquisition opened the way for Oedipus, who *converts* unconscious desire to the realm of individual belief. What Deleuze calls "schizoanalysis" is the attempt to "ensure the contrasting *reversion:* restoring the syntheses of the unconscious to their immanent use. De-oedipalizing, undoing the daddy-mommy spider web, undoing the beliefs so as to attain the production of desiring-machines, and to reach the level of economic and social investments where the militant analysis comes into play" (*AO* 123). The triangle is not actually closed. It may seem that first a child has issues with daddy-mommy and then projects this onto boss, police, etc., but in fact the socius is so structured as to be projected into the family, so that desire is locked into it. As we will see in the next section, capitalism is the social machine that creates the double bind, inciting desire by creating lack while at the same time opening up new desires that can never be fulfilled.

For Deleuze, desire is not a mental or psychic reality separate from material production. It is "mechanic," producing the real in the field of the natural and the social. The process of production within and among desiring-machines also consumes (or consummates) by connecting, conjoining, and disjoining. Desiring-machines are systems of interruptions or breaks *(couperes),* i.e., function as breaks in the flow of relations between machines; "everywhere there are break-flows out of which desire wells up, thereby constituting its productivity and continually grafting the process of production onto the product" (*AO* 39-40). He spells this out in terms of three types of syntheses of the unconscious, a "connective" synthesis that withdraws from the whole, a "disjunctive" synthesis that detaches, and a "conjunctive" synthesis that engenders a residuum, "has something left over."

All of these together are what it means to produce, to "carry out real operations of desire in the material world" (*AO* 45). Deleuze and Guattari argue that nature is a process of production and that production is itself already consumption and recording without any mediation by representation (or anything else). Recording and consuming determine production immediately within the process itself. "Hence everything is production: *productions of productions,* of actions and of passions, *productions of recording processes,* of distributions and of coordinates that serve as points of reference; *productions of consumptions,* of sensual pleasures, of anxieties and of pain" (*AO* 4). Consumptions are produced and recordings are consummated immediately within all processes, so that in a very real sense everything is production.

What about the second curse? Deleuze's metaphysics of desire as production (recording-consumption) is also meant to overcome the oedipalizing force of *law-guilt*. Like Nietzsche, he affirms a kind of transvaluation of all values, insisting that any morality that begins with prohibition and the subjection of people to guilt (resignation and ressentiment) is "slave morality." Such desire is saturated by sadness and weakness, while Deleuze celebrates the constructive power of joyful desire (*AO* 123). One way to contrast Deleuze's understanding of desire from one based on *prohibition* is by explaining his idea of constructing a "body without organs." It is no accident that his treatment of the triple curse of "the priest" who inscribes law and prohibition occurs in a chapter called "How Do You Make Yourself a Body without Organs?" in *A Thousand Plateaus*. You cannot desire without making a body without organs (BwO). What is it? "[Y]ou're already on it. . . . On it we sleep, live our waking lives, fight — fight and are fought, seek our place, experience untold happiness and fabulous defeats; on it we penetrate and are penetrated; on it we love."[16]

The BwO is not something we interpret or from which we interpret; it is that which "causes intensities to pass," that in or on which experimentation of desiring-machines occurs. It is not a belief or a concept, but a set of practices. Making a BwO does not mean constructing a subject, a self with an "identity," an *organized* body. It is experimentation with the lines of forces that escape organization; it involves relating, connecting, deciding, consummating, in short — producing. The BwO is not defined by any external measure that prohibits or lures desire, any more than by a lack that hollows it out. It is "the *field of immanence* of desire, the *plane of consistency* specific to desire" (*TP* 170). Resisting external limits to desire, Deleuze writes of the joy that is immanent to the flow of desire itself. This is a joy "that implies no lack or impossibility and is not measured by pleasure since it is what distributes intensities of pleasure and prevents them from being suffused by anxiety, shame and guilt" (*TP* 172).

Deleuze's opposition to the third curse on desire — the *ideal signifier* — can also be illustrated by pointing to the idea of the BwO. "Signifiance" is one of the "strata" that attempt to bind us. We are told, "You will be signifier and signified, interpreter and interpreted — otherwise you're just a deviant" (*TP* 177). But against this power of stratification, this dualistically construed "interpretation" of external (ideal) signs, the BwO

16. Deleuze and Guattari, *A Thousand Plateaus*, p. 166. Hereafter, this book will be cited in the text as *TP*.

opposes an "experimentation on the plane." Instead of searching for the signifier or signified, we are to enjoy the connection of desires, conjunction of flows, and continuum of intensities that is the BwO. This challenges the idea of simple distinction between desires (or objects of desire) that are objectively true or false. But Deleuze does not mean that there is no need for discernment, no distinctions at all in desiring-production. Rather, the task is "distinguishing within desire between that which pertains to stratic proliferation, or else too-violent destratification, and that which pertains to the construction of the plane of consistency (keep an eye out for all that is fascist, even inside us, and also for the suicidal and the demented)" (*TP* 183).

It is important to note that Deleuze does not deny all structure or all signing. Rather, he is against models of signification that are dominated by the ideal, by an allegedly transcendent signifier that "means" something the subject must "recognize." Deleuze takes this dualistic semiotics to be a negative vestige of Platonism. The body without organs is not a "subject" who searches for what a transcendent signifier "means." Significance is not about abstract representation of meaning that transcends the subject, but about doing, experimenting, producing. Even reading a text is production. Reading is not a "search of what is signified, still less a highly textual exercise in search of a signifier. Rather it is a productive use of the literary machine, a montage of desiring-machines, a schizoid exercise that extracts from the text its revolutionary force."[17]

In *The Logic of Sense* Deleuze argues that the Stoics developed a theory of logic and language which allows for the play between signifier and signified, but recognizes that the conditions for this interplay include that the heterogenous series be converted toward a paradoxical element, which is their "differentiator."[18] Sense is that which disposes the conditions for such signification. This appropriation of the Stoics is part of his program of the reversal of Platonism, which he believes requires a transcendent notion of the divine (or God) as the representational Idea that secures knowledge of the Signified. Before outlining the contours of this philosophical program

17. Deleuze and Guattari, *Anti-Oedipus*, p. 116. Deleuze prefers a pragmatic view of semiotics, and interestingly engages Charles Peirce at several key points in some of his other writings. Cf. *Proust and Signs* (New York: Continuum, 2008), as well as *Cinema I* and *Cinema II*. Like Peirce, he aims for a semiotics that overcomes idealism. A "symbol" for Deleuze is a "desiring-machine that functions within the social machine, an investment of the social machine by desire" (*Anti-Oedipus*, p. 197).

18. Deleuze, *The Logic of Sense*, p. 60; cf. 164.

(§§6-7), along with its challenges and opportunities for de-oedipalizing Christian theology (§§8-9), let us explore the way in which Deleuze's understanding of desire is inextricably entangled with the *social*.

5. Capitalism and Schizophrenia

"All that exists is desire *and the social.*" Social machines and desiring-production become together. In *Anti-Oedipus,* Deleuze and Guattari explain that "the social and the metaphysical arrive at the same time, in accordance with the two simultaneous meanings of *process,* as the historical process of social production and as the metaphysical process of desiring-production" (*AO* 392). The business of the socius is "to code desire — and the fear, the anguish of decoded flows" (*AO* 153). Capitalism is the social machine that has an intrinsic relation to Oedipus; both are forces that work to colonize us. "We are all little colonies and it is Oedipus that colonizes us" (*AO* 287). If we follow Deleuze on this point, this means that any postcolonial theology will also need to be post-oedipal theology.

To make sense of this connection, we must back up and understand the three types of social machine postulated by Deleuze: the primitive, the despotic, and the capitalist socius, or "savages, barbarians and civilized men." Deleuze is well aware of the "orientalist" overtones of such terminology; his adoption of such phrases is initially shocking but his use of them is ironic — serving his own purposes of constructing a postcolonial, minoritarian, and micropolitical approach to social theory. If one can get past the initial offensiveness (which seems intentional), the radicality of his critical analysis of capitalism quickly begins to emerge. Deleuze argues that each type of social machine produces a *representation,* organizing elements at the "surface" of the socius: "the system of connotation-connection in the savage territorial machine, corresponding to the coding of the flows; the system of subordination-disjunction in the barbarian despotic machine, corresponding to overcoding; the system of coordination-conjunction in the civilized capitalist machine, corresponding to the decoding of the flows" (*AO* 284).

To oversimplify greatly, the "primitive" territorial machine is incapable of coding all the flows of desire, which leads to the "despotic" machine, which overcodes the desires. However, such barbarian or imperial overcoding crushes desire, leaving no escape for the flows, breaks, and "schizzes." The capitalist machine is faced with the task of "decoding and deterritorializing" the flows (*AO* 35-37). This is not understood as a simple linear evolution, for all the forces are present together in every society in different ways. Capitalism presupposes the conditions present in the other social machines. The savage social machine begins the process of coding, having inscribed *lack* within the consciousness of the socius. The despotic social machine overcodes by enforcing *law* in various ways (e.g., imperialism), which results in the ressentiment of the subjects. However, this overcoding is too restrictive and the flows of desires inevitably break out. Capitalism, or "civilized" society, allows and even encourages this schizzing, this deterritorializing and decoding, but at the same time "represents" and internalizes desire as both lack and law. Oedipus lurks within the other social machines, but it is established fully in capitalism.

In other words, capitalism is the social machine that incorporates lack, law, *and the signifier* into desire. How can capitalism decode (allow for schizzes) while simultaneously reterritorializing (colonizing) desires? How can it inscribe both lack and law without overcoding? On the one hand, capitalism decodes the flows that the other social machines code and overcode by effecting "relative breaks," by substituting its own axiomatic, which maintains the energy of the flows "on the body of capital." Through the abstraction of "money," capitalism "axiomatizes" the decoded flows. In capitalism, "representation no longer relates to a distinct object, but to productive activity itself. The socius as full body has become directly economic as capital-money; it does not tolerate any other preconditions." Capitalism substitutes the abstraction of "money" for the very notion of a code, creating an "axiomatic of abstract quantities that keeps moving further and further in the direction of the deterritorialization of the socius" (*AO* 36). We think we are free because we do not see the inscribing instrument; that which has replaced the code is its displaced representative — money. The Signified is hidden but everywhere.

On the other hand, to avoid "barbarism" the social machine of capitalism must *also* reterritorialize the deterritorialized flows. It must avoid letting the flows of desire reach their absolute limit (schizophrenia).[19] It must

---

19. Schizophrenia is the "absolute limit" of every society, because "at the bounds" of all social production it "sets in motion decoded and deterritorialized flows that it restores to desiring-production" (*Anti-Oedipus,* p. 288). It resists the inscription of the socius. The use of the term "schizophrenia" may seem odd, but he does not have in mind what he calls the "artificial" schizophrenics housed in modern mental institutions (*Anti-Oedipus,* p. 5). He means a "healthy" schizophrenia whose "madness" is the result of its resistance to the oedipalizing forces of the capitalist socius.

control the very tendency which it at the same time gives free rein. Against the production of "an awesome schizophrenic accumulation of energy" capitalism brings to bear the powers of repression, inhibiting the tendency by struggling to reterritorialize desires in the form of bureaucracy, war, etc. Capitalism "axiomatizes with one hand what it decodes with the other" (*AO* 267). In other words, it produces a double bind; arousing and opening desire-flows that can never be (must never be) satiated. Capitalism works only when it simultaneously excites desires (by inscribing lack) and prohibits desires (by inscribing law), both of which are "represented" by capital (inscribing the significance of "money").

Deleuze and Guattari argue that the "family" plays a special role in the capitalist social machine, which helps to explain why it is so intimately tied to Oedipus. The capitalist socius needs an agent that is capable of inscribing the recording surface of desire, an agent that records social production and its consumption. Only such an agent would allow the socius to inscribe a mechanism that both represses desire's potential for revolt and revolution, while masking that inscription. "Such an agent exists: the family" (*AO* 131). Capitalism produces a colonizing triangle within which lack is created along with prohibition of decoded flows, both of which are "represented" and displaced within and by Oedipus. Capital takes upon itself the relations of alliance and filiation. There ensues a "privatization of the family according to which the family ceases to gives its social form to economic reproduction; it is as though disinvested, placed outside the field" (*AO* 285). Placed outside the social field, the family simply applies the social axiomatic.

The proposed solution in *Anti-Oedipus* is "schizoanalysis." Deleuze and Guattari reproach psychoanalysis for stifling the order of production by forcing desire into the order of representation, especially oedipalization within the privatized family (*AO* 334). The negative task of schizoanalysis is de-oedipalizing, decastrating, decoding, deterritorializing. The positive task of schizoanalysis is "learning what a subject's desiring-machines are, how they work, with what syntheses, what bursts of energy in the machine, what constituent misfires, with what flows, what chains, and what becomings in each case" (*AO* 371). Because the unconscious *produces* rather than *means,* schizoanalysis foregoes all "interpretation" and embraces "experimentation" with the decoding of flows and the process of desiring-production. The Deleuzian project is the replacement of colonization with nomadology, a process that does not have an idealized goal, but "is always and already complete as it proceeds, and as long as it proceeds" (*AO* 417).

How is this related to *theology* and its negative construal of desire? On the one hand, insofar as Christian organizations are implicated within the capitalist socius, they participate in the colonization of desires. Traditional Christian formation practices have certainly leaned more toward inscribing the repression of desire than experimenting with desiring-production. On the other hand, insofar as Christian doctrine has embraced and reinforced Platonic idealist metaphysics, it has participated in the oedipalization of thought itself. Overcoming this comfortable addiction to Plato will involve more than simply rethinking the focus on individual souls, refiguring the role of sexuality in salvation, and resisting the temptation to project the object of desire onto an ideal transcendent plane. Producing a de-oedipalizing theology will also require a conceptual struggle against the constraints of the Platonic domain of representation that has dominated western philosophy.

6. The Reversal of Platonism

This chapter is not the place for a full engagement with Deleuze's attempted philosophical revolution; our focus here will be on outlining the general contours of those aspects of his proposal that are most relevant for understanding the task of de-oedipalizing theology. These are, first, his privileging of the Different over the Same (this section) and, second, his metaphysical construal of the genitality of thought, of that which engenders or creates temporal consciousness (next section). Both of these have explicitly theological bearing. The two key texts in this regard are his earlier (single-authored) books *Difference and Repetition* and *The Logic of Sense.*

Everything depends, argues Deleuze, on a basic decision between two formulas: "only that which resembles differs" or "only differences can resemble each other." These are two distinct readings of the world. "The first formula posits resemblance as the condition of differences . . . according to the other formula, by contrast, resemblance, identity, analogy and opposition can no longer be considered anything but effects, the products of a primary difference or a primary system of differences."[20] In other words, the first invites us to think difference from the standpoint of a prior simili-

20. Deleuze, *Difference and Repetition*, p. 116. Hereafter, this book will be cited in the text as *DR.*

tude or identity, while the second invites us to think sameness as the product of a deep disparity.

Plato began with the first formula, interpreting the world within the domain of models and copies through "representation." The model is the Same, the copy is the Similar, and knowing occurs when one recognizes that the latter re-presents the former. Aristotle deploys representation in relation to the limited and finite. He extends representation from the "highest genera to the smallest species" in his own distinctive way, but he remains within the representational domain of sameness. Deleuze argues that some Christian theologians attempted to extend representation to the infinite, to render representation itself infinite. This attempt to conquer the infinitely great (Hegel) and the infinitely small (Leibniz) still operates within the domain of representation (*DR* 297). Whether he interprets these authors correctly on every point is less important for our purposes than observing his basic critique: they failed to see that the distinction between finite and infinite does not apply to "the different" in the way it applies to "the same."

In the milieu of representation "difference is posited on the one hand as conceptual difference, and repetition on the other hand as difference without a concept" (*DR* 302). Deleuze believes this is the disastrous confusion: "assigning a distinctive concept of difference is confused with the inscription of difference within concepts in general — the determination of the concept of difference is confused with the inscription of difference in the identity of an undetermined concept" (*DR* 32). When reason is mediated through representation, it is shackled or subjected in four ways: identity, analogy, opposition, and resemblance (*DR* 29). He also refers to this as a quadruple yoke (*DR* 302) or the four iron collars (*DR* 262) of reason. The "quadripartite fetters" that bind difference, or upon which it is crucified, are based on the assumption that "only that which is identical, similar, analogous or opposed can be considered different: *difference becomes an object of representation always in relation to a conceived identity, a judged analogy, an imagined opposition or a perceived similitude*" (*DR* 138).

Deleuze begins differently, arguing for the second formula: "It is always differences which resemble one another, which are analogous, opposed or identical: difference is behind everything, but behind difference there is nothing" (*DR* 57). Difference "must relate different to different without any mediation whatsoever by the identical, the similar, the analogous or the opposed" (*DR* 116-17). This is hard for most of us to understand because our very "thinking" operates within (but oblivious to) the presupposed categories of identity. We conceive of difference as primarily negative, as that which is not the same, that which depends on a prior sameness. Deleuze reverses the priority so that "resemblance is said of internalized difference, and identity of the Different as primary power" (*DR* 300). The shift to the second reading of the world changes everything; Deleuze develops new ways of construing thought, idea, universality, etc. For our purposes, the important point is Deleuze's claim that Plato's idea of knowledge as recognition, which presupposes the resemblance of a copy to a model, makes it impossible to conceive of difference in itself or of repetition for itself.

Platonism is usually understood as the attempt to distinguish between essence and appearance, intelligible and sensible, original and copy, etc. But the real task that drives Plato's project, according to Deleuze, is "selecting among the pretenders, distinguishing good and bad copies," between copies that are well founded in the original idea and the simulacra that are engulfed in dissimilarity.[21] The reversal of Platonism involves the "rising" of the simulacra, which subverts the world of representation. His purpose is not to turn Plato's height-depth distinction upside down, but to challenge the whole domain of representation, which presupposes the categories of up-down, model-copy, etc. For Deleuze, as for the Stoics, everything happens on "the surface" (*LS* 145). "It is a question of simulacra, and simulacra alone. . . . Simulacra are those systems in which different relates to different *by means of* difference itself" (*LS* 299). Nothing is behind or above difference.

All creative process is "the consequence of a difference which is originary, pure, synthetic and in itself. . . . If difference is the in-itself, then repetition in the eternal return is the for-itself of difference" (*LS* 125). The "rising" itself is the distribution of intensities on the surface, the play of simulacra in which desiring-machines operate. For Deleuze, the absolute is not a represented transcendent ideal, but that which "returns," namely, the intensity of the force of the Disparate that encounters and engenders thinking through a *complex* repetition of *pure* difference. "The ultimate element of repetition is the Disparate, which stands opposed to the identity of representation" (*LS* 57).

The "dark precursor" of Disparity is the differentiator of differences; "it is the in-itself of difference or the 'differently different' — in other words, difference in the second degree, the self-different which relates dif-

---

21. Deleuze, *The Logic of Sense*, p. 294. Hereafter, this book will be cited in the text as *LS*.

ferent to different by itself" (*LS* 119). The presentations of difference have effects; they produce opposition, resemblance, identity, and analogy. The latter do not subordinate difference; rather, they are *effects* of difference. Difference is not something negative said about similars, about identities that are opposed or analogous, but rather an affirming, positive power that engenders thought, that makes Ideas productive.

7. The Genitality of Thought

What is it that dramatizes temporality, animates language, liberates desire, and awakens thought? Traditionally the answer to these questions is the placeholder for the divine, for God. For Plato, knowing has to do with the recognition of ideal Forms, the identification of the similarity between model and copy. The immortal soul returns from the material to the intelligible realm, drawn by the Idea of the Good. Aristotle refigured the relation between form and matter, but sameness and representation continued to dominate his physics, his metaphysics, and his theory of language. For him the "final cause" of human knowledge is the unmoved mover, thought thinking itself (the same). Insofar as Christian theology has adopted and adapted these categories, it too has operated for the most part under the domain of sameness and representation, which Deleuze argues produces and sustains the oedipalization of desire.

Following Nietzsche, Deleuze replaces "God" with the "eternal return" as that which engenders thought. According to Deleuze, Nietzsche's *speculative* teaching is that "becoming, multiplicity and chance do not contain any negation; difference is pure affirmation; return is the being of difference excluding the whole of the negative." This is clarified in the *practical* teaching, which is that "difference is happy; that multiplicity, becoming and chance are adequate objects of joy by themselves and that only joy returns."[22] Deleuze asserts that thought is awakened by the arrival of a difference in intensity, the complex repetition of the element of pure difference itself. For him, knowledge is not about *recognizing* something but about being encountered. "Something in the world forces us to think. This something is an object not of recognition but of a fundamental *encounter*" (*LS* 139). Thought arises in the encounter with difference.

Deleuze's reading and appropriation of Nietzsche's theory of the eter-

22. Deleuze, *Nietzsche and Philosophy*, p. 190.

nal return is complicated and controversial, but for our purposes the key point is how Deleuze's own construal privileges the *future* among the modes of time. In *Difference and Repetition*, he spells out the complexity of repetition in terms of the three "syntheses" of time.[23] Building on Bergson's analysis of the passive and active syntheses of time (derived and refigured from Hume), Deleuze writes of the first synthesis in relation to the living present, the second in relation to the pure past, and the third in relation to the future. These three syntheses are Repetition in different modes. The present is the repeater, the past is repetition itself, but the future is that which is repeated.

The future, however, is the royal repetition; it "subordinates the other two to itself and strips them of their autonomy." Making the category of the future primary involves making repetition "not that from which one 'draws off' a difference, nor that which includes difference as a variant, but making it the thought and the production of the 'absolutely different'" (*DR* 94). The future has an essential relation to the eternal return because it is the arrival of the different; "the future is the deployment and explication of the multiple, of the different and of the fortuitous, for themselves and 'for all times'" (*DR* 115). The difference between the classical Greek "eternal return" and the Deleuzian is that the latter is the complex *re*-petition of the different rather than the *re*-presentation of the same. The prefix (re-) shifts its meaning because "in the one case difference is said only in relation to the identical while in the other it is the univocal which is said of the different. Repetition is the formless being of all differences, the formless power of the ground which carries every object to that extreme 'form' in which its representation comes undone" (*DR* 57).

In *The Logic of Sense,* Deleuze discusses the genitality of thought by engaging Immanuel Kant's paralogisms of reason. In Deleuze's reading of Kant, the *self* is the idea that conditions the attribution of the category of substance to phenomena; it is the principle of the categorical syllogism. The *world* is the idea that conditions the attribution of the category of causality to phenomena and so functions as the principle of the hypothetical syllogism. The idea of *God* ensures the attribution of the category of community, and so conditions or founds the disjunctive syllogism (*LS* 335). For

---

23. Cf. *Difference and Repetition*, pp. 71, 85, 69, 90, 94, 115, 41, 57, 292-301. Deleuze gives a more careful treatment of Bergson in his book *Bergsonism* (New York: Zone Books, 1990), and of Hume in his book *Empiricism and Subjectivity* (New York: Columbia University Press, 1991).

Deleuze, the death of God comes with the death of the (oedipal) self and the world, all understood in terms of Identity. This completely alters one's sense of that which engenders thinking.

However, the important point here is that Deleuze explicitly places the eternal return in the same philosophical slot that God once held for Kant; "the eternal return expresses this new sense of the disjunctive synthesis" (*LS* 340). The Christian repetition, he argues, which is founded on God, makes only a negative or exclusive use of the disjunction; difference is negative and said only of the Same, which returns or to which we return. Deleuze's own understanding of the disjunctive syllogism is tied to his affirmative view of the intensity of difference, which is not simply negative and exclusive but inclusive, so that disjunctions remain disjunctions. The "eternal return" is the arrival of the Disparate, the affirmative (creative) disjunctive synthesis of disjunctions that generates intensities and actualizes intentionality.

Deleuze even hints at a new way of understanding "theology," which does not require "belief" in the idea of God or any other forms (structures) that must be filled with beliefs. The "structure" has no need to be filled, he argues, to be called "theological." We may now think of theology as "the science of nonexisting entities, the manner in which these entities — divine or anti-divine, Christ or Antichrist — animate language and make for it this glorious body which is divided into disjunctions" (*LS* 322). The authors of *Anti-Oedipus* insist that the body without organs is not God, but "the energy that sweeps through it is divine . . . the sole thing that is divine is the nature of an energy of disjunctions." To the question, "Do you believe in God?" Deleuze answers: "Of course, but only as the master of the disjunctive syllogism . . . as the *Omnitudo realitatis,* from which all secondary realities are derived by a process of division" (*AO* 14).

What are we to make of such an idea of "God"? How can Christian theology respond to the idea of "nonexisting entities" that engender thought and liberate desire? What kind of experiments might theology produce in response to the Deleuzian invitation to reverse Platonism and break free of the (sexual and social) forces of Oedipus?

8. De-Oedipalizing Theology

Like Nietzsche, Deleuze tends to unfairly characterize all religious people as saturated by ressentiment, and to portray Christianity in particular as wholly trapped within "slave morality," imprisoned within the "priestly curse" on desire which it played such a pivotal role in casting. It is tempting at this point to embark upon a defense of Christian theology, to enumerate the diverse voices in the tradition that have celebrated the encounter with infinite qualitative difference and opened up anti-oedipal lines of flight in relation both to family and economic life. Priests are not the only kind of religious person. Many prophets, sages, shamans, poets, and mystics throughout the ages have resisted repression and oppression. Indeed, not even all priests are obsessed with Oedipus!

The focus of this chapter, however, has been on finding resources in Deleuze for opening up new possibilities for the positive production of de-oedipalizing theology. The task is not only exploring opportunities for liberating *theology* from its own (partially self-imposed) oedipalization but also finding ways in which theological-production might itself become a more powerfully *de-oedipalizing* force in contemporary society. Like other religious traditions, Christian theology will increasingly be faced with the task of tending to otherness, of dealing with the tensions that arise with late modern fascination with difference. This will require more attention to the demands of and opportunities for interreligious and interdisciplinary dialogue.

As we move forward, I would like to suggest some directions for de-oedipalizing theological experimentation. Following these directions will indeed challenge the value and validity of some traditional doctrinal formulations, especially those that are couched within the categories of substance and sameness that dominated most ancient and early modern philosophy. However, it will also open up new opportunities for strengthening and clarifying some of the most significant late modern trajectories in Christian theology. In *Reforming the Doctrine of God*, I outlined and illustrated three of these trajectories: the retrieval of intensive infinity, the revival of trinitarian doctrine, and the renewal of eschatological ontology.[24] I do not have the space here to explore all the creative disjunctive syntheses that might emerge in a longer critical engagement between Deleuzian philosophy and the constructive proposals I outlined in that book, but I can begin to follow some of these lines of flight.

---

24. F. LeRon Shults, *Reforming the Doctrine of God* (Grand Rapids: Eerdmans, 2005), Part II.

F. LeRon Shults

De-Oedipalizing Infinity

In a sense Deleuze is right when he suggests that theology is the "science of nonexisting entities." It has to do not with one of the things that exist in the world, but with the "infinite," with that which conditions or engenders finite "existing" things or processes. Deleuze's proposed concept of the infinite is the Disparate, i.e., the complex repetition of pure difference, the *a priori* positive principle of disjunction. He equates the false infinite with the infinity of religion, and suggests that "Being, the One and the Whole are the myth of a false philosophy totally impregnated by theology."[25] We can admit that many, perhaps most, forms of western religious speculation and practice (including those in Christianity) do in fact work with idealized representations of the infinite that are problematic for the reasons that Deleuze identifies. In fact, we could add to his litany of complaints.

However, this is not the *only* way of being religious or doing theology. Even Christian theology has not always been bound to or by this unifying of God with Being, this "representation" of God as "the One." Especially (but not only) within the apophatic streams of the Christian tradition one finds theological approaches that link infinity to *intensity* (which Deleuze himself wishes to do), and insist that the (divine) infinite cannot be grasped or represented by the human mind. The idea that "God" is "non-existent," in the sense that the divine is not one of the things that exist but that which conditions existence, has been embraced by mystical theologians throughout the centuries. The encounter with intensive infinity is not like our encounters with other finite (existing) intensities. This being-encountered constitutes the conditions for all of our finite encountering, opening up the possibilities of our dynamic ek-sistent coming-to-be.

Under the reign of sameness and substance metaphysics, Christian theology was too often tempted to think of the divine as one kind of substance (immaterial) in distinction from another kind of substance (material). The problem, on this model, is the difference between them, which somehow must be overcome. Indeed, it is hard to explain a real encounter between such substances, especially since immaterial substance is eternally the same. Moreover, the simple opposition of the two types is already philosophically problematic, for it defines an allegedly unlimited (infinite) substance in a way that is essentially limited — bounded by its difference from finite substance. Shifting our conceptual focus from sub-

25. Deleuze, *Logic of Sense*, p. 315.

98

stance to relation, from sameness to difference, from extension to intension in our articulation of the encounter with infinity, does not mean leaving behind the Christian tradition. But it does mean refiguring it in ways that overcome its reliance on categories that too easily tempt it toward the false infinite.

De-Oedipalizing Trinity

This doctrine might seem to be the most problematic of Christian concepts and the one that ought to be jettisoned first in dialogue with late modern philosophy. However, if "theology" is the science of the nonexistent, i.e., discourse on that which creates existence, dramatizes language and engenders thinking, etc., then the doctrine of the Trinity can have an important de-oedipalizing function. It can remind us of the dangers of imagining the divine (infinity, "God") as a single subject, as *a* person who thinks and wills. Thinking of the infinite as *a* subject easily collapses into a false infinity, in which the in-finite is not truly unlimited because it is defined in relation to its objects of cognition and volition. The temptation to develop what we might call an *analogia mentis*, a resemblance between the divine and the human soul, is difficult to resist; the anthropomorphic illusions against which Lucretius, Spinoza, and Deleuze warn us are difficult to dispel.

Reinvigorating and refiguring trinitarian concepts in ways that privilege relationality and differentiation can help us resist the deleterious effects of the metaphysics of substance and sameness, which has sometimes oedipalized the Christian articulation (and experience) of being encountered by the truly infinite. Deleuze criticizes the Christian reliance on *simplicatio* and calls for an understanding of the eternal return that involves *complicatio*. However, why should we think that neo-Platonic and Aristotelian conceptions of "simplicity" are necessary components of any presentation of Christian theology? It is interesting that Deleuze has his own "trinitarian" conception of the complex repetition of pure difference: complication, explication, and implication.[26] The human experience of being-limited — of encountering infinity — leads to philosophical reflection on the ultimate conditions of finite differentiation. The truly infinite must be understood in some way as the ground of our coming-to-be dif-

---

26. Deleuze, *Difference and Repetition*, p. 123.

ferentiated. It was difficult to do so under the dominance of the categories of simplicity, unity, sameness, etc. Today Christian theology has a fresh opportunity to articulate a trinitarian conception of the infinite that makes sense of our experience of becoming-personal.

Many theologians seem to feel they are forced to choose between these options: *either* God is "a" person *or* God is in no way related to personhood. Why not think of "God" as the ultimate origin, condition, and goal of creaturely becoming-personal? The ("nonexistent") divine is not one member of the genus "existing persons," not even the best, most intelligent, most powerful person, but rather that which generates existence, creatively encountering it in a way that engenders and liberates the finite desire for well-differentiated intimacy, making possible the coming-to-be of human persons. The doctrine of the Trinity has been an attempt to articulate this intuitive sense that God is the ground of human personhood. However, it will not work simply to think of God as three persons, who are more or less like us, yet mysteriously one and the same substance. Instead, we can imaginatively engage the mysteriously differentiating force of intensive infinity that constitutes our desire to become-personal precisely by incursively energizing and evocatively liberating our differentiated and temporal coming-to-be.

De-Oedipalizing Futurity

Deleuze is right to criticize theology for its tendency to think of God as a first cause, which led to (or reinforced) a reliance on categories such as necessity, foreknowledge, predestination, etc. Such theological modeling seems to crush human freedom, to deny the reality or responsibility of human desiring. However, this is not the only tendency one finds in theology. Many of the leading theologians of the twentieth century recognized and renewed what we have called an "eschatological ontology" within the Christian tradition. Here we have a recovery and refiguring of resources in the tradition that think of the *being* of the world as constituted by the *advent* of God. Deleuze is critical of (what he takes to be) Søren Kierkegaard's view of "repetition" and "the Eternal," but he never engages the appropriations of Kierkegaard (and other resources in the Christian tradition that emphasize futurity) by late modern theologians such as Jürgen Moltmann, Wolfhart Pannenberg, and Eberhard Jüngel. This theological shift (Futurity) may be the most difficult to understand, but it is as important as the others (Infinity, Trinity) for de-oedipalizing theology and saving desire.[27]

In this context I limit myself to pointing out two issues that require special attention in a theological articulation of divine Futurity. One is the danger of collapsing into a spurious conception of infinity (or false eternity) in which "the future" as one mode of time is defined in relation to the others. If this (creaturely) mode of time, which dialectically presupposes the other modes, is *identified* with the divine, then the latter would be defined by its essential opposition to the past and the present, upon which it would be dependent for its "existence." On such a model, it would be hard to protect against the appearance of a kind of backwards determinism, predestination in reverse. We can avoid this by insisting on the *absolute* Futurity of God, which is not *relative* to (defined over against) the past and the present, but that which "defines" all the existential modes of the open flow of time. The concept of Absolute Futurity can serve to indicate an understanding of Eternity as the all-enveloping and all-pervading arrival of the intensively infinite differentiating reality that opens up what we experience as a temporal trajectory.

A second issue is the relation of futurity to the formation of persons. As we saw above, Deleuze makes a special link between the eternal return and the future in his understanding of the arrival of the Disparate that generates intensities and engenders thought. However, it is not always clear how (or whether) memory of the past ought to play a role in the present construction of a body without organs, on the desiring production of human life. Not surprisingly, Deleuze himself does not deal significantly with the theme of messianic expectation, which captured the attention and shaped the thought of many other participants in the philosophical shift to alterity, such as Derrida, Levinas, and others. For those of us who want to contribute to the formation of desire within a particular religious community, it will be important to make more explicit the way in which anticipations of transformation should be shaped by remembrances of the concrete narrative that has and continues to engender faith, love, and hope. Deleuze's preference for Dionysius over the Crucified will naturally give us pause, but it should not keep us from engaging his metaphysical prioritizing of the arrival of "the new," which might add to the ongoing

---

27. For a fuller discussion of the philosophical dimensions of this shift, see Shults, "The Philosophy of Time: The Turn to Futurity in Late Modern Philosophy," *Studia Theologica* 61 (2007): 47-60.

conversation about temporality and eschatology in theology. Moreover, such an engagement could also have an explicitly de-oedipalizing effect, freeing us from a conception of time as that which lacks Eternity because of a past or present failure of human subjects to measure up to an idealized external rule of pleasure.

Such development of the concepts of Infinity, Trinity, and Futurity could have a further and broader de-oedipalizing effect. For example, what about de-oedipalizing *ecclesiology?* The traditional "marks" of the church (one, holy, catholic, apostolic) were formulated during the patristic period under the influence of the neo-Platonic philosophical privileging of the categories of unity and sameness, which contributed to the political resistance to plurality and difference.[28] The church as an *organization* has invested much of its energy in holding together those who constitute its *body*. Much of Christian ecclesiology (in theory and practice) has been obsessed with clearly demarcating and controlling who is "in" and who is "out," policing the boundaries of the (social) body of Christ using particular cultural construals of law and justice; this has had a profound effect on atonement theory.[29] What would it look like to explore modes of ecclesial life that celebrate the construction of a "body without organs," to produce (consume and register) joyfully on the plane of consistency in ways that resist the inscription of desire by the capitalist socius?

Might we produce a de-oedipalizing *soteriology?* The Christian tradition has too often limited its understanding of salvation to the transportation of individual souls to an idealized future paradise. However, salvation is not merely a future external ideal for individual subjects but a present experience of the fullness of life that energizes our production and creation of the good life for and with concrete, embodied others.[30] Christianity has always insisted that salvation is by *grace,* and yet so often this is defined in a way that presupposes an external *ideal* that is bound to the concept of *law;* divine regulation and redemption are necessary because of human *lack.* Soteriological de-oedipalization will involve attending to the way we record our libidinal investments, to the ways in which our

28. Cf. Shults, "Reforming Ecclesiology in Emerging Churches," *Theology Today* 65, no. 4 (January 2009): 425-38.

29. Cf. Shults, *Christology and Science* (Burlington, VT: Ashgate; Grand Rapids: Eerdmans, 2008), ch. 3.

30. Cf. Shults, *Reforming Theological Anthropology* (Grand Rapids: Eerdmans, 2003), Part III, and Shults and Steven J. Sandage, *The Faces of Forgiveness* (Grand Rapids: Baker Academic, 2003), ch. 4.

consumptions produce forms of life that are not salutary for many of the desiring-machines with which we find ourselves more or less connected.

9. Theology after Oedipus?

Do we really want to escape Oedipus? For all its tragedy and repression, oedipalization can make us feel safe. A theology of desire that provides an individual with delayed fantasies of a future asexual heavenly pleasure, which promises to satiate the existential dis-ease (lack) he or she has allegedly contracted by transgressing the divine law, can feel comforting in its own way. Deleuze's attack upon Oedipus can be disturbing, and it is tempting to immediately counterattack or defend the organs of Christianity that make us feel safe. But there are ways of protecting ourselves that are not healthy. Some modes of experiencing safety (and salvation?), some ways of repressing desire, hinder our capacity for true transformation and intimacy.

In this context I have attempted to indwell Deleuze's critique as deeply as possible, to listen carefully to his "prophetic" challenges to the "priestly" curse on desire. We can and should also acknowledge that de-oedipalization can be taken too far, or take place in inappropriate ways. Liberating desire is not sufficient, for there are forms of "free" desire that can be destructive, as Deleuze himself admits.[31] Engaging his radically positive conception of desire theology will require a great deal of wisdom and discernment within community. De-oedipalizing theology will surely be terrifying, as meaningful transformation always is, but it might also open us up to new experiences of saving desire that are more delightful than we could imagine to ask or think.

Fear and desire come together, and go together. We cannot liberate our desires without facing our fears. Although he imprisons us, we desire "Oedipus" and fear losing him, because he saves us from those desires

---

31. I have not focused here on the problems in Deleuze's philosophy and psychology. It is not clear how his call to respond to the encounter with the infinite in a particular way — affirm difference, embrace chance, employ willpower, love fate — leaves any significant place for compassion or altruistic love, which he views (with Nietzsche) as weakness or ressentiment. Another problem is his focus on psychoanalysis; his approach would have been fuller if he had engaged other psychological schools that are not oedipalizing in the same way, that tend to relationality quite differently (e.g., self-psychology, differentiation, object relations, and attachment theories).

which we are afraid will lead to our abandonment and absorption by significant others. To the extent that our theology is saturated by the categories of lack, law, and idealization, we will — like Oedipus — be driven by these finite fears and bound to repression and self-destruction. However, becoming-oedipal is not the only way of being pious. Encountering infinity can also evoke a delightful response, one in which the power of love conquers the fear of death. The ongoing conceptual task of theology is explicating the ultimate origin, condition, and goal of our experience of being-encountered by an ever-arriving presence that opens us up to and for the intensity of loving and being loved in relation to finite others.

However, this conceptual task is inherently pragmatic. The genitality of thought and the liberation of desire are intertwined. Whether consciously or unconsciously, theology makes its own libidinal investments in the social field. These investments are sometimes repressive, but they can also connect, diverge, and conjoin in ways that intensify our experience of the binding, healing, restoring, liberating, and *productive* power of love. De-oedipalizing theology can produce a difference precisely as it *makes* love (and not "Platonic" love!) in the world. The infinitely creative force of love engenders the freedom of finite desire. The saving creativity of love makes a difference, the infinite difference of the world. Lack, guilt, and idealization. Poor Oedipus. Despite his pious intentions, he is colonized and colonizes others. Is it crazy to think that his — and our — liberation could come from theology, from the joyful production of *saving* desire?

Mothers Just Don't Do It

Cristina Grenholm

The title of a novel has lingered in my mind for many years: *My Mother Gets Married.*[1] I do not even recall reading the novel while in school, but the title has stayed with me. The book was published in 1936 and the author, Moa Martinson, was one of the few female writers even mentioned at school.[2] That could be one reason for the title remaining with me, although strangely unrelated to my reading experiences and — something that became apparent quite recently — even to the power of this expression. It was not until last year, when my own mother told me that she was getting married, that I realized the full power of the title. Mothers do not get married. Mothers are married to fathers. The stereotype became clear to me once again: mothers are loving, but not lovers. They are neither desiring subjects nor appropriate objects of desire.

Leafing through the newspaper one early summer morning, I was thinking about how times have changed. Nowadays children are used to parents breaking up and getting into new relationships — although it is still rare that mothers remarry at the age of 74, as my mother did.[3] Moa

1. Moa Martinson, *Mor gifter sig: Skildring* (Stockholm: Bonnier, 1936); *My Mother Gets Married,* trans. Margaret S. Lacy (New York: Feminist Press at the City University of New York, 1988).

2. In fact, she was one of the most popular writers of her time, bringing a woman's perspective to the flourishing realistic literature produced by her male colleagues Artur Lundqvist, Ivar Lo-Johansson, Eyvind Johnson, Jan Fridegård, Harry Martinson, and others. *My Mother Gets Married* is the first book in an autobiographical trilogy.

3. However, almost half (47 percent) of Swedish women aged 70-74 are single women (never married, divorced, or widows) according to official statistics of 2007. The corresponding figure for men is one third (32 percent). The difference is explained by the fact that

Martinson's title would not have been as powerful today, I thought. Then my eyes fell on an article about a children's book exhibit where "some unusual themes" were presented, such as a book about mum's new husband.[4] The stereotype seems to be alive also in third-millennium Sweden. Mothers are not usually thought of as lovers and potential brides.

We find the same stereotype of the nonerotic mother in theology, of course. The strong connections between Christianity and western culture at large when it comes to desire were clearly depicted in the previous chapter. According to the logic of the Oedipus myth, we are here touching upon the spell of the Western Man and his inevitable and forbidden desire for his mother in competition with his father. Seen in the light of LeRon Shults's chapter, one could perhaps view my contribution as a de-oedipalized theology of the mother. Still, my starting point is different; my companions are Eve and Mary. I am less concerned with the possible assassination of the father than with liberating the joy of the mother.

This chapter contains a gender analysis of a general image of Christian motherhood, the specific case of Mary, mother of Jesus, and an analysis of the function of motherhood in a patriarchal society. I will present an overall picture of the Christian tradition of motherhood, although I am aware of the limits of such generalizations. These sections close with a statement about "the message" conveyed by Christian tradition and by society at large, respectively. This is bad news, somewhat at odds with the goal of this book, which is aimed at clarifying the importance for theology of a positive conception of desire. Yet clarifying the conflict between desire and the traditional view of motherhood also has a constructive role.

The aim of "saving desire" calls for a reinterpretation of motherhood. I briefly present the model of "scriptural criticism" that both motivates and helps us in this endeavor. Returning to the Christian tradition with this model, I find resources for a constructive feminist interpretation of motherhood and desire. In a similar way, societal expectations on motherhood are corrected by reference to an alternative interpretation of the experience of motherhood. I can thus claim that this creative feminist reflection is rooted in theology and experience.

In sum, I point in the direction of reinterpretations of three themes: Christian motherhood; Mary; and the function of motherhood in society.

---

men die earlier. Twenty-four percent of women and 7 percent of men are widowed. *Women and Men in Sweden: Facts and Figures 2008* (Stockholm: Statistics Sweden, 2008), p. 20.

4. *Svenska Dagbladet,* 7 July 2008.

I try to open a window upon the vision of a world where mothers' desires are welcomed for the benefit of flourishing Christian communities in contemporary society, where the richness of life is enjoyed although its difficulties are not hidden.

Motherhood Saves from Desire

Welcoming desire means that we need to confront the negative role of desire in Christian ethics, the common Christian view of desire as something purely individual, and the disembodied character of much theological reflection. Christian motherhood has been clearly constrained by traditional Christian views of desire and the corresponding ethics. Mothers have been seen as models for a life that is fulfilled without sexual and — one is tempted to say — any other kind of personal desire. Furthermore, motherhood is primarily understood individualistically, and its public and communal aspects are often hidden. Finally, motherhood has been understood spiritually, although it is indeed an embodied experience. For the majority of mothers it implies sexual intercourse followed by nine months of pregnancy.[5]

To make a very long story short, within Christianity motherhood has been the primary way of putting adult women in their place.[6] Let me remind us of this heritage by referring to two biblical passages. The first is quite long, but both central and telling.

> Be subject to one another out of reverence for Christ. Wives, be subject to your husbands as you are to the Lord. For the husband is the head of the wife just as Christ is the head of the church, the body of which he is the Savior. Just as the church is subject to Christ, so also wives ought to be, in everything, to their husbands. Husbands, love your wives, just as Christ loved the church and gave himself up for her, in order to make her holy by cleansing her with the washing of water by the word, so as to present the church to himself in splendor, without a spot or wrinkle or anything of the kind — yes, so that she may be holy and without

5. This is not to deny that there are other ways of being a mother, through adoption or in same-sex relationships, for example. I just want to point to a characteristic of much mothering, if not all.

6. For a fuller exploration of this theme see Cristina Grenholm, *Motherhood and Love: Beyond the Gendered Stereotypes of Theology* (Grand Rapids: Eerdmans, 2011).

blemish. In the same way, husbands should love their wives as they do their own bodies. He who loves his wife loves himself. For no one ever hates his own body, but he nourishes and tenderly cares for it, just as Christ does for the church, because we are members of his body. "For this reason a man will leave his father and mother and be joined to his wife, and the two will become one flesh." This is a great mystery, and I am applying it to Christ and the church. Each of you, however, should love his wife as himself, and a wife should respect her husband. (Eph. 5:21-33)

Although there are some exhortations of mutuality in this text, the subordination of women to men as well as the asymmetrical character of the relationship is obvious. Since the wife and the church are parallel, it is a little difficult to interpret this text from a gender perspective. Still, when we focus on the symbolic level, we need not keep the two apart. Let us turn to some details. Husbands are to love their wives, since loving them also implies self-love for the husband. "He who loves his wife loves himself" (v. 28). Furthermore, mutuality is punctuated by husbands loving their wives with the expectation of respect in return. "Each of you, however, should love his wife as himself, and a wife should respect her husband" (v. 33). It is appropriate to ask how "love" is defined here — whether this is a love relationship at all or rather the intimate version of patriarchal society.[7] The wife belongs to her husband and should be at his disposal. She is there to enhance his self-esteem and let herself be cleansed so as to have no "spot or wrinkle" (v. 27) as a result of being the object of his care.

When Ephesians 5:21-33 is read from the perspective of the ethical constraints put on mothers by Christianity, the modest glimpses of mutuality seem weak. Men's desires are accepted. Men need to leave their parents to become one flesh with their wives. Women's desires are at best hinted at, but the prospect of fulfilling them is limited from the very beginning by the exhortation to women to be subject to their husbands. Let us move on to another text:

I desire . . . also that the women should dress themselves modestly and decently in suitable clothing, not with their hair braided, or with gold, pearls, or expensive clothes, but with good works, as is proper for

7. Cf. Werner Jeanrond, "Love," in *The Cambridge Dictionary of Christianity*, ed. Daniel Patte (Cambridge and New York: Cambridge University Press, 2010).

women who profess reverence for God. Let a woman learn in silence with full submission. I permit no woman to teach or to have authority over a man; she is to keep silent. For Adam was formed first, then Eve; and Adam was not deceived, but the woman was deceived and became a transgressor. Yet she will be saved through childbearing, provided they continue in faith and love and holiness, with modesty. (1 Tim. 2:9-15)

According to this text, the ideal Christian woman should become a mother in order to make up for the sin of Eve. Motherhood will even save her: "and Adam was not deceived, but the woman was deceived and became a transgressor. Yet she will be saved through childbearing, provided they continue in faith and love and holiness, with modesty" (vv. 14-15).

Disregarding the strange theology of this passage (opening a way to salvation for mothers that is not related to Christ), we can see that motherhood is a solution to sexual desire, both for the woman, who fulfills her duties by becoming a mother, and the man, who will be rescued from further temptations by having one woman who belongs to him. In addition, she is not to be devoted to sexual pleasure, but to promoting the spiritual virtues of "faith and love and holiness" (v. 15). We can understand the message as a disembodiment of women even in motherhood.

Although these biblical passages are marginal in scripture, they have played an important role in the history of the church. If we take into account that Christianity, although affirming the importance of true teaching,[8] is primarily a practice, a faith lived in ordinary families, we can understand the power of this family construction in the lives of Christian women.[9] Adult Christian women should turn away from sin by becoming wives and mothers and by converting their sexual desire into modestly

8. Cf. Frances Young, *The Making of the Creeds* (London: SCM Press; Philadelphia: Trinity Press International, 1991), p. 1: "In practice, Christianity has all the characteristics mentioned in common with other religions, and like other religions it has taken many different forms and developed many different lifestyles over the centuries as it has been incarnated in different cultures; but in theory Christianity is homogeneous and its homogeneity lies in orthodox belief. Despite the ecumenical movement, Christian groups still claim that their truth is the truth, betraying that this is something they all have in common: namely, a distinction between true belief and false belief. There may in practice be a number of different orthodoxies, but 'orthodoxy' seems characteristic of Christianity."

9. See, for example, Rosemary Radford Ruether, *Christianity and the Making of the Modern Family* (Boston: Beacon Press, 2000), and Rita Nakashima Brock, "Marriage Troubles," in *Body and Soul: Rethinking Sexuality as Justice-Love*, ed. Marvin M. Ellison and Sylvia Thorson-Smith (Cleveland: Pilgrim Press, 2003), pp. 352-74.

practiced love modeled by faith. By adhering to these ideals, women are supposed to contribute to the character of the Christian community. Not least are they saving men from giving in to their lusts by bringing them to the safe haven of matrimony. Their embodied power as mothers and wives is transformed into spiritual modesty, perhaps even weakness.

The general message from Christian tradition is clear: mothers have been moved away from desire and from sin and placed in the realm of the fulfillment of subordination and maternal bliss. One important aspect of this is that the mature woman is supposed to give up her autonomy, being at the service of husband and children. Her voice is silenced and she remains in the background.

Mary Fulfills the Desires of Others

Mary, Mother of Jesus, is the model mother in Christian theology. Although her position in theory and praxis varies between denominations and traditions, she remains central. Mary identifies the norm. It is not uncommon that Mary be taken as an example also by non-theologians. Swedish feminist philosopher Ulla M. Holm expresses a widespread image of Mary as mother: "she who puts her own will aside in unconditional obedience to her almighty Lord, carries out his orders, worships and serves both him and the Son. She is given worth as container for the divine, a vessel of grace."[10]

We see here a mother who is totally emptied of herself and filled with tasks imposed on her. She is the maid of both the Father and the Son. She is not only deprived of her voice and autonomy but is intensely subordinated. Traditional Christian ethics put the mother of mothers within strict limitations.

Although Mary is central as a mother in Christian faith, the position of mothers in general is heavily marginalized in tradition. Sallie McFague has analyzed this fact. She depicts God the Father as a dominant metaphor or model in Christianity.

> [God the Father as metaphor] suggests a comprehensive, ordering structure with impressive interpretive potential. As a rich model with

---

10. Ulla M. Holm, *Modrande & praxis: En feministfilosofisk undersökning* (Göteborg: Daidalos, 1993), p. 257.

many associated commonplaces as well as a host of supporting meta-phors, an entire theology can be worked out from this model. Thus, if God is understood on the model of "father," human beings are under-stood as "children," sin is rebellion against the "father," redemption is sacrifice by the "older son" on behalf of the "brothers and sisters" for the guilt against the "father" and so on.[11]

The mother is strangely put outside the dynamics of the relationship be-tween the father and his children. Mary is necessary for the relationship between the Father and the Son to occur, but once it is established she van-ishes. Of course, traditional Christian theology cannot have Mother Mary put on a par with God the Father. Still, the quote from McFague shows that there is more to it than just guarding the distinction between the divine and the human. In Christian theology the space of mothers is very limited. When the life of the father and his children is depicted, the mother is no longer visible. The disembodiment of all Christian mothers is further en-hanced in the model Mother Mary. Following Sallie McFague, we see a communal life characterized by asymmetry. Although venerated, mothers are just the prerequisite for male interaction.

Another theologian that has worked on the theme of Mary is John Macquarrie. His interpretation of the virginal conception can be under-stood as radical in the sense that he does not believe in a biological miracle. He rather points to the existential dimension of Mary's motherhood.

> She had to conceive him not only in her womb but in her heart, she had not only to bring the child forth but to rear him, to awaken him as any mother must to the meaning of love, to impart to him a constant orien-tation to God, and these things were possible only if she lived herself in the closest relation to God (that is, in grace) and was perfectly respon-sive to him. In other words, she had to be truly and utterly woman.[12]

Macquarrie points to what Mary does as what should be done by "any good mother" and in doing this she is "truly and utterly woman" and "per-fectly responsive." The model Mother Mary not only gives up her auton-omy by neglecting her own desires and needs, but she is totally devoted to

---

11. Sallie McFague, *Metaphorical Theology: Models of God in Religious Language,* 2nd ed. (Philadelphia: Fortress Press, 1984 [orig. 1982]), p. 23.

12. John Macquarrie, *Mary for All Christians,* 2nd ed. (Edinburgh: T. & T. Clark, 2001 [orig. 1990]), p. 26.

fulfilling the desires of others: her children and God (nothing is said about the husband).

This is an illustration to the character of God the Father as a dominant metaphor that prevails in contemporary Christian theology. Although Mary and other mothers are parts of the relational web of life — between God and humans and between humans — they are not there on equal terms with their fellow men. In fact, they are not part of the relational web, but only its facilitators. Mary gives, but is not offered anything in return. The relational web is not built on mutuality, but on the mother providing the life conditions for the others. The expectations put on the model Mother Mary and all of her sisters also become unrealistic.

As is well known, the demands on a mother are very high. Paula Cooey even characterizes the concept "ordinary mother" as an oxymoron:

> If being ordinary involves characterological flaws, making serious, sometimes tragic mistakes while bearing or rearing children, or leaving one's children while working outside the home, then mothers must be extraordinary. Due to cultural romanticizing of both motherhood and childhood, U.S. society expects nothing less than extraordinary mothers as normative.[13]

Why has the extraordinary been made ordinary for mothers? Motherhood has been culturally constructed so as not to refer to actual mothers, but to ideal mothers. Consequently it is considered futile to try to become a good mother; rather you should be content to aim at being "good enough."[14]

The message of the traditional interpretations of Mary as the model mother is unambiguous and clear: Motherhood implies letting go of your own desires, while fulfilling those of others. Hereby mothers play an important role in forming human relationships, while true mutuality is excluded from the dynamics of life, not only for the mothers but for everybody. Disembodiment also entails a marginal position in social life, a "dissocialization," reinforced by the unrealistic idealization of mothers.

---

13. Paula M. Cooey, "'Ordinary Mother' as Oxymoron: The Collusion of Theology, Theory, and Politics in the Undermining of Mothers," in *Mother Troubles: Rethinking Contemporary Maternal Dilemmas*, ed. Julia E. Hanigsberg and Sara Ruddick (Boston: Beacon Press, 1999), pp. 229-49, here 229.

14. The concept of "good enough" mothers was launched by the British psychoanalyst Donald Woods Winnicott.

Society Depends on Neglecting the Desires of Mothers

I have already touched upon the communal dimensions of motherhood. In this section, I will go one step further by reflecting on a possible explanation for the mechanism through which the extraordinary demands on mothers have become regarded as ordinary. What is the role of women's sexuality in society? From the model Mother Mary we have learned that motherhood is structurally disembodied and hidden behind the interaction of the father and the son. This implies that the model Mother in Christianity — a mother outside the dynamics of the relationship between the father and his children — does not fit into the general patriarchal understanding of women as bodies and men as minds. Rather than being clear-cut, the notion of woman is highly ambiguous in patriarchal thinking.[15] We have the two stereotypes of the Madonna and the whore. An analysis of motherhood needs to deal with both sides of this ambiguity. The sexuality of mothers is kept secret, but it is active all the same.

A helpful clarification of the role of the sexuality of mothers and other women has been given by political scientist Anna Jónasdóttir in her book *Why Women Are Oppressed.* Her point is that a basic mechanism in a patriarchal society is that it exploits the love women give to men. Men never get enough and keep asking for more, thereby actually exploiting women's power to love and literally demanding more than could reasonably be expected.

> [P]revailing social norms, accompanying us from birth and constantly in effect around and in us, say that men not only have the right to women's love, care and devotion but also that they have the right to give vent to their need for women and the freedom to take for themselves. Women, on the other hand, have the right to give freely of themselves but have a very limited legitimate freedom to take for themselves. Thus men can continually appropriate significantly more of women's life force and capacity than they give back to women. Men can build themselves up as powerful social beings and continue to dominate women through their constant accumulation of the existential forces taken and received from women. If capital is accumulated alienated labor, male authority is accumulated alienated love.[16]

15. Cf. Grace M. Jantzen, *Becoming Divine: Towards a Feminist Philosophy of Religion* (Bloomington and Indianapolis: Indiana University Press, 1999), pp. 27-58.

16. Anna G. Jónasdóttir, *Why Women Are Oppressed* (Philadelphia: Temple University Press, 1994), p. 26.

This can be understood as a plausible explanation for the extraordinary demands made on women, among whom a majority are related to men through motherhood. In a patriarchal society, it is normal for men to ask for more than they are prepared to give themselves. Again, we can notice the asymmetry and the lack of mutuality. The needs and desires of men can never be satisfied. They need the extra power given to them by women to become the powerful social beings they are. The ambiguity of women's sexuality relates to the fact that it is both used — confirming men's desires — and neglected — making women's desires invisible.

Jónasdóttir's analysis covers more than motherhood. It includes many different kinds of love-giving. At the same time, it fits well with the description of model Mother Mary discussed in the previous section. The perfect responsiveness of motherhood is transferred to the whole of women's lives on a structural level. Following Jónasdóttir we can say that women "have a very limited legitimate freedom to take for themselves," that is, to have their desires fulfilled.

Let us for a moment return to Ephesians 5. Could the commands that spouses be subject to one another (v. 21) and that husbands should love their wives (v. 25) be helpful correctives to the mechanisms described by Jónasdóttir? On the contrary, I think that this analysis clarifies the patriarchal character of Ephesians 5. The husband is not asked to love his wife in return for her love. He is asked to love her in order to cleanse her from sin. He is not asked to love her for her own sake.

What about the specific issue of sexuality? We noticed that the only desire clearly present in the passage is the man's desire to become one flesh with his wife. Still, her body is not totally absent. First, it is mentioned as a parallel to Christ and the church. Christ is the head of the church, which is the body. Likewise the husband should be the head of his wife. Her body is not explicitly mentioned, but we are led to ponder the relationship between a head — the man — and a body — the woman. The subordination is clear.

The woman's body is mentioned one more time in Ephesians 5. The man is urged to nourish and tenderly care for (v. 29) his wife as he does for his own body. Here the male reader is given a chance to realize the mutual needs of women's and men's bodies. However, it requires a strategy of "reading against the grain" of the passage as a whole. The passage is saturated with the message requiring the subordination of the woman, and after all, her body is just dimly seen behind the man's care for his own body, which is used as a norm.

Ephesians 5 can in fact serve as a textbook example of the role of sexuality in a patriarchal society. This text is barely visible when decent relationships are discussed, but still it is very effective. Jónasdóttir's thesis is that sexuality is the arena where social and political power relations are at play. Sex transfers power between people in a way that shapes society. "I imagine that the specific realities of sexual life (eroticism) entail a particular strength/power development in human beings and a transference of power between people that has great significance for how we are with each other and how we organize our societies."[17] Thus, following Jónasdóttir, our society is dependent on the neglect of the desires of women as men's partners, that is, as potential and real mothers. I believe she has a point here. I will bring nuances into this picture later, also following Jónasdóttir, but let us first face the stereotype of the patriarchal society that affects us all.

Women provide love for the benefit of society by transferring power to men, which helps them reach social positions. However, women are not given as much in return. Love flows from women to men in a communication that is not characterized by mutuality. Rather, women let go of their love and lose control over its power and it does not return to them in a sufficient degree.

This implies that there is more to the mechanisms of motherhood than a weak and unbalanced mutuality. The structure of a patriarchal society places women in a situation of inverted autonomy, that is, a situation characterized by heteronomy. A little etymology helps us clarify what is at stake here. The original meaning of the Greek word *auto* is self and *nomos* means law. *Hetero* means the other or another. An autonomous person can set her own standards, while a heteronomous person is controlled by the law of the other.[18]

Let us pause and ponder the consequences of what has just been said. I believe that the results of Jónasdóttir's analysis have to be taken into account when we try to create space for welcoming desire into contemporary theology. Once again, it will not be sufficient or effective just to "add women and stir."[19] It is not only the disembodiment of women and the

17. Jónasdóttir, *Why Women Are Oppressed*, p. 21. See also p. 12.

18. Cf. Daphne Hampson, "On Autonomy and Heteronomy," in *Swallowing a Fishbone? Feminist Theologians Debate Christianity,* ed. Daphne Hampson (London: SPCK, 1996), pp. 1-16.

19. Cf. Sandra Harding, *Whose Science? Whose Knowledge? Thinking from Women's Lives* (Ithaca, NY: Cornell University Press, 1991).

transfer of their desires into "faith and love and holiness" (1 Tim. 2:15) that forms part of traditional Christian ethics. Women's embodied desires have thereby been dealt with too. Their desires are to be taken into account to a significantly lower degree than those of men. Furthermore, this is not just a church problem, but a problem of society at large.

The message from patriarchal society is that women's desires can be met to a far lesser degree than those of men.[20] Society demands not only that mothers give up their autonomy and enter into unequal relationships, but that they actually lose control of the empowerment that they give to others without expecting anything in return.

Motherhood as a Misfit When Saving Desire

This book, *Saving Desire,* testifies to the growing insight into the role of desire in our lives. Fulfilling desires can indeed be harmful, but not being guided by them is just as dangerous. Desire is also what connects us with the goodness and richness of life, and ultimately with God. This was pointed out already in the first chapter. Simultaneously, it must be stressed that it is a characteristic of the human condition, that our desires can never be fulfilled. Rather, desires eventually point to God as the giver of a life that is richer than we can possibly imagine. Desire belongs to the heart of theology. Henriksen claims that life must be lived in a simultaneous acceptance of desire as a gate opener to the goodness of life and awareness of the fact that we will never reach total satisfaction in this world.

Motherhood stands out as a human position that is very difficult to combine with accepting desire in this sense:

(a) Motherhood entails neglecting the desires of the subject and giving up autonomy.
(b) Motherhood entails fulfilling the desires of others and excluding mutuality in relationships.
(c) Motherhood entails losing control over empowering love, ending up in a heteronomous position without protection.

20. For the neglect of children's needs see Bonnie J. Miller-McLemore, *Let the Children Come: Reimagining Childhood from a Christian Perspective* (San Francisco: Jossey-Bass, 2003).

Desire is an important issue in theology that calls for a severe critique of motherhood in theology and in a patriarchal society. Anyone striving for justice needs to confront the injustice revealed in motherhood. We can understand autonomy, relationality, and heteronomy respectively as three modes of life.[21] All three necessarily are parts of our lives. They are not to be understood as positions that individuals hold. Under normal circumstances — disregarding the complexity of normality — we all move between speaking our mind (autonomy), engaging in conversation (relationality), and listening to others (heteronomy).

The stereotypical position of motherhood in Christianity and society at large is intertwined with the negative poles of autonomy, relationality, and heteronomy. The autonomy of mothers is strongly restricted. Mothers do not really form part of the relational interactions, while they provide much of its resources. Finally, their lack of power has become a more or less permanent status, instead of being the positive heteronomous experience of letting go of responsibilities, resting from the demands of life, and regaining strength. A good balance between the positive aspects of the three life modes should be our goal.

Motherhood, Subjectivity, and Emotional Capacity

As we have seen since the first chapter, desire simultaneously shapes us as individuals and relational beings. For relationships to be mutual and flourishing, individuals have to get out of their egocentrism and interact. With Henriksen, we realize the danger of egoism blocking our potential for communication with the other. The husband of Ephesians 5 must be warned for turning the potential love for the other into self-love, which makes him basically unable to love his wife. To borrow Henriksen's terminology, his desire risks being closed instead of open.

However, as I hope is clear from this chapter, egoism is not the problem of the mother. She does not need exhortation to opening as opposed to closing desires; rather, she needs exhortation to redirect her open desires to include care for herself as an individual. Christian mothers have been

21. See Cristina Grenholm and Daniel Patte, "Overture: Receptions, Critical Interpretations and Scriptural Criticism," in *Reading Israel in Romans*, ed. Cristina Grenholm and Daniel Patte, Romans Through History and Cultures 1: Receptions and Critical Interpretations (Harrisburg, PA: Trinity Press International, 2000), pp. 1-54.

taught to turn away from their own desires, while caring for those of their husbands and children. Their problem is a lack of subjectivity, or rather, of recognizing and appropriating their own self-related desires. Their problem is not the individualism that men display in a patriarchal society.

A quotation from Henriksen can be used as a reminder to Christian mothers not to follow traditional, exclusively altruistic ethics of motherhood. Rather they should explore how they can fulfill their desires. "By acting on desires, we become someone specific — both to ourselves and to others. Hence, if we do not relate to our desires in one way or another, we lose some of our chances for becoming a self for ourselves as well as for others. To become a self is a necessity in order to be something for others."[22]

This insight calls for change also among those with whom mothers interact. It calls for a change of ideals in childrearing. We need to criticize the mechanism that leads children (also grownup children) to tend not to see the autonomy of their mothers. Peggy Cooper Davis holds that children need to learn to recognize and accept the autonomy of others, and they need to start with their mother.[23] Accepting her autonomy implies accepting her desires. Thus Cooper Davis has criticized theories that emphasize the importance for mothers not to stretch their ties to their children. On the contrary, mothers need to stand out as subjects also vis-à-vis their children. Mothers are not there just to keep their children satisfied; they are there also to teach children true mutuality. They are not there just to develop their own capacity to let go of themselves in heteronomy, but also to teach their children that they have to let go. A loving relationship is actually characterized by its capacity to protect the vulnerability of the other.[24]

Feminist scholars have pointed to the tension between motherhood and maturity. Paula M. Cooey says that "[b]eing a good mother by definition precludes acting like an ordinary, mature adult subject to moral and emotional complexity."[25] The personal growth of both the mother and the child is inhibited.

Desire is more than sexual desire. However, since motherhood and sexuality form a hidden unified theme in theology and society at large, it is

22. Henriksen, "Desire: Gift and Giving," p. 10 in this volume.

23. Peggy Cooper Davis, "A Reflection on Three Verbs: To Father, to Mother, to Parent," in Hanigsberg and Ruddick, eds., *Mother Troubles*, pp. 250-78, here 258: "cognitive and emotional growth require encouragement of child-caregiver relationships in which the child learns to recognize and accept the autonomy of others."

24. Grenholm, *Motherhood and Love*, ch. 6.

25. Cooey, "'Ordinary Mother' as Oxymoron," p. 238.

interesting to see what happens if we spell it out. Following Brock, and considering Eros as the very basis for the power of life, we have every reason also to explore sexuality in this context.[26]

The World Association of Sexual Health defines sexuality thus: "Sexuality is an integral part of the personality of every human being. Its full development depends upon the satisfaction of basic human needs such as the desire for contact, intimacy, emotional expression, pleasure, tenderness and love."[27] This quotation points in much the same direction as Henriksen's remark on the need for acting on desires in order to become a self, that is, an integrated personality. Furthermore, the examples given in this quote remind us of what is at play. It concerns much more than the sexual act itself. Eventually acknowledging sexual desires is crucial to our capacity for emotional expression and love.

A Rationale for Reinterpreting Tradition

What can we do about this situation? How can we handle such a heritage? With biblical exegete Daniel Patte I have developed a model for describing the process of biblical interpretation.[28] It does not claim to be innovative, but it clarifies that each interpretation involves choices of three kinds. What is focused in the *text*? Which *contextual* factors (historical or contemporary) are brought into play? What *theological* concepts are used? The interpretive choices made in each case often remain invisible and are taken for granted in tradition. But there are other options! The same model helps us when we need new creative interpretations of Christian tradition. Indirectly, the model can also be applied to a general analysis of a phenomenon in society. Society too has its authoritative texts (written or not, formally accepted or not), its descriptions of its setting, and its key concepts.

We labeled the model "scriptural criticism." By this we wanted to signal that it remains within the tradition of critical biblical exegesis and thus forms part of the academic community at large. But we also wanted to

26. Rita Nakashima Brock, *Journeys by Heart: A Christology of Erotic Power* (New York: Crossroad, 1995 [orig. 1988]), p. 25: "The fundamental power of life, born into us, heals, makes whole, empowers, and liberates. . . . This power heals broken-heartedness and gives courage to the fainthearted. It is the feminist Eros, what I call erotic power."

27. http://www.worldsexology.org/about_sexualrights.asp, 15 October 2008.

28. See Grenholm and Patte, "Overture," pp. 1-54. For a development related to systematic theology and gender theory, see Grenholm, *Motherhood and Love*, ch. 3.

state that it is important to take into account the claims made for religious authority by the interpreters-believers. In the history of biblical exegesis there has been a clear tendency merely to account for historical or philological or other kinds of "facts" while the presumed religious dimension of the texts has been left aside. As a systematic theologian I also care about a thorough analysis of beliefs in religious settings.

Eve Revisited

What are the options for finding resources for a reinterpretation of a Christian view of motherhood in general? For a reinterpretation that allows for desire? It is obvious when 1 Timothy is compared to Genesis 1–3 that its use of the reference to Eve is selective. In Genesis we can read that it has been entrusted to Eve to be the mother of humanity and the co-creator with God. We are also told that she is both doomed to desire her husband and to experience the pain of giving birth.

What does this mean? Eve is caught between lust and pain. This is, of course, the fundamental dilemma that traditional Christian ethics has dealt with by moving the mother away from lust and leaving her with a rationale for her pain in giving birth. However, we can go back to the original dilemma and get a flavor of a good desire — good but not uncomplicated, just the kind of desire that we are familiar with. It is a relief that also the naked body has its place within tradition and not only the body that is hidden by decent clothing. We should also notice that Genesis 3 tells us nothing about sin or guilt. Those words are absent from the text. The connection between the episode in the Garden of Eden and sin develops through the Wisdom tradition and is fully expressed by Paul, for example in Romans 5:12.[29] However, read with reference to a situation in which the theme of motherhood and sexuality needs to be approached by means of a new positive understanding of the concept of desire, the text opens up new possibilities.

We need to try to open a window upon the vision of a life where mothers' desires are welcomed. If we continue to read the story of Adam

---

29. James Barr, *The Garden of Eden and the Hope of Immortality: The Read-Tuckwell Lectures for 1990* (London: SCM Press, 1992), pp. 6, 49-51, 75-78. Cf. my analysis in Cristina Grenholm, *The Old Testament, Christianity and Pluralism*, Beiträge zur Geschichte der biblischen Exegese 33 (Tübingen: Mohr/Siebeck, 1996), pp. 167-71.

and Eve, we can actually find a hint of a self-assertive mother, integrated also in her sexuality. A presentation of Eve's actual motherhood less ambiguous than the one depicted in Genesis 3 is given in Genesis 4:1. The passage is indeed short, but it conveys nothing of the tension between desire and pain; rather, it communicates the joy and empowerment of Eve: "Now the man knew his wife Eve, and she conceived and bore Cain, saying, 'I have produced a man with the help of the Lord.'"[30]

Eve's exclamation is at least something to start with when creatively developing a contemporary theology of motherhood. She stands out as an autonomous person, trusting her intimate relationship with God and — we can assume — with Adam. Her self-assertive claim "I have produced a man" suggests that she was less passive than the first words of the verse might suggest to us; that she actually longed for and enjoyed knowing Adam; that she learned intimacy, emotional expression, pleasure, tenderness, and love. We can envision Eve as an autonomous subject, as empowered and joyful.

Mary and Mothers as Real People

We need more than a reinterpretation of motherhood in general, opposing the subordinate position of mothers, the demand put on them to exchange embodied pleasure for holiness and a limited autonomy. In view of a theology of desire it also becomes clear that Mary, as the icon of Christian motherhood, runs the risk of becoming an idol in the biblical sense, a misleading object of faith. In Christian life the fact that mothers face extraordinary demands is not only a problem for them, but also for those making the demands.

Following the postmodern turn in theology of John Caputo, it has to be emphasized again and again that what humans desire can neither be met by immanent objects, nor encapsulated in a metaphysical description of God as the fulfillment of all desires. Rather, desire has to be directed to something else, to what is and remains unknown, although we can relate to it. This is what Caputo has termed "eschatological desire."[31] Of course,

---

30. Cf. Leila Leah Bronner, *Stories of Biblical Mothers: Maternal Power in the Hebrew Bible* (Dallas: University Press of America, 2004), pp. 2-4.

31. John D. Caputo and Michael J. Scanlon, *God, the Gift, and Postmodernism,* Indiana Series in the Philosophy of Religion (Bloomington: Indiana University Press, 1999).

this is characteristic of apophatic theology all through history, and with Caputo we find many other contemporary thinkers who point in the same direction. Still, this insight needs to be repeated, for example in terms of absolute futurity, as LeRon Shults did in the previous chapter.

The venerated Mary and the venerated mothers tempt people to imagine the possible fulfillment of all their needs by somebody within reach. This is true also of those who are discontent with their mothers' ability to fulfill their desires. The problem is how their expectations are directed away from the eschatological fulfillment of desire. The idea of the perfectly responsive mother is dangerous to our spiritual health, preventing the development of faith in God beyond understanding.

The perfectly responsible mother is also a danger to our capacity for building healthy relationships. To acknowledge mothers as subjects and as desiring human beings means to bring them out of their hidden position as providers of the life conditions of others. We have to rid ourselves of the false apprehension that somebody exists among us who is a perfect provider of all we need. Rather, we are part of a web of social relationships that is not characterized by perfection. This is in fact what ties us together. We need each other in coping with this imperfect life. We need to support the growth of mutual relationships, where the richness and challenges of life can be shared. Our desires will never be fulfilled, but still they will continually lead us to explore more of the good of life and direct us towards the necessary webs of relationships, since we cannot manage on our own.

Accepting that mothers will not fulfill our desires and recognizing their need to be part of a relational web of mutuality challenges not only the egoism of modern man, but also his conviction that he can escape vulnerability. According to the stereotype of patriarchal society, those in power are invulnerable. One of the rationales for their right to power is that they protect those who are weak. This means that the modes of life are distributed among people, hiding the fact that we all share in each one of them.

Let us return to the icon of the perfectly responsive Mother Mary. Such an interpretation of her reflects interpretive choices. There are other options. If we turn to the story of the annunciation in Luke 1:26-38 we can confirm that Mary is totally at the disposal of the Lord, but she is also promised the protection of the Holy Spirit.[32] I believe this is an essential point made in the text that risks being hidden by the theological notion of

---

32. I have written extensively on this interpretation in *Motherhood and Love,* ch. 4.

the virginal conception. Being at the disposal of somebody — be it a human or divine figure — contains a potential danger of exposure and — in the long run — oppression. The protection of the Holy Spirit, i.e., the protection of a loving God, does not necessarily have to be interpreted as making Mary the vessel of somebody else. Mary can be understood as a respected, vulnerable human being, open to one of the deepest challenges of life, i.e., procreation. There is a big difference between being open and being empty. As Mary opens up to giving life she is vulnerable, but the fact that she is not in control does not mean she has to be characterized in negative categories, i.e., who she is *not* or what she does *not* have.

We need to look at the general implications of this interpretation. Although the mother of Jesus is unique, Luke 1:26-38 has more to tell us about life. We get a clear image of the fact that the life we share includes frightening experiences of not being in control. Mary worries about what others can do to her. She also fears the presence of God and where it will take her. This is something we all can relate to. Everybody — not only mothers — has to face situations in which we are at somebody else's disposal, that is, heteronomous situations in which our vulnerability is exposed. The announcement of a child-to-be-born has parallels in other news being brought to us that connects us to other people in ways we cannot control. Still, the message is "Do not be afraid" (Luke 1:30), along with the promise of God's protection. Although lack of control is frightening to the ego of modern man, it constitutes an option for those who do not fear their own vulnerability and who can rely on the care and love of others. The ability to share vulnerability is also the ability to share love. This shows the way to relational empowerment. Carter Heyward has expressed it beautifully:

> In the beginning is the relation, not sameness.
> In the beginning is tension and turbulence, not easy peace.
> In the beginning, our erotic power moves us to touch, not to take over; transform, not subsume. We are empowered by a longing not to blur the contours of our differences, but rather to reach through the particularities of who we are toward our common strength, our shared vulnerability, and our relational pleasure.[33]

Heyward depicts a community where desires are mutually acknowledged. Eros includes sexual desire, but it is not limited to intimacy. Living accord-

---

33. Carter Heyward, *Saving Jesus from Those Who Are Right: Rethinking What It Means to Be Christian* (Minneapolis: Fortress Press, 1999), p. 100.

ing to this vision means "to god" in Heyward's terminology.[34] She invents a new verb. We need not interpret this in a reductionist sense — that there is no other god than our communal life and how we act in it. Rather, we can understand it to mean that God is present where desire is truly at play in strength and vulnerability. The point is that we should neither leave the vulnerable mother outside relational interaction, nor let her be the ideal provider of all we need. She should be invited as one of us in her vulnerability and her capacity for love.

Motherhood in a Society of Mutuality

A society built on the giving of love by women eventually makes us all losers. It is a consumer society, which neither cares for justice nor values wisdom. Letting the stream of goods move only in one direction eventually leads to the destruction of life, since life implies real communication and sharing, that is, mutuality. However, what we need is not to stop the flow of love, but a change of vision that somewhat redirects it.

The patriarchal society feeding from the love of women rests on the idea that the one who receives more lives more. Life is something you need to possess and enhance. This is the logic of the isolated ego, which will be further described in the next chapter. Its mistake is in taking as a given that fulfilling desire means to possess the object of desire and that giving away implies giving up on desire.

According to Bonnie Miller-McLemore, our ways of thinking are caught within an economic framework.[35] The basic mechanism in economic thinking is, first, that everything can be given an exact value and, second, that this value makes exchange possible. By exchanging value, business life makes sure that balance can be kept despite constant change and exchange. You can always balance the accounts. However, this economic framework does not fit well with human life when it is understood in a broader perspective. First, life cannot be given an exact value. Second, life is not exchangeable. Third, life does not come to a balanced bottom line. It functions in a different way.

We can see that the analysis of Anna Jónasdóttir brings motherhood into this economic framework. Mothers, as key providers of love, empower

---

34. Heyward, *Saving Jesus from Those Who Are Right*, p. 96.
35. Miller-McLemore, *Let the Children Come*.

men by a mechanism whereby they let men, so to speak, possess the love that was given to men and use its power to obtain other positions and resources. Love is used, not enjoyed.

Social structures are powerful and hard to change, both in church and in other parts of society. Where can we find resources for change? For this, I turn to experiences that do not fit with the economic framework and that break out of the depressing pattern Jónasdóttir provides. We have to find a more nuanced interpretation of the experience of mothers and consider its social implications. Becoming a mother in a patriarchal church and society is associated with many limitations, but there is more to it than limits. Why do women become mothers in the first place? Lynn Paltrow has a mind-blowing list of reasons why drug-using mothers give birth that shows how multifaceted the motherhood experience is. This list can be applied to other circumstances.

> But drug-using pregnant women become pregnant and carry to term for the same range of reasons all women do. Because contraception failed. Because they fell in love again and hoped this time they could make their family work. Because they are "pro-life" and would never have an abortion. Because when they found out the beloved father of the baby was really already married, they thought it was too late to get a legal abortion. Because they do not know what their options might be. Because they have been abused and battered for so long they no longer believe they can really control any aspect of their lives including their reproductive lives. Because they wanted a child. Because their neighbors and friends, despite their drug use, had healthy babies and they believed theirs would be healthy too.[36]

Although women give birth against their will, it also occurs — and among western well-to-do women quite frequently — that women enjoy getting pregnant and giving birth. Also the interpretation that women are alienated by loving others is selective. Jónasdóttir testifies to this experience too. Letting go of your control by having a baby and by giving it love can be a valuable experience.

> The satisfaction of many values in life presumes that one loses, or restricts considerably, control over future conditions of choice — being

---

36. Lynn M. Paltrow, "Punishment and Prejudice: Judging Drug-Using Pregnant Women," in Hanigsberg and Ruddick, eds., *Mother Troubles*, pp. 59-80, here 69.

pregnant and giving birth to children, for example. . . . Pregnancy carries us into a union with nature (which always varies with different social forms); we enter into a process the course of which we can influence ourselves only to a minimal degree (and of course this degree differs socially and historically); we run risks to life and health both during and after pregnancy and birth; and to all this are added the ties and responsibilities during the child's upbringing and for the rest of his or her life. But the value of bearing life and helping it to be is so enormous that many happily restrict their own autonomy for its sake.[37]

Here we catch a glimpse of a positive experience of heteronomy, our lack of control. Pregnancy is a process that we can influence only to a minimal degree. It brings us into relationship with a child and a father, and we do not know of its concrete challenges. Still, many of us happily accept this and consciously restrict our autonomy. To many it is an experience of being brought into the center of the power of life, which is not controllable but is still worthy of our trust. We enjoy giving love; we do not always fear it will make us losers.

This is a logic of Eros, the love that goes out of its way to reach its beloved, forgetting about her self, yet not losing anything. Rita Nakashima Brock describes the erotic power, the feminine Eros that moves us and heals us.

The fundamental power of life, born into us, heals, makes whole, empowers, and liberates. Its manifold forms create and emerge from the heart, that graceful, passionate mystery at the center of ourselves and each other. This power heals broken-heartedness and gives courage to the fainthearted. It is the feminist Eros, what I call erotic power.[38]

We need to change from a pattern of possession to a pattern of mutual giving and receiving. Mothers should not stop giving, but they need also to receive. Such a change of vision will not turn losers into winners, but it will change the framework for approaching life. Life is more about sharing than winning or losing. The point is that we are all here to enjoy the goods and face the challenges. That I love you means that I desire to be with you and that I want that you are. On a societal level, we need to expand the "you" that we can encounter without a will to take over or own. Such a

37. Jónasdóttir, *Why Women Are Oppressed*, p. 174.
38. Brock, *Journeys by Heart*, p. 25. Cf. pp. 39-40.

change would replace traditional Christian ethics with the aid of a theology that is not disembodied, but rather experienced in and through embodied social interaction.

Welcoming Mothers' Desires

A society that depends on dismissing desire is potentially harmful to all of us. We need a change of vision and we must start exploring what will happen if mothers' desires are openly welcomed, made visible, and fulfilled. "Motherhood and desire" should not be understood as a contradiction in terms. On the contrary, mothers should welcome their own desires in order to clarify their own autonomy. Mothers should also make clear that they neither can nor should fulfill the desires of others. Rather than making us poorer, this would enrich the whole community by promoting truly mutual relations. Such a change would mean that we could share both the richness and the challenges of life in vulnerability and empowerment. Mothers should simply not accept a society that is not prepared also to make them receivers.

What does this entail for theology? First, theology must clearly turn away from the long tradition of subordination of mothers. We can begin by pondering Eve desiring Adam and rejoicing in giving life. Second, theology must stop nurturing the false belief that there are perfect providers in this world and accept that we are friends in an imperfect world, sharing both vulnerability and the capacity to love. Finally, theology must bring to a close the mechanism of exploiting the love of mothers and take the lead in exploring mutual joy and delight.

Desire makes us approach what is good in life. We need not fear that desire will always lead us astray; rather, we should be wary of the risk of avoiding the good things that God wants to give to us. A vivid image of an expression of such joy can be found in the movie *Mamma Mia*. Many women of all ages found themselves empowered by that movie. There is a scene when the Abba song "Dancing Queen" is sung. In the movie, Mamma herself, played by Meryl Streep, takes the lead in a crazy and joyous dancing in which all the women she passes by join in. In the midst of grieving with broken hearts and of doing housework they just let go and dance down the hill. A hundred women are dancing by the sea and eventually jump into the water, smiling. Is this not part of "the great adventure of ec-stasis" that Wendy Farley explores in the next chapter? In the movie, we are brought back to the Greek archipelago, but Oedipus seems to be long gone.

Beguiled by Beauty: The Reformation of Desire for Faith and Theology

Wendy Farley

Cristina Grenholm's image of the grieving, working, middle-aged women who break into a glorious dance is a good one to carry forward in these reflections on desire. At the heart of Christianity is the astonishing revelation of the outrageous, unrestrained outflow of divine love, not only into the potential beauty of creation but in the stained and wounded body of humanity. Looking at the hideous defacement of the divine image through a history filled with suffering and oppression, we might think that a more reasonable deity, one more like us, would have lost hope for humanity. But, as Luther suggested long ago, divine love comes to us as grace: we do not have the power to turn God against us. Christianity teaches us that the divine continues to long for us as we long for God. This union of desire lies beneath all of the distortions of desire that create so much suffering.[1] Because desire can be dangerous, Christianity has often been nervous about it. But if we root our understanding of desire in this union of longing between humanity and God, we might find a way out of an impasse between indulgence and repression — toward what Jan-Olav Henriksen has called an "incarnal experience" of the good life.

The divine desire for humanity suggests an alternative way of casting the distinction between law and grace, which haunts and torments Protestantism. Divine desire is a kind of prevenient grace that constitutes our creation and calls us to redemption. Confident of the divine desire for us, we circumvent the anxiety that propels us toward moralism and judgmen-

---

1. Eckhart provides one example of this nonduality of desire: "The eye with which I see God is the same eye with which God sees me. My eye and God's eye are one eye, one seeing, one knowing, one love." Meister Eckhart, German Sermon Number 12.

talism. This anxiety is, paradoxically, particularly acute among Protestants. Although we like to claim a faith particularly proximate to grace, reflections on desire allow us to see how a preoccupation with law distorts our own faith traditions. As Henriksen points out, it is easy for us to become tangled up in a legalism that thwarts our deepest religious impulses and stifles our flourishing as persons and communities.[2]

The detrimental effects of law on religion are played out in the atonement theory, as Rita Brock makes clear.[3] At its worst, this theory envisions a divine sovereign himself enslaved to a penal code that offers the death penalty as the only possible solution to crime. The difficulty in envisioning mothers as desiring beings, as Cristina Grenholm makes clear, is only one example of the impoverishment of life and faith when law gains priority in our faith.[4] In the absence of a theological account of human and divine desire, we are forced to conceive of God in harsh terms that stifle the yearning of the heart. Augmenting the discourse of law and grace with that of desire may allow a richer language for exploring the spiritual journey to divine love.

This chapter contributes to the effort to "save" desire by arguing that its exile from Christianity results in a distortion of faith. We should remember that "Eros" has been one of the names of God from the time of the Song of Songs.[5] As a name of the divine it is also an aspect of the divine image. Proverbs makes this explicit by characterizing erotic desire as also a "vital element of the moral life," crucial to the "wisdom and discipline" that form our relationship to the Beloved.[6] Retrieving Eros as an ancient name of the divine opens a way to integrate desire into faith and to identify the formation of desire as a central task of Christian life.

A theology of desire provides an antidote to the formation of desire by consumer society preoccupied with individual satisfactions. Perhaps it can assist us in conceiving of motherhood in more realistic and humanizing

2. Jan-Olav Henriksen, "Desire: Gift and Giving," p. 4 in this volume.

3. Rita Nakashima Brock's chapter in this volume, "Paradise and Desire: Deconstructing the Eros of Suffering." See also her book, *Journeys by Heart: A Christology of Erotic Power* (New York: Crossroad, 1991), e.g., pp. 55-57.

4. Cristina Grenholm, "Mothers Just Don't Do It," p. 107 in this volume.

5. Origen and St. Hippolytus were among the first interpreters of the Song of Songs in Christianity, but they are far from the last. R. P Lawson, "Introduction," *Origen: The Song of Songs, Commentary and Homilies* (Westminster, MD: Newman Press, 1957), p. 8.

6. Christine Roy Yoder, "The Shaping of Erotic Desire in Proverbs 1–9," p. 148 in this volume.

ways. Christian community provides an alternative apprenticeship of desire, emphasizing the relational quality of human life and nourishing our capacities for compassion and justice. Faithful desire is limited to individual satisfactions, even religious ones. It is genuine delight in our own good and the good of others. A theology of desire is a counterweight to legalistic and individualistic religion even as it displaces the false satisfactions of consumerism with the fullness of life lived in relationship to others.[7] But let us begin with an image of the repression and liberation of desire.

Desire in Exile

Sweet Land, a recent film set in a Lutheran community in Minnesota just after World War I, sympathetically displays the redemption that comes to a community when it is able to overcome its fear of desire. A bride is sent from Norway to marry a recently immigrated bachelor farmer. She is rushed from train station to church, but when the minister realizes she is German, he is horrified and refuses to marry them. His view of her further deteriorates when he drinks her too strong (and delicious) coffee and, worst of all, discovers her dancing to a phonograph she lugged on her lap through the long journey from Europe. The minister is not a hard-hearted man, but he is caught between contradictory demands of his faith. "I believe in a God of love and compassion," he preaches, but he also believes in the importance of order and homogeneity to keep the fragile community safe. In strange obedience to this God of love and compassion, he expels her and her would-be husband from the farming community, knowing that without the aid of the community it is nearly impossible to survive. He is afraid of the threat of her lawless sensuality. But when a ruthless banker evicts the couple's friends, including a pregnant wife and nine children, the German woman and her would-be husband appear and put up the money for the mortgage. This spontaneous and extravagant generosity saves the family, but simply shifts the threatened foreclosure to their own farm. And yet, the extravagant act inspires the community to overcome its passivity toward the bank: the other farmers collectively put up the money

7. Grenholm is particularly eloquent about the distortions that arise when a Christian ideal of self-sacrifice displaces the need to nurture oneself (e.g., "Mothers Just Don't Do It," p. 112 in this volume), a theme that echoes Brock's argument in *Journeys by Heart,* e.g., p. 25. Desire undermines this zero-sum game by revealing the radical ways in which happiness, good, and redemption require us to live into our mutuality and interdependence.

to save the farm. One reckless act of generosity provokes another, and in this way the woman is finally incorporated into the community.

Two ideas of community are present here. One is based on a law-like commitment to order but harbors a destructive anxiety provoked by difference and sensuality. Exiling the upright young man and his bride seems a reasonable price to pay if it protects the community from the vague threats of desire and difference. Another kind of community emerges when it is vivified by the extravagance of desire. The film is a beautiful evocation of the way the community is transformed by this German woman — even with her strong coffee, waltzes, and good cooking. Desire, far from destroying community, deepens its bonds.

That Christianity has tended toward the pastor's initial hostility has resulted in a tragic inattention to the formation of healthy and life-giving forms of desire. This inattention means that simple joys become occasions of contorted guilt and communities are rifted by exclusion and violence. In our eagerness to preserve the purity of community, we amputate our own members.[8] I think, for example, of the self-righteousness with which churches break communion over questions of sexuality and defraud ourselves of the gifts of those who seem different.[9] I would like to keep in mind the pastor's conversion to a deeper appreciation of desire as we consider ways to reintegrate desire into Christian thought and practice. The pastor was kind but needed to stretch his faith to overcome his anxieties. It is natural for human beings to be anxious and hostile as we encounter sexual and cultural differences. Though the *godhatesfags* website may illustrate a particularly horrifying extreme, many of us, like the pastor, find it preferable to exile our minority companions if it preserves the integrity of the community.[10] But I take

---

8. Rita Nakashima Brock describes how this spirit of repression serves a culture of domination that objectifies those different from ourselves by projecting negative aspects of ourselves onto others (*Journeys by Heart*, p. 57). A similar point is echoed by Cynthia Bourgeault: "Unfortunately, feelings unacknowledged do not go away; they just go deeper." *Centering Prayer and Inner Awakening* (Cambridge, MA: Cowley, 2004), p. 129.

9. Many books witness to the pain of this; examples include Richard Cleaver, *Know My Name: A Gay Liberation Theology* (Louisville: Westminster/John Knox, 1995); Carter Heyward, *Speaking of Christ: A Lesbian Feminist Voice* (New York: Pilgrim Press, 1989); or Horace L. Griffin's *Their Own Receive Them Not: African American Lesbians and Gays in Black Churches* (Cleveland: Pilgrim Press, 2006).

10. See Michael Cobb's *God Hates Fags: The Rhetoric of Religious Violence* (New York: New York University Press, 2006) for a discussion of religious violence and the rhetoric that supports it. Less dramatic but nonetheless quite touching was a term paper I received describing the exclusion of young gay men from the Methodist church in which they were raised.

the gospel to be an invitation to release from these anxieties and enter more deeply into the reckless and extravagant love of the divine.

Christianity is in the strange position of condemning and denigrating minority sexual desires, maternal desires, and (in some cases) safe sex and birth control, while remaining almost entirely porous to consumerism. In the series of reflections in this book, all of the authors reflect on ways in which repression of desire disconnects us from the compassionate power of divine love.[11] Jan-Olav Henriksen is disturbed by the repressive interpretation of desire within Christianity, whose association of desire with cupidity and anxiety contrasts with the biological basis of human consciousness.[12] Henriksen's analysis reminds us that Christianity puts itself at odds with the basic facts of our existence as embodied, biological beings.

Rita Brock's analysis reminds us that repression, rather than purifying us for life with the divine, projects impurity onto others to justify their domination. Like Cristina Grenholm, I am concerned that capitalist culture seeps into Christian formations of desire. In addition to her analysis of the strange alliance between patriarchal Christianity and the privileging of capitalistic economies, I would add another dimension: the *de facto* colonization of desire by secular culture. That is, one problem with the exile of desire from faith is that, without desire, human life, community, and religion are impoverished and unjust. A second problem is that the actual formation of desire is tacitly taken out of the hands of the Christian community and handed over to the marketplace. Christian theology has failed faith by what it does and by what it leaves undone.

The United States, like the world, is faced with a number of severe and potentially catastrophic problems, which I hardly need rehearse here. But in the face of suffering and danger, Christianity's most public moral discourse has been consumed with the effort to control and condemn sexual behavior.[13] This preoccupation leaves unchallenged the shaping of desire by a consumer culture. Advanced capitalist societies include "the most sophisticated systems for forming and inciting desire that the world has ever

11. Brock, *Journeys by Heart*, p. 108.

12. Desire, from this perspective, functions to direct us "toward objects that satisfy our primary biological aims: to continue to live and to bring forth further life." Jan-Olav Henriksen, "Desire: Gift and Giving," p. 5 in this volume.

13. Mark Jordan's *Ethics of Sex*, New Dimensions to Religious Ethics (Malden, MA, and Oxford: Blackwell, 2002), provides a detailed analysis of the history of these attitudes as well as helpful constructive suggestions for rethinking sexual ethics.

seen."[14] Consumer culture shapes desire quite freely, dictating not only the contents of desire but also the quasi-theological claim that the almost exclusive correlate to human happiness is what can be purchased and consumed. One satisfies desires for novelty with a trip to Best Buy, for prestige with a new car. But when the consumption of objects fails to bring satisfaction, consumer culture has its own way of responding to the restlessness of desire. The marketplace accepts the axiom of Christian anthropology that the goods of this world are intrinsically unsatisfying; but, instead of redirecting desire, it simply proliferates possible, if temporary, fulfillments. "We never tire of our earthly pleasures because their disproportion to our desire is constantly promised fulfillment by something else."[15]

The market operates out of a more realistic understanding of the human spirit than much contemporary Christianity. It understands that we humans are fundamentally oriented by desire.[16] The ache in the human breast for happiness is mediated through embodied experiences of hunger, sexuality, an enjoyment of color, sound, pleasure, beauty, adventure. We human beings crave relationship, affirmation, self-respect, hope, creative expression, wonder, novelty, security, family, freedom. These desires are infinite, as the human spirit is infinite, and finite, as we humans direct the infinity of desire to particular satisfactions. The genius of advertising is to connect these very real dynamics of desire to objects that can be purchased. Shampoo produces orgasmic pleasure while beer quenches lust and loneliness along with thirst.[17] The marketplace correctly diagnoses the dynamics of desire but incorrectly prescribes relief. It is granted the power to shape the content of desire, the images by which we navigate who we are, what it means to be successful, happy, secure. The understanding of

---

14. Vincent J. Miller, *Consuming Religion: Christian Faith and Practice in a Consumer Culture* (New York: Continuum, 2005), p. 107.

15. Miller, *Consuming Religion,* p. 128. Miller's book presents a particularly fine and subtle analysis of the dynamics of desire as these are appropriated by consumerism; see especially ch. 4, "Desire and the Kingdom of God."

16. This point is made in the introduction to Henriksen's chapter: "desire is the phenomenon that perhaps more than any other phenomenon relates us both to the world and to ourselves, and orients us, directs us, and *individualizes* us." "Desire: Gift and Giving," p. 2 in this volume.

17. The film *Advertising and the End of the World* is particularly articulate about this "misdirection" of desire (Miller, *Consuming Religion,* pp. 119ff.) in which genuine human desires are directed toward commodities. Thus the desire for camaraderie is directed toward drinking a particular beer, the desire for a happy family directed toward a brand of camera film, and so on.

oneself as part of a larger community, which is essential to social justice, is displaced by individual satisfactions disconnected from social or environmental relations.

Oddly, Christianity has almost nothing to say about this. Its repression of desire blinds it to the pervasive appropriation of desire by markets. Disinterest in the main engine of desire-formation dramatically limits Christianity's influence on spiritual formation. Because of our context in a capitalist and consumer economy, it is especially urgent that we recover resources for shaping desire in positive ways. But a repetition of Christianity's dour suspicion of desire and its pleasures is not the way to do this. Returning to parts of the tradition that link human and divine desire is one way of considering alternatives to Christianity's oppressive sexual moralities and uncritical embrace of consumer values.

The Divine Eros: Good Beyond Being

Notwithstanding the exile of desire from faith, Christian theology includes extraordinarily rich and profound reflections on desire. Both classical and contemporary theologians have interpreted desire as an aspect of divine being through which the divine flows toward humanity and humanity yearns toward the Beloved.[18] By interpreting desire in connection with its divine origin, we see more clearly how essential it is for faith. We can explore new ways to form desire that create identity and community rooted in compassion, justice, and joy.

Pseudo-Dionysius and Mechthild of Magdeburg are two theologians who have focused on the divine desire as key to Christian faith. The anonymous Dionysius uses Eros as a name of God to express the paradoxical kenosis through which creation occurs. He is "so bold as to claim also that the Cause of all things loves all things in the superabundance of his goodness, that because of this goodness he makes all things, brings all things to perfection, holds all things together, returns all things. The divine longing is Good seeking good for the sake of the Good. That yearning which creates all the goodness of the world preexisted superabundantly within the Good and

---

18. Even a partial list of these erotic theologians would take up many pages — one thinks of Gregory of Nyssa, Bernard of Clairvaux, Hadewijch, Eckhart, Schleiermacher, Tillich. Recent theology also includes many names, starting with Rita Nakashima Brock, but also including Catherine Keller, Carter Heyward, and Gerard Loughlin, among others.

did not allow it to remain without issue."[19] Dionysius describes God as "beguiled" by creation, drawn out of sterile perfection to radiate the divine love throughout all of creation. "[T]he very cause of the universe in the beautiful, good superabundance of his benign yearning for all is also carried outside of himself in the loving care he has for everything. He is, as it were, beguiled by goodness, by love, and by yearning and is enticed away from his transcendent dwelling place and comes to abide within all things, and he does so by virtue of his supernatural and ecstatic capacity to remain, nevertheless, within himself."[20] Through these images, Dionysius displays the distinctively creative power of love. Shaped by the logic of the ego, we tend to think that possession is the natural teleology of desire and that generosity is its least obvious expression. But for Dionysius the most natural flow of desire is toward the other, beguiled by its beauty, eager to share the good.

Several hundred years later, we find Mechthild of Magdeburg complementing the metaphysics of Pseudo-Dionysius with a poetic picture of God the Father enticed by the delight of love to move out of the perfect but limited love within the Trinity. Mechthild mixes feminine and masculine imagery as she envisions the Holy Spirit, "plucking the Holy Trinity" like a harp and singing, "Lord, dear Father, I shall give you out of yourself generous advice. We no longer wish to go on thus, not bearing fruit. We shall have a created kingdom. . . . For, dear Father, that alone is true joy, that in great love and infinite happiness one gather them in your sight." The Son picks up the theme: "Dear Father, my nature shall also bear fruit. Now that we want to undertake wondrous things, let us make man in my image. Even though I foresee great tragedy, still I shall love man forever." The Father concurs: "A powerful desire stirs in my divine breast as well, and I swell in love alone. We shall become fruitful so that we shall be loved in return, and so that our glory in some small way shall be recognized. I shall make a bride for myself who shall greet me with her mouth and wound me with her beauty. Only then does love really begin."[21]

Mechthild, like Dionysius, depicts Eros as the energy through which creation emerges from the divine. This cosmic eroticism is also the occasion for the kenosis of divine power: for Mechthild, God becomes divine when he surrenders control for the vulnerability of love.

---

19. Pseudo-Dionysius, *Divine Names*, 708B.

20. Pseudo-Dionysius, *Divine Names*, 712A-B.

21. Mechthild of Magdeburg, *Flowing Light of the Godhead*, III.9. Mechthild of Magdeburg was a beguine who lived in what is now Germany c. 1260–c. 1282/94.

> Then a blessed stillness
> That both desire comes over them.
> He [God] surrenders himself to her [the soul],
> And she surrenders herself to him.[22]

What Dionysius describes metaphysically, Mechthild displays poetically. But she, too, portrays love as fulfilled in its flow toward others. The security and supremacy possible when there is no competing power and no vulnerability is surrendered because it is only then that "love really begin[s]." To the astonishment of the ego, it is this vulnerable fecundity of Eros that is the foundation of creation and of redemption.

In this branch of theology, divine love breaks the hold of self-enclosed unity so that the sublime joy of relation can emerge. Cynthia Bourgeault notes the use of kenosis "to describe the internal life of the Trinity. It speaks of the self-emptying love with which the Father spills into (or gives himself fully into) the Son, the Son into the Spirit, the Spirit into the Father. This complete inter-circulation in love is called *perichoresis*." Through this erotic self-giving the Beloved reveals the divine nature and "bestows this vital energy upon the world in a cascade of divine creativity."[23] It is a divine love ceaselessly, infinitely pouring out the good, exuberantly sharing the beauty of being with all that can be. Eros is this paradoxical "zeal" of love that abandons itself in order to express itself. Self-enclosed love is not love at all. It is the nature of love to be dialectical, to have an object other than itself. In the case of the divine, this self-othering of love is the act of creation.

Scripture applies to the human spirit the words that most profoundly describe the paradox of love: the one who loses her life will gain it and the one who keeps her life will lose it (Matt. 16:25; Luke 9:24). By clinging to the egocentric structure of consciousness, we lose our spiritual life: we protect ourselves, but lose our real identity as love for all reality. When we think about this fundamental spiritual reality we can understand that it is a pale and distorted reflection of the reality of the divine life: a so-called god that would retain its life would not be god. A god self-enclosed in eternal and imperious majesty would be a projection onto the divine of the ego's ultimate fantasy of glory and security. If only, the ego thinks, I could be impervious to all, a rock, an island that touches nothing, as Paul Si-

---

22. Mechthild of Magdeburg, *Flowing Light of the Godhead*, I.44.
23. Bourgeault, *Centering Prayer and Inner Awakening*, p. 153.

mon's song puts it. Or in the words of Bruce Springsteen: "Every man wants to be rich and every rich man wants to be king and a king ain't satisfied until he rules everything."[24] These fantasies of the ego are projected onto God, and we imagine that God is the kind of supreme "I" that the ego wishes for itself. According to the logic of the ego, the best description of erotic surrender in mutual love is "self-sacrifice," that is, the painful loss of self, the martyrdom of one's one good for another.[25]

But in writers like Dionysius and Mechthild the divine Eros inhabits an entirely different economy. It is supreme joy to escape from the sterility of isolation and release oneself into the beauty of relationship. Rather than a subject suspiciously sparring with another ego in mutual efforts of domination, Eros is the ceaseless surrender of possession in favor of the emptying of love toward, for, with, through its beloved. As Rita Brock put it: "Erotic power is the energy that produces creative synthesis, and is enhanced by the relationships that emerge from creative synthesis. It produces not fusion and control, but connectedness."[26] This magic of connection she sees as "the confirmation of divine presence in human life."[27] The infinitely fecund emptying of the divine in surrender to love is creation. Erotic love draws into being the reality of something other than God, created by love in order to be loved and to love in return. The emptiness and emptying of the divine is the arc of desire that calls us into existence and

24. See Ola Sigurdson's article, "Songs of Desire: On Pop-Music and the Question of God," in *God, Experience, and Mystery,* ed. Werner Jeanrond and Christoph Theobald, *Concilium* 2001/1 (London: SCM), pp. 34-42. Dr. Sigurdson also has articles in Swedish on this subject.

25. Ann Carson's *Eros the Bittersweet* (Princeton: Princeton University Press, 1986) points out the omnipresence of this understanding of the loss of self as "bitter" in Greek poetry and as characteristic of a particular way of construing selfhood in which relationship, even — especially — love relationships, could only be a kind of assault on the integrity of the self. Dionysius's display of eros as the ecstatic fulfillment not only of human but of divine being requires that we shift our logic in the entirely opposite direction.

26. Brock, *Journeys by Heart,* p. 39.

27. Brock, *Journeys by Heart,* p. 45. This point is echoed by Carter Heyward: "The erotic is our most fully embodied experience of the love of God. As such, it is the source of our capacity for transcendence, the 'crossing over' among ourselves, making connections between ourselves in relation. The erotic is the divine Spirit's yearning, through our bodyselves, toward mutually empowering relation, which is our most fully embodied experience of God as love (First Letter of John, 4:7ff). Regardless of who may be the lovers, the root of the love is sacred movement between and among us. This love is agapic, philial, and erotic. It is God's love and, insofar as we embody and express it, it is ours." *Touching Our Strength: The Erotic as Power and the Love of God* (San Francisco: HarperSanFrancisco, 1989), p. 99.

beguiles us with its beauty. Eros is kenosis not as a loss of self but as the great adventure of ec-stasis: becoming real by standing outside of oneself, where selflessness is not loss but delight.[28] We see in the ecstatic metaphysics of Dionysius and Mechthild a theological foundation for Grenholm's and Brock's insistence that self-sacrifice is an inadequate and destructive model for Christian life.

This theology explodes the logic of egocentrism not only for interpreting the divine but also for understanding ourselves. Through creation in the divine image we bear this erotic structure within ourselves. Our truest and deepest reality is the self-emptying ecstasy of love. It is our ultimate nature to love, not as a collector loves possessions, but rather with divine abandon. It is our deep nature to relinquish the tyranny of subjectivity and flame with the ecstasy of erotic love, love that dissolves the claims of the ego and becomes itself most perfectly in union with the Beloved — and thus in community with all of creation upon which divine love is lavished. In Eros, we die to the relentless demands of the ego so we can live in the nothingness of intimate love. Luminosity is a root metaphor for this: light is itself by giving itself away; it illumines everything with the intimacy of its touch by being nothing at all. This is the structure of Eros, creative because it possesses nothing, touching everything because it holds nothing back: infinitely empty, fecund, and joyous.

It is our tragic and mysterious destiny to bear this divine Eros under the conditions of finitude. It is important to remember both the luminosity at our core and the harshness of finitude as we attempt to reintegrate desire into Christian faith. If we do not, we may allow Eros to degenerate into another version of sacrifice. We might, for example, return to berating mothers for their selfish desires. After all, erotic love for others is a sign of our divine image. "Good" mothers would find it sufficient to delight in their children. As a mother of three children, I can testify to the delights motherhood can offer. But loving one's children does not remove the conditions of finitude that include patriarchy and oppression, physical fatigue and spiritual yearnings that are irreducible to the delight of maternal and other forms of Eros. We bear the divine Eros and yet live in the midst of suffering, death, and confusion. We are seduced by self-defeating forms of

---

28. Pseudo-Dionysius is, of course, only one thinker representing this metaphysics of eros. Other examples in the ancient world include Gregory of Nyssa and John Palamos. Paul Tillich is indebted both to this tradition and to the Lutheran contemplative Jacob Boehme in his use of eros for the doctrine of God.

desire and torn apart by the riptide of unbearable beauty. As Henriksen has pointed out, we are also biological beings, and our desires are oriented to the impertinent demands of flesh and emotion. We are wrapped up in nerve endings, hormones, skin, muscle, emotion, and endlessly restless thought. This biological being is also formed and deformed by oppressive social structures, as Brock and Grenholm make clear. In the chapter that follows this one, Christine Yoder alerts us to Proverbs' way of deciphering some of the oscillations of desire in the service of wisdom or foolishness.

It may sometimes be difficult for us to practice wisdom in this kind of existence. Consumer culture entices us to forsake our erotic nature and sicken ourselves in an isolated, drunken frenzy of possession. Moralism would have us condemn humanity: unattractive, disordered, capable of unimaginable cruelty and stupidity. These confusions make it tempting simply to repress or condemn desire. And yet, as Julian of Norwich noted, the erotic nature of the divine may be seen even in the midst of suffering and anguish. Envisioning an underlying tenderness that cherishes creation as unconditionally as our ideal mothers cherish their children, she writes: "And so Jesus is our true Mother in nature by our first creation, and he is our true Mother in grace by his taking our created nature. All the lovely works and all the sweet loving offices of beloved motherhood are appropriated to the second person." She expounds on this metaphor in her next chapter: "[O]ur great God, the supreme wisdom of all things, arrayed and prepared himself in this humble place, all ready in our poor flesh, himself to do the service and the office of motherhood in everything. The mother's service is nearest, readiest and surest: nearest because it is most natural, readiest because it is most loving, and surest because it is truest. No one ever might or could perform this office fully, except only him."[29]

It may be difficult for us to cherish the beauty of the earth: amoral, terrifying, vast beyond our control or imagination, violent and incomprehensible. But if we are to love God, we must love what God loves: ourselves, one another, and the earth. We must try to cherish one another as bearers of the divine Eros, in admittedly maimed and often horrifying

29. Julian of Norwich, *Showings,* trans. with an introduction by Edmund Colledge and James Walsh (New York: Paulist Press, 1978), chapters 59 and 60 of the Long Text, pp. 296-97. In light of Grenholm's analysis, it might be interesting to investigate whether Julian's depiction of the erotic nature of the divine mother's love could be helpful. It might also be useful to explore her celebration of human motherhood, which recognizes that human mothers also need protection and cannot be expected to embody the perfect mothering possible only by the divine mother.

forms. For "we are his bliss, we are his reward, we are his honor, we are his crown."[30] For Julian, the limitless desire of the divine for humanity means that Christ must come to us in our suffering. In stark contrast to Mel Gibson's depiction of the Passion, we do not suffer because we must imitate Christ; Christ suffers because it is only in this imitation of our suffering that the divine can come to us in our genuine need. Julian describes the face of Christ, utterly disfigured by anguish and torment, as the most beautiful face in the world. This face is the face of humanity in our long crucifixion. Julian, awakened to the solidarity that joins the human to the divine and all humans to one another, sees in the contortions of our condition the most beautiful face in the world. This is a beauty Christianity too often disdains or transmutes into a penal theology that obscures the radicality of divine love in favor of punishment that buys forgiveness. But for Julian, mother Christ adores us even in our suffering, and our condition is made luminous by the unconditional nearness of the divine.

It is the vocation of Christian communities to participate in the love by which the divine Eros cherishes the world. We imitate Christ not in our suffering but by being beguiled by the beauty of humanity, tricked neither by the meretricious pleasures of the market nor by the despised mask of suffering. Inhabited by divine desire, we can hope to recognize the face of humanity as the most beautiful in the world, the face of Christ, beautiful and tormented.

Biology prods us with amoral impulses toward the variety of pleasures that maintain life. A consumer culture entices us with a glittery fantasy world in which every craving finds satisfaction. We find joys in romantic relations, in love for our children, in the pleasures of friendship; and we find consolations in a hot cup of coffee, a good meal, a new dress. At the root of our being we are emptied into the abyss of divine Eros. Whether it is directed toward the divine Mother and Lover or the neighbor's wife, desire can feel as unmasterable as the sea. Whether we see this force playing out in a toddler's tantrum, a saint's passion, or a CEO's humiliating fall, we might as well try to pin back the waves as deny the force of desire in us. Somehow Christianity must acknowledge all of these aspects of desire and witness to ways to live in this kind of world, pulled apart by these crashing cross-currents, faithful to the luminous image of God we must bear within us.

30. Julian of Norwich, *Showings*, p. 216.

"God is also in the pots and pans" (Teresa of Avila)

If we think of Christianity not only as belief but as desire, practices that shape desire will be crucial to a life of faith. Everything we do, see, think, reject, and seek shapes our desire.[31] To the extent that we separate our daily actions from Christian practice, most of our formation, spiritually and socially, will be handed over to secular society. To wish to jettison this world as inherently evil would be to submit to a kind of contemporary Manichaeism. And yet to remain dominated by it betrays the counter-cultural message of the gospel. In this concluding section, I will make some proposals for thinking about the formation of desire through every-day practices of prayer and mindfulness. Naturally, there are many other practices one might explore. I offer these only as examples.

The subjection of desire to egocentrism and to market capitalism finds a parallel in the ancient theological wisdom that desire is hindered by a bondage that is hard to see and harder to break.[32] The absence of true freedom is made all the more tragic because we retain the illusion of freedom in our capacity for choice. Because agency is a "misleading description of what desire fundamentally is," the reformation of desire cannot be located simply in ideas.[33] I would suggest that we consider the significance of contemplative prayer as a bridge between what we consciously choose and believe and our preconscious habits and desires. Through contemplative forms of Christianity there is an accumulated wisdom about how we can reshape desire in ways that liberate us for love, even though many of our habits and desires remain hidden from us and are not directly subject to our control.[34]

---

31. Thomas Aquinas's analysis of habitus remains as insightful as any for reflecting on how our actions shape us in ways of which we are not fully conscious (*Summa Theologica* I ii, questions 49-54).

32. "I do not understand my own actions. For I do not do what I want, but I do the very thing I hate. . . . I do not do the good I want, but the evil I do not want is what I do" (Rom. 7:15, 19). This theme is systematized in the writings of Augustine, and after him, Luther and Calvin, who believed that "true *libertas* — that is, freedom in the sense of the ability to love God fully, and hence will the good with complete righteousness — perished as a result of the Fall." Aaron Stalnaker, *Overcoming Our Evil: Human Nature and Spiritual Exercises in Xunzi and Augustine* (Washington, DC: Georgetown University Press, 2006), p. 104.

33. Henriksen, "Desire: Gift and Giving," p. 11 in this volume.

34. Pierre Hadot's work is a particularly good description of the role of spiritual practice in ancient Christian and non-Christian communities, which envisioned that the human being could be transformed for equanimity and love through practices that focused the

Prayer is a particularly powerful practice for the reforming of desire because it can quiet, however briefly, the incessant demands of the ego. When conscious thought is calmed, the mind opens up upon its depths. From a Christian point of view, these depths are where the apophatic "self" and the apophatic divinity exist in the unity of love. Near the end of her life, Mechthild of Magdeburg described this prayer as the intimacy of human and divine love: "Our Lord said: 'I longed for you before the beginning of the world. I long for you and you long for me. Where two burning desires meet, there love is perfect.'"[35] There are a number of techniques for silent prayer. They usually involve methods for focusing the mind so that it does not lose itself entirely in the internal chatter that constantly preoccupies our mental attention. The anonymous author of *The Cloud of Unknowing* recommends that we use a short word to focus our mind, but reassures us that "a naked intention directed to God, and himself alone, is wholly sufficient."[36] We might focus on our breath or on a sacred word. We might attend especially to the effort of concentration or the more gentle direction of attention.[37]

But whatever its form, contemplative prayer allows us to dwell in silence, nourished by the immediacy of love, and so recognize that the claims of the ego and the world are not ultimate. We might use Augustine's distinction to say that silent prayer helps us to enjoy rather than to merely use the world.[38] Prayer allows us to live in the world neither despising it

---

mind on the divine. See especially Part II of *Philosophy as a Way of Life: Spiritual Exercises from Socrates to Foucault* (Malden, MA: Blackwell, 1995).

35. Mechthild of Magdeburg, *Flowing Light of the Godhead*, VII.16.

36. *The Cloud of Unknowing*, trans. with an introduction by Clifton Wolters (Baltimore: Penguin Classics, 1961), ch. 7 (p. 61).

37. There are now many books about Christian contemplative practice, including, for example, James Finley's *Christian Contemplation: Experiencing the Presence of God* (New York: HarperOne, 2004). Guidance in centering prayer can be found in the work of Fr. Thomas Keating, Basil Pennington, and Cynthia Bourgeault. Mary Jo Meadow's *Christian Insight Meditation: Following in the Footsteps of John of the Cross* (Somerville, MA: Wisdom Publications, 2007) draws connections between St. John of the Cross and Buddhist meditation. An example of the practice of *lectio divina* is found in Martin Smith's book *The Word Is Very Near You: A Guide to Praying with Scripture* (Cambridge, MA: Cowley, 1989).

38. Although if we were to use Augustine in this way we might have to reinterpret what he means. See Sigurdson's discussion of Augustine in his chapter in this volume. Carlo Carretto offers a somewhat gentler reflection on the importance and difficulty of loving creatures as well as the Creator in a genuinely life-giving way, in *Letters from the Desert* (Maryknoll, NY: Orbis Books, 2002), pp. 26-27.

nor addicted to its goods. We dwell in the multidimensionality of our lives more spontaneously. We weave together and integrate the deep truth of our being with the everyday realities of incarnate, social existence. This is not renunciation but a fuller, deeper immersion into the world. Integrating prayer into daily life, day by day and even moment by moment, is a way of constantly orienting oneself to the ground of one's joy and desire. By pausing, however briefly, for silent prayer, we build a reservoir — or perhaps connect to this reservoir — of calm from which we return refreshed for our normal activities. We rest in the divine Eros even as we are preoccupied with daily life.

Another dimension of the formation of desire is the practice of mindfulness. This kind of prayer is not the concentrated silence of contemplative prayer but the reorientation of mind and heart through everyday tasks. Jon Kabat-Zinn's development of mindfulness-based stress reduction (MBSR) has made the discipline of mindfulness more available to the medical establishment as a component of healing.[39] But mindfulness practice is deeply rooted in the practices of the ancient Christian ascetics. Evagrius Ponticus gives much advice regarding the practice of watching the way emotions and passions arise in us. One of the main practices he describes is to "keep careful watch over [one's] thoughts."[40] Dorotheus of Gaza emphasizes the practice of mindfulness as simply paying attention to what we are doing and feeling, so we notice feelings of anger or jealousy or lust as they arise and before they overpower us. This practice also weaves mindfulness into everyday activities.[41] We can send up prayers of intercession or thanksgiving as we listen to the car radio. We can twine our suffocating frustration with consciousness of a dimension of calm. We can weave the layers of con-

39. Jon Kabat-Zinn founded the Stress Reduction Clinic at the University of Massachusetts Medical Center and is the author of a number of books, including *Full Catastrophe Living* (New York: Delta, 2005), and, with his wife, *Everyday Blessings* (New York: Hyperion, 1997); also see his audio CD *Mindfulness for Beginners* (Sounds True, 2007). Another contemporary interpreter who puts together Buddhist and Christian traditions of mindfulness is B. Alan Wallace, *Mind in the Balance: Meditation in Science, Buddhism, and in Christianity* (New York: Columbia University Press, 2009).

40. Evagrius Ponticus, *The Praktikos and Chapters on Prayer*, Saying 50. A modern reader should not be unduly put off by the personification of interior mental events as demons, which is characteristic of this period.

41. Dorotheus of Gaza is a good example of mindfulness as a way of watching our emotional reactions to everyday life, in *Dorotheus of Gaza Discourses and Sayings: Desert Humor and Humility*, trans. with an introduction by Eric P. Wheeler (Kalamazoo: Cistercian Publications, 1977).

sciousness together in every act and dedicate every emotion — fear, wonder, anger, anxiety, thanks — into our life with the divine.[42]

Basil Pennington reminds us that *lectio* is the reception of revelation in whatever form it comes to us. Normally it is understood to refer to the meditative reading of scripture, but it can also occur in relation to art and the much "larger book of revelation; the whole of the work of the Creator." He notes that Bernard of Clairvaux "found God more in the trees and brooks than in the books."[43] The integration of Christian practice with everyday life should not be understood as a repression of ordinary human desire in favor of a fantasy about purity. Instead, we pour ourselves out for God in the minutiae of our lives, consciously weaving all of our everyday attachments, fears, and anxieties into our faith. This practice allows us to view our desires in a fresh way that challenges anything that harms us, including the normalized predations of a consumer society and teachings of the church that fail to be life-giving.

Through mindfulness practice we become clearer about what we actually believe and desire without leaping to judgment or condemnation. By releasing the habit of moralizing, mindfulness provides a space in which what is actually harmful to us can be seen more clearly. What we discover may surprise us. Mindfulness may be a way for mothers to recognize that the voice that represses their desires is not the voice of God but of patriarchal society. Mindful consumption may alter our purchasing patterns. Instead of moralistically rejecting things we enjoy, we might discover how anxieties and frustrations have been channeled into consumption. We are less bound to destructive patterns of consumption even while we are able to enjoy things that we had denied ourselves. When the wounds of anxiety or guilt are integrated into our desire for God, we can inhabit our consumer world with a greater degree of freedom.

---

42. This interpretation of a judgmental piety as a symptom of sin rather than faith is found in Schleiermacher's *Christian Faith,* especially in his analysis of the work of Christ and the doctrine of regeneration. "The assumption into vital fellowship with Christ, therefore, dissolves the connexion between sin and evil, since morally the two are no longer related to each other, even if from the merely natural point of view the one is the consequence of the other. . . . Now here the beginning is the disappearance of the old man, and so also of the consciousness of deserving punishment. Consequently the first thing in the reconciling aspect is the forgiveness of sins. For in the unity of life with Christ all relation to the law ceases" (*Christian Faith,* 101.2).

43. Basil Pennington, *Centering Prayer: Renewing an Ancient Christian Prayer Form* (New York: Doubleday/Image, 1982), p. 14.

The weaving of ordinary desire into Christian practice might also change our relations to others. The reformation of desire that allows us to see and delight in others may translate indifference or duty into genuine compassion. We may experience more deeply a desire to ameliorate harm and to protect the beauty of other people, their cultures, and our world. We cannot escape the web of connections that relate us to oppressive and polluting activities. But when we consider our consumption as a practice of faith, our erotic attunement to the world may give us energy to support humane rather than destructive practices. At the same time, the reformation of desire may clarify our deepest vocation. By focusing our energies we renounce obligations inconsistent with the realities of our time and energy. Thinking about everyday practices of cleaning, purchasing, parenting, and entertainment as reformations of desire might clarify how we, as Christians, want to inhabit this world. It might empower a discipline to live responsibly and justly that is rooted in joy. Pierre Hadot notes the tension in spiritual practice between equanimity and the intensified sense of commitment to the human community. This concern for justice is essential to spiritual practice, but "is probably the hardest part to carry out. The trick is to maintain oneself on the level of reason, and not allow oneself to be blinded by political passions, anger, resentments, or prejudices. To be sure there is an equilibrium — almost impossible to achieve — between the inner peace brought by wisdom, and the passions to which the sight of the injustices, sufferings, and misery of [humanity] cannot help but give rise. Wisdom, however, consists in precisely such an equilibrium, and inner peace is indispensable for efficacious action."[44]

By trying to engage desire more directly as a Christian practice, we might also break out of the dichotomy between secular hedonism and oppressive morality. Bringing our sexuality directly into the life of faith through mindfulness and prayer makes it possible to better distinguish what is life-giving from what is debilitating. We might have a chance to notice the ways in which a socially acceptable hedonism — prevalent on college campuses, for example — turns out to be rather empty, perhaps even self-destructive in ways we had not recognized. This is not the application of a repressive, even antiquated, morality. It is the discovery of how harmful alienated sexuality can be, not least as it serves patriarchal interests at the expense of one's inner wisdom. When we become more attuned to what is destructive and what is healing, we might also acknowledge a wider

44. Hadot, *Philosophy as a Way of Life*, p. 274.

range of eroticism and love that is life-giving and healing. Gay and lesbian Christians integrate their sexuality with their faith by attending to the nearness of the divine that is mediated through all genuine love, including their own.

These are only a few examples of how a reformation of desire might be present in everyday life. Faith is always unpredictable, apophatic, but, as Brother Lawrence puts it: "At any moment and in any circumstance, the soul that seeks God may find God and practice the presence of God."[45]

Conclusion — "Whatever Is Gracious": Faith and the Divine Eros

Through desire we are linked to God's desire for us. But we bear this divine image in bodies and in societies that confuse as well as delight us. Culture and even religion embody power structures, patriarchy, ignorance, prejudice, hedonism, and intolerance that cannot be assumed to be consistent with faith. By attempting to integrate faithful desire into ordinary life we modify the way we interact with culture and religion. We can replace normalized, if harmful, interpretations of desire with a more deeply experiential awareness of the life-giving power of faith. This frees us to navigate our social world with greater compassion for suffering and joy in the beauty of the world.

Perhaps the more significant consequence of saving desire is the reorganization of the very categories through which we interpret faith. A reformation of desire dissolves polarities between law and grace and between renunciation and attachment. These categories are inconsistent with the realities of our biological lives and also with the tender mercies of the gospel. Erotic Christianity attends to what is life-giving and what is healing. What ways of life make our bodies and spirits strong, joyous, and compassionate? What ways of life darken our sympathy for others and thwart the expression of our gifts? What are the social structures that contribute to the amelioration of suffering? What can the church do to live out a compassionate embrace of all creation?

Saving desire is rooted in longing for God. Attention to the divine Eros

45. Brother Lawrence, *The Practice of the Presence of God* (Grand Rapids: Baker, 1967). He is quoted as saying, "The time of business does not with me differ from the time of prayer; and in the noise and clatter of my kitchen, while several persons are at the same time calling for different things, I possess God in as great tranquility as if I were upon my knees at the blessed sacrament" (p. 30).

destabilizes our egocentric pleasures and anxieties. It works with the realities of our minds and of our communities. It does not deliver much in the way of universal standards or apodictic certainty. To the contrary, when we attend to the particular by cherishing God's creation in its unique embodiments, the messiness of life is more rather than less obvious. But if we are bereft of certainty we lean toward a sparking of the love that animates faith. Suffering may become both more egregious as compassion is intensified and at the same time more bearable because it is not ultimate.

In our disorientation by the divine Eros we can pray with St. Paul: "whatever is true, whatever is honorable, whatever is just, whatever is pure, whatever is lovely, whatever is gracious, if there is excellence, if there is anything worthy of praise, think about these things" (Phil. 4:8). We have here no clear standards or rules, only an invitation to delight in the mysterious and omnipresent goodness of the divine, scattered throughout creation and discovered in the most unexpected places, not least in the faces of all those who bear the divine image.

The Shaping of Erotic Desire in Proverbs 1–9

Christine Roy Yoder

As many contributors to this volume note, history abounds with portraits of erotic desire as dangerous coupled with efforts to control and repress it. Some philosophers and theologians would eliminate desire, particularly erotic desire, at least as part of an ethical life. The Greek Stoics believed that the attainment of virtues brought freedom from passions. Paul encouraged believers not to marry unless they lacked self-control ("it is better to marry than to be aflame with passion," 1 Cor. 7:9).[1] And Immanuel Kant argued that sexual desire leads to "using" people and thereby degrading their humanity — a tendency that only marriage with its promises of mutual concern might limit.[2] Implicit in these points of view is the notion that desire lacks intentionality and cannot be redirected: desire is, so to speak, "hardwired" into human psychology and, as a result, is contrary to knowledge and good judgment. Intense and impure, desire is a danger, "a disease that good thought ought to cure."[3] It is no wonder that, as Wendy Farley observes, Christianity has long been nervous about it.

So it is striking that Proverbs 1–9, the hermeneutical key to a book that aims to teach wisdom and to form "fearers of the LORD" (1:2, 7), engages

---

1. D. B. Martin, "Paul without Passion: On Paul's Rejection of Desire in Sex and Marriage," in *Constructing Early Christian Families: Family as Social Reality and Metaphor,* ed. H. Moxnes (London and New York: Routledge, 1997), pp. 201-15.

2. I. Kant, *Lectures on Ethics,* trans. L. Infield (Indianapolis: Hackett, 1980), pp. 163-64.

3. M. C. Nussbaum, *Upheavals of Thought: The Intelligence of Emotions* (New York: Cambridge University Press, 2001), p. 461. See also J. Butler, *Subjects of Desire: Hegelian Reflections in Twentieth-Century France* (New York: Columbia University Press, 1987), esp. pp. 1-15.

An abbreviated version of this chapter appeared in *Journal for Preachers* 33 (2010): 54-61.

erotic desire as a vital element of the moral life. Framed as a father's instruction to his son or sons,[4] these chapters place an "extraordinary emphasis" on erotic desire — an emphasis "out of all proportion" with treatment of the topic elsewhere in the book[5] — not with hope of repressing or eliminating it, but rather of pointing the youth's desire toward the "right" *objects*. Desire itself is assumed; the concern is the power of desire rightly or wrongly directed. And whereas we may anticipate correctly that "right" objects of desire include one's lifelong companion ("the wife of one's youth," 5:18) and "wrong" objects include another person's spouse ("the wife of another," 6:26), the parent's extension of erotic desire to talk about our relationship with the abstract concepts of "wisdom" and "folly" is unexpected.[6] Suddenly, the pursuit and attainment of knowledge is not about the extirpation of passion. Rather, it requires cultivation of it.

Not surprisingly, the parent's teaching about desire is entwined with similarly abundant language of emotion.[7] Proverbs 1 alone, for example, refers to greed (1:19), love and delight (1:22), hate (1:22, 29-30), terror, distress, and anguish (1:26-27, 33). Personified wisdom identifies herself as "delight" and rejoices before God and in the world (8:30-31). And God is said variously to love like a parent (3:12), to hate (6:16), and to revel with wisdom (8:30). Although typically considered distinct phenomena, desire and emotion (along with appetites) have been grouped and analyzed together since Aristotle. Recent studies in philosophy, ethics, psychology, and

4. The father-to-son setting is common in ancient Near Eastern wisdom literature. For example, the epilogue of the Egyptian *Instruction of Anii* is a dialogue between a father and son (M. Lichtheim, *Ancient Egyptian Literature,* 3 vols. [Berkeley: University of California Press, 1973-80], 2:144-45), and the Sumerian *Instructions of Shuruppak* are lessons that Shuruppak teaches his son (W. G. Lambert, *Babylonian Wisdom Literature* [Winona Lake: Eisenbrauns, 1996], pp. 92-94). Elsewhere in the Old Testament, Ecclesiastes addresses "my son" (12:12). In Proverbs, the father-to-son setting continues throughout chapters 1–9 and is assumed occasionally later in the book (19:27; 23:15, 19, 26; 24:13, 21; 27:11). Twice, the father associates his teaching with that of his wife (1:8; 6:20), but she never speaks directly to the son.

5. R. Murphy, "Wisdom and Eros in Proverbs 1–9," *Catholic Biblical Quarterly* 50 (1988): 600.

6. Other ancient Near Eastern wisdom texts address marital infidelity but only briefly (see the Egyptian *Instruction of Ptahhotep* and *Instruction of Anii*). The extension of desire to personified wisdom recurs in Sirach 4:11-19; 6:18-31; 14:20–15:8; 51:13-30; and Wisdom 6:12-16; 7:7-10; 8:2-6; 9:4-10 — texts subsequent to Proverbs and arguably informed by it.

7. See my "The Objects of Our Affections: Emotions and the Moral Life in Proverbs 1–9," in *Shaking Heaven and Earth: Essays in Honor of Walter Brueggemann and Charles B. Cousar,* ed. C. Roy Yoder et al. (Louisville: Westminster John Knox, 2005), pp. 73-88.

neurobiology emphasize their close connection.[8] Far from irrational impulses or animalistic energies, emotions are increasingly considered forms of intelligence and discernment.

As Martha Nussbaum argues, emotions have objects; they are "about something." Emotions embody a person's perception of and beliefs about the object and invest the object with value — as significant for some role it plays in the person's life.[9] As such, emotions appear to be eudaimonistic,[10] namely, concerned with a person's flourishing. Desire, in turn, is an aspect or consequence of emotion.[11] Emotion frequently inspires a desire to act. So, for example, fear may prompt a desire to run away; anger may spark a desire for retaliation; and love may stir a desire to protect and be with the beloved. Of course, not all emotions motivate a definite plan of action (e.g., happiness may prompt a desire simply for more happiness; grief may prompt the wish that the person one loves did not die), but the connection — that emotion gives rise to desire — suggests that desire is also intentional and eudaimonistic.

Erotic desire is admittedly more complex, exhibiting elements of push and pull. On the one hand, it is a drive that arises independently of the presence of an object and *pushes* for satisfaction. On the other hand, erotic desire may be *pulled* into being by the value of the object, and thereby exhibit "rich and selective intentionality."[12] The parent of Proverbs 1–9 assumes the push: not once is erotic desire itself labeled a vice; not once is the youth told to repress it. Instead, the parent seizes on the pull of erotic

8. For example, see Nussbaum, *Upheavals of Thought;* and R. C. Roberts, *Emotions: An Essay in Aid of Moral Psychology* (New York: Cambridge University Press, 2003), esp. pp. 160-67.

9. For more of Nussbaum's argument, see her "Emotions as Judgments of Value and Importance," in *Thinking about Feeling: Contemporary Philosophers on Emotions,* ed. Robert C. Solomon (Oxford: Oxford University Press, 2004), pp. 183-99; and *Upheavals of Thought,* pp. 19-88. See also N. Sherman, "Wise Emotions," in *Understanding Wisdom: Sources, Science, and Society,* ed. W. S. Brown (Radnor, PA: Templeton Foundation Press, 2000), pp. 319-37.

10. Nussbaum favors the Greek spelling of this term instead of the English (eudaemonistic) because the former broadly includes distinct conceptions of what is good while the latter, in her view, is too narrowly associated with the notion that the supreme good is happiness (*Upheavals of Thought,* p. 31 n. 23).

11. Roberts, *Emotions,* pp. 160-67; Nussbaum, *Upheavals of Thought,* pp. 135-36.

12. Nussbaum, *Upheavals of Thought,* p. 131. Consider, for example, that Eve, at the serpent's urging, comes to see the fruit of the forbidden tree differently and to desire it: when she "saw that the tree was good for food, and that it was a delight to the eyes, and that the tree was to be desired to make one wise, she took of its fruit and ate" (Gen. 3:6).

desire — its intensity and partiality — and attempts to direct the youth's desire by teaching about the value or danger of its potential objects. The attempt reveals a conviction that desire may, at least in part, be socially formed or constructed.

That is, the youth learns desires in much the same way one learns one's beliefs, namely, through interactions with others — predominantly with parents or other caregivers in the beginning, and then later with a wider community. With the parent(s) as his first model (cf. 1:8; 6:20), the youth "tries on" various desires that in due course will hopefully become his own. Desires develop over time and, arguably, even as an adult may be modified — by changes in the environment (e.g., customs, institutions, laws), relationships, or changes in thought, for instance.[13] Indeed, inasmuch as Proverbs conceives the quest for wisdom to be a lifelong endeavor (e.g., 1:4), the possibility of learning something new in adulthood — including something that modifies one's emotions and desires — is assumed. Moreover, the inclusion of both persons *and* concepts (such as wisdom) as potential "objects" signals an understanding that erotic desire includes but is not limited to sex; it is a potent metaphor for how one comes to know the world, others, oneself, and God.[14]

My contribution to our common work is to consider how the parent of Proverbs 1–9 characterizes erotic desires as rightly and wrongly directed. By desiring "right" objects, the wise gain knowledge and flourish; they become interdependent[15] with God, wisdom, and others. Conversely, the fool's misplaced desires result in isolation and alienation from others and spark violence and rage in the community. Finally, I reflect briefly on some implications of desire so conceived for thinking about moral formation in our own time.

It is important to note up front that the parent of Proverbs 1–9 aims to shape the erotic desire of young men of relatively privileged circum-

---

13. See Roberts, *Emotions*, p. 351; M. C. Nussbaum, "Narrative Emotions: Beckett's Genealogy of Love," *Ethics* 1 (1988): 234-35; *Upheavals of Thought*, esp. pp. 139-237. This is not to dispute that there may also be evolutionary origins for emotions and desires.

14. Other contributors to this volume emphasize the orienting function of desire. See especially Henriksen and Farley.

15. By "interdependent" I mean (a) recognizing that those whom we love are separate from us and not mere instruments of our will; (b) depending on them in certain ways (without insisting on omnipotence); and, in turn, (c) inviting others to depend on us and committing ourselves to be responsible to and for them in particular ways (see Nussbaum, *Upheavals of Thought*, pp. 224-29).

stances, perhaps the sons of affluent and moderately wealthy members of an urban commercial class.[16] As several studies highlight, the portrait of erotic desire in Proverbs 1–9 is thus clearly male, and the text reflects and reinforces a context that is patriarchal in structure and androcentric in bias.[17] For example, the juxtaposition of personified wisdom and folly perpetuates the stereotyped polarization of women as wholly good or wholly evil, with men as either their beneficiaries or their victims; a woman outside of one's household who initiates sex is cast as a dangerous aggressor (7:6-23; cf. 6:23-26[18]); and men are attributed ownership of their brides (e.g., 5:15-19). Moreover, the parent's construction of desire assumes that self-centeredness (being "wise in your own eyes," 3:7), arrogance, and autonomy are key obstacles to a wise, ethical existence — an assumption that a description of women's erotic desire might well not share.[19] Alert to the parent's particularity and the possibilities and perils of his pedagogy, I turn now to consider the parent's construction of erotic desire as essential to the moral life.

Desire Directed Rightly

As the parent describes it, the wise person is a desiring subject — one who longs for the right object: wisdom. The youth is urged repeatedly to "seek" wisdom (1:28; 2:4; 7:15; 8:17), to cry out for it (2:3; cf. 1:28), to search for it as for hidden treasures (2:4), and to watch and wait daily at personified wisdom's door (8:34). Moreover, even when the youth "finds" wisdom (e.g., 2:5; 3:13; 8:9, 17, 35), even when he "acquires" it (3:13; 4:5, 7), his pursuit of

16. Note, for example, that the parent assumes that the youth has ownership of or access to agricultural production (3:9-10) and money (5:10; 6:35), and that the youth needs guidance about the proper management of that money — including the dodging of get-rich-quick schemes (1:11-19), responsible giving (3:9-10; cf. 3:27-28), and the avoidance of certain financial risks (6:1-5).

17. See, e.g., C. A. Newsom, "Woman and the Discourse of Patriarchal Wisdom: A Study of Proverbs 1–9," in *Gender and Difference in Ancient Israel*, ed. P. Day (Minneapolis: Augsburg Fortress, 1989), pp. 142-60; G. A. Yee, "'I Have Perfumed My Bed with Myrrh': The Foreign Woman (*'iššâ zārâ*) in Proverbs 1–9," *Journal for the Study of the Old Testament* 43 (1989): 53-68.

18. Reference to the intoxicating power of a wife's lovemaking leaves open the possibility that she may initiate sex with her husband (5:19).

19. See W. Farley, *Eros for the Other: Retaining Truth in a Pluralistic World* (University Park: Pennsylvania State University Press, 1986), pp. 105-10; and the contribution by C. Grenholm to this volume.

wisdom continues. The book's prologue, for example, beckons the discerning to learn more (1:5-6), the wise are to be ardently receptive to instruction (e.g., listening, watching, inclining their hearts), and personified wisdom's invitation to her home and the feast she prepares is in the present tense, that is, perpetual and immediate (9:4-5). Paradoxically, one can never wholly possess wisdom; there is no moment of "stable perfection,"[20] no arrival at or achievement of intellectual or contemplative purity. Instead, the predominant metaphor for life in Proverbs 1–9 — a path or way — indicates that the wise (and foolish) are on a journey, while active verbs convey unremitting movement *toward* the good (so "walk," "run," "stumble," "enter," "avoid," "go," "turn away," and "pass by" in 4:12-19 alone). Assumed is a lifelong yearning for and pursuit of wisdom — a hunger that is not satisfied ultimately, a thirst that is not quenched. Compare personified wisdom's self-revelation in Sirach 24:21: "Those who eat of me will hunger for more, and those who drink of me will thirst for more." Desire for wisdom is intrinsic to the virtuous life. And because that desire is never sated, the wise never cease reaching for the good.[21]

The parent's emphasis on desire locates what is good for the human *outside the self.* Desire *opens* a person. Inherent is an understanding of the human as limited and in need of knowledge from beyond oneself for wholeness. Conversely, wisdom is pictured as independent, not simply part of its pursuer. The parent underscores wisdom's independence variously, calling wisdom a divine gift (2:5-6), personifying wisdom as a woman who takes her stand in the heart of the city, in the bustle of everyday life (1:20-21; 8:2-3), extolling wisdom's preeminent and mysterious relationship with God (8:22-31), celebrating wisdom as the means by which God formed the world (3:19-20), and, with only one exception (5:1), never referring to wisdom as belonging to a person (that is, with a possessive suffix). Furthermore, by designating God as the source of wisdom (2:5-6[22]), the parent couples desire for wisdom with desire for God — so that waiting and longing for wisdom become expressions of worship. Indeed, Proverbs repeatedly insists that the wise are, first and foremost, "fearers of the LORD"[23] and,

---

20. Nussbaum, *Upheavals of Thought*, p. 537.

21. Henriksen observes similarly in this volume that because desire is not satisfied once and for all, "it makes us able to participate more fully and more continuously in the goodness of the world" (p. 6). See also Farley, *Eros for the Other*, p. 69.

22. Disrupted word order in Prov. 2:6a emphasizes that God is the source of wisdom: "For *YHWH* gives wisdom."

23. The so-called "motto" of Proverbs declares: "the fear of the LORD is the beginning

by implication, that there are no distinctions between "sacred" and "secu-lar," "spiritual" and "rational" ways of knowing.[24] The parent thus portrays the wise as incomplete in and of themselves, and wisdom — the good they seek — as elusive, mysterious, wholly and holy "other." Not surprisingly, humility is a hallmark of wisdom (e.g., 3:34; 15:33).

The characterization of desire for personified wisdom as *erotic* signals its partiality and intensity. The parent encourages partiality by celebrating wisdom's intrinsic and incomparable value — she is more precious than jewels, gold, and choice silver (3:14-15; 8:10-11, 19); twice the parent insists, "nothing you desire can compare with her" (3:15b; 8:11; and "with all you possess, get insight," 4:7). The use of particular verbs, often as imperatives, demonstrates that desire for wisdom prompts acts of emotional and physi-cal intensity: seize her (3:18; 4:13), take hold of her (3:18), do not abandon or divorce her (4:6), guard her (4:6), embrace her (4:8; cf. 4:13), watch over her (4:13), and do not let her go (4:13). The parent implores the youth to love wisdom (4:6; cf. 8:17, 21) and cherish her (so 4:8) — the emotions most likely to prompt desire to be with wisdom — and to "acquire" her (so 4:5, 7), a verb that can connote possession and/or marriage (cf. Ruth 4:5, 10). The youth should call wisdom his "sister," an expression of romantic endearment (Prov. 7:4; cf. Song 4:9, 10, 12),[25] and wait expectantly, as lovers do, "day by day" outside wisdom's house (Prov. 8:34; cf. Job 31:9; Song 2:9; Sir. 14:20-25). At every turn, the parent seeks to inculcate in the youth a passion for wisdom that is comparable to the erotic desire of a lover for the beloved — a passion that wisdom promises to reciprocate ("I love the one who loves me," Prov. 8:17; cf. 4:6, 8-9).

Such desire for wisdom, the parent contends, is *necessary* for human flourishing. Not only does the desire itself inspire happiness ("happy is

---

(*rēʾšît*) of knowledge" (1:7a). The term *rēʾšît* may be interpreted temporally as "beginning" or "starting point" (cf. Gen. 10:10; Jer. 26:1), suggesting that "fear of the LORD" is the prerequi-site or foundation for knowledge. The term may also be read qualitatively, so that this fear is the "first," "best," or "epitome" (e.g., Jer. 2:3; Amos 6:6) of knowledge. Understood as such, "fear of the LORD" is the quintessential expression of what it means to be wise. Either way, and the ambiguity may well be intentional, there is no wisdom without it.

24. As G. von Rad famously observed, "It was perhaps [Israel's] greatness that she did not keep faith and knowledge apart. The experiences of the world were for her always divine experiences as well, and the experiences of God were for her experiences of the world" (*Wis-dom in Israel*, trans. J. D. Martin [London: SCM, 1972], p. 62).

25. Egyptian love poetry also employs "sister" as a term of romantic endearment (e.g., Lichtheim, *Ancient Egyptian Literature*, 2:181-93).

the one who . . . watches daily at my gates," 8:34), but wisdom herself bestows it ("happiness" or "blessing," 3:13, 18; 8:32, 34).[26] Moreover, wisdom identifies herself as sheer "delight" (8:30b). Before God and in the world she "rejoices," a verb that refers broadly to "making merry" — playing (Job 40:20; Zech. 8:5), singing and dancing (e.g., 1 Sam. 18:6-7; 2 Sam. 6:5, 21), telling jokes and performing tricks (e.g., Prov. 26:19; Ps. 104:26; Jer. 15:17). God and humanity revel with her as she does with them. Learning so conceived is neither tedious nor burdensome, but a joy-filled, love-inspiring, and playful relationship with knowledge and God that, in turn, fosters health and long life (Prov. 3:16, 18; cf. 3:8), dispels fear and anxiety (1:33; 4:6; cf. 2:11), and makes possible honor and prosperity (3:14, 16; 4:9; 8:15-16, 18-19, 21).

Whereas philosophers and theologians have long cautioned that the partiality and intensity of erotic desire make it adverse to general social concern — that passionate attachment to another person fosters exclusivity — the parent of Proverbs 1–9 contends exactly the opposite with regard to desire for wisdom. Desire for wisdom *turns one outward;* it dismantles preoccupation with oneself (being "wise in one's eyes," e.g., 3:7), and prompts one to regard others and the world not as things for one's enjoyment but as independent and divinely wrought. Desire for wisdom thus engenders a fierce commitment to neighborliness and justice: *it empowers one's moral agency.* At the heart of the prologue of Proverbs, for example, the sages claim that wisdom motivates "righteousness, justice, and equity" (1:3b; cf. 2:9) — terms that together refer comprehensively to ethical and honest conduct in personal and communal relationships. The wise are said to "understand righteousness and justice and equity, every good path" (2:9), and to walk, as does personified wisdom, on "paths of justice" (e.g., 2:8; 8:20; cf. 2:20; 4:11) and peace (*shalom,* 3:17). Indeed, the terms "wise" and "righteous" eventually become interchangeable,[27] and the wise person's sphere of concern is said to include the land and all creatures, animal and human (10:5; 12:10; 24:27; 27:23-27).

The parent offers concrete examples of how those who desire wisdom engage the "neighbor" and/or "friend." The wise speak honestly (4:24). They do not withhold good from those to whom it is due, plot harm

---

26. Indeed, the term "happy" or "blessed" forms an *inclusio* around the tribute to wisdom in 3:13-18.

27. So, for example, the righteous are juxtaposed with fools in 10:21, not with the wicked as we expect.

against the neighbor, quarrel without cause, or participate in violence (3:27-32; cf. 1:10-19; 4:17; 6:12-19). They avoid risky economic entanglements (6:1-5), honor the relationships of others (6:29-35), and refuse to "sow discord" (6:14, 19). Wisdom also inspires rulers of every people and nation to "decree what is just" and govern rightly (8:15-16). Later in the book, the sages describe the wise as knowing the "rights of the poor" (29:7a) and being generous with them — motivated by the conviction that God created everyone, and God is concerned particularly for the vulnerable (e.g., 14:21, 31; 15:25).[28] By orienting a person outward, desire for wisdom awakens one to the beauty (the createdness) and to the suffering of others, and compels one to act with compassion and justice.

At the same time, the parent urges the youth to nurture intimate relationships. Longing for wisdom does not necessitate "rising above" or gradually purging oneself of erotic desire for another person, but rather claims such desire as part of the moral life when directed rightly — here to "the wife of one's youth" (5:18). The parent's use of water as a metaphor for her in 5:15-18a, an association made similarly in the Song of Songs,[29] conveys the wife's considerable value and mystery.[30] Water is primeval and essential for life (Gen. 1–2); limited and precious, particularly in a desert climate such as Palestine, water is the purest, most effective means to quench thirst and cleanse oneself.[31] The metaphor thus suggests the wife's unmatched ability to slake her husband's thirst, to quench his sexual desire. At the same time, water is also mysterious and chaotic, even when, as several of the parent's descriptions denote, it is channeled or contained ("cistern . . . well . . . fountain," Prov. 5:15-16, 18).[32] The sense may be that the "wife of one's youth," like wisdom, is never fully known. More explicit, however, is the parent's conviction that a husband's passion for and fidelity to his wife is essential to the wellbeing of the couple and the community. Without it, whether by choice or by force, his wife will eventually abandon him, a fate

---

28. See also 17:5; 19:17; 22:2, 22-23; cf. 11:24-25.

29. Note the lover calls his bride "a sealed cistern" (4:12), "a garden fountain, a well of living water, and flowing streams" (4:15).

30. Meeting a woman, often a future wife, at a well is also a motif. Recall, for example, the stories of Rebekah (Gen. 24), Rachel (Gen. 29), Zipporah (Exod. 2:15-22), and the Samaritan woman (John 4:6-15).

31. Water's considerable value is indicated also by the extent to which people argue and rejoice about it (e.g., Gen. 21:25-26; 26:17-22; Num. 21:16-18; Ps. 104:10-13; 114:8).

32. The Egyptian *Instruction of Anii* similarly describes a "stranger" woman as "deep water whose course is unknown" (Lichtheim, *Ancient Egyptian Literature*, 2:137).

the parent depicts in brushstrokes of chaos — waters "scattered outside" and flowing "in the city squares" (5:16-17).[33]

The parent thus implores in 5:18b-19:

> May you rejoice in the wife of your youth,
>   a lovely deer, a graceful gazelle.
> May her breasts quench your thirst at all times;
>   may you ever stagger by her love.

Focusing on the wife's sexual desirability, the parent first compares her, as was common in ancient erotic speech, to certain animals.[34] The parent then makes a pun, referring to the woman's *daddîm* ("breasts" or "nipples") — a word remarkably similar to *dōdîm* ("lovemaking," 7:18; cf. Song 1:2, 4; Ezek. 23:17). The parent's hope is that the woman's breasts/lovemaking will so "quench" her husband's thirst that he "staggers" around like a drunkard. Whereas elsewhere in the Old Testament the verb "to stagger" is always used negatively, as in "to stray," "make a mistake," or "do wrong" (e.g., Prov. 5:20; 19:27; 1 Sam. 26:21; Ps. 119:21, 118), the parent uses it here positively. Rather than admonishing the youth never to "stagger" (that is, to stray), despite the excitement and passion that connotes, the parent encourages him to do so and regularly — "at all times" — *with his wife.* Erotic desires for one's life companion and for wisdom, it seems, are two parts of the same story: the wise human as desiring subject.

In sum, the parent characterizes the moral self as dependent and independent, as susceptible and accountable. The wise desire the good that lies beyond themselves — namely, wisdom, a good they never ultimately control — and, "pulled" by that desire, they make decisions about how to act in ways that best enable them to attain it. Desire for the right object(s) is constituent of human flourishing, arguably its very source, and striving through good choices and efforts of the will are acts of dignity. For the parent of Proverbs 1–9, desire for wisdom is not a means to an end, a state of being that moves one eventually to some perfect and abstract realiza-

---

33. The parent thus assumes, as was common in patrilineal cultures, that the husband has charge of the wife's sexuality. The husband's loyalty is necessary to preserve sexual and social order.

34. In the Song of Songs, for example, the woman's breasts are likened to "two fawns, twins of a gazelle" (4:5; cf. 2:7; 3:5), her eyes to doves, her hair to a herd of goats, and her teeth to a flock of freshly shorn ewes (4:1-2; 6:5-6); similarly, the male lover is compared to a gazelle and young stag (2:9, 17; 8:14).

tion of knowledge, but an enduring passion that grounds one firmly in the human situation by inspiring acts of justice and kindling intoxicating loves.[35]

Desire Directed Wrongly

Woven tightly with this portrait of the wise person as a desiring subject is a cautionary tale about erotic desire directed wrongly. On center stage are fools[36] who, unlike the wise, live according to what is "wise in [their] own eyes" (3:7).[37] Trusting their wits alone, fools are smugly self-sufficient, willful, complacent, and careless. What is good for them is whatever they deem to be at the moment. Not surprisingly, their emotions and desires are skewed: fools loathe objects they should love (e.g., "fools despise wisdom and instruction," 1:7b) and esteem objects they should hate (so wisdom asks, "how long . . . will you love being naïve?" 1:22). Their moral universe is upside down, characterized by antipathy for God, wisdom, other people, and even themselves (e.g., 1:7, 22, 29, 30; 5:12; 8:36; 9:8).

The fool's erotic desire is pulled into being by physical appearance and the possibility of an illicit encounter. Unlike the descriptions of personified wisdom that mention only her hands (1:24; 3:16), lips, and mouth (namely, her speech, 8:6-8),[38] the parent's depiction of the "strange woman" or personified folly teems with visual cues about her body and mannerisms. Moreover, much about her appearance is misleading — hence the "*seeming* beauty of Folly."[39] Although explicitly identified as married in 7:6-27, for example, she wears the garments of a prostitute — perhaps a veil that covers her face (Gen. 38:14-15; cf. Job 24:15). "Guarded" of heart, she does not readily reveal her thoughts and intentions (Prov.

---

35. Indeed, one might argue that desire for wisdom leads to an intensification of emotions rather than extirpation of them, including happiness, delight, and hatred of evil (e.g., 8:13).

36. For a helpful discussion of the terms used for "fool" in Proverbs 1–9, see M. V. Fox, *Proverbs 1–9*, Anchor Bible 18A (New York: Doubleday, 2000), pp. 38-43.

37. See also 26:5, 12, 16; 28:11; 30:12.

38. Similarly, the tribute to a woman of substance in 31:10-31, who is to be identified with personified wisdom, celebrates her strength and works rather than her physical attractiveness.

39. R. C. Van Leeuwen, "Liminality and Worldview in Proverbs 1–9," *Semeia* 50 (1990): 116.

7:10). She is noisy, rebellious, and restless (7:11; 9:13); indeed, her brazenness is written across her "hardened" face (7:13), an expression used for people who lack appropriate sensibilities such as circumspection (21:29), respect (Deut. 28:50), and humility (Dan. 8:23). Her "feet," which may also be a euphemism for her genitalia (cf. Deut. 28:57; Ezek. 16:25), do not stay at home. Instead, she is out and about, "in the street . . . in the squares" (Prov. 7:12) — where lovers seek each other (Song 3:2) and prostitutes wait (Jer. 3:2; Ezek. 16:30-31). And, as is true of the lover in Song of Songs, folly's lips (or speech) drip with honey (cf. Song 4:11b) and her palate is oily smooth,[40] although here what is initially smooth and sweet turns bitter, poisonous, and sharp as a two-edged sword (Prov. 5:4). The fool's longing ignites at the possibility of such a mysterious companion — one who is "out of bounds," as two of the terms used to name her indicate.[41] Not surprisingly, the parent cautions, "do not desire *her beauty*" (6:25).[42]

What the fool desires is a one-night stand, passions indulged immediately and without consequence — a "frenzy of possession."[43] Not at all interested in a relationship such as that offered by personified wisdom[44] and

40. Compare "May your palate be like the best wine that goes down smoothly," Song 7:9a (Heb. v. 10a; cf. Song 5:16a).

41. See, for example, 2:16. The first term is *zārâ*, a word that elsewhere in the Old Testament designates an "outsider," someone not of one's family (e.g., Deut. 25:5), tribe (e.g., Num. 1:51; 18:4, 7), or community (i.e., "foreigners," e.g., Hos. 7:8-9; Isa. 1:7). Such a "stranger" is often considered illegitimate (e.g., Hos. 5:7), forbidden (e.g., Jer. 2:25), and/or an enemy (e.g., Isa. 29:5; Jer. 30:8). The second term is *nokrîyyâ* which, contrary to many modern translations ("adulterous," cf. NRSV), typically denotes a "foreigner," usually a non-Israelite (e.g., Deut. 17:15; Judg. 19:12; 1 Kings 8:41) but at times anyone outside a person's family (e.g., Gen. 31:15). With *zārâ* and *nokrîyyâ*, the parent identifies the woman as "other" without specifying exactly what makes her so. She is "strange": someone "outside" socially accepted categories, whether ethnic, legal, social, or sexual.

42. Compare Proverbs 31:30a, "Charm is deceitful and beauty is *hebel*" — namely, ephemeral and unreliable.

43. See Farley's use of this phrase in her contribution to this volume, p. 139.

44. Proverbs assumes that wisdom's companionship with those who love her endures. Note, for example, that the nature and extent of lexical and thematic parallels between the descriptions of personified wisdom in Proverbs 1–9 and of the woman of substance in 31:10-31 suggests that the two figures essentially coalesce (cf. C. Roy Yoder, *Wisdom as a Woman of Substance: A Socioeconomic Reading of Proverbs 1–9 and 31:10-31* [Berlin: Walter de Gruyter, 2001], pp. 91-93). As such, the silent youth of Proverbs 1–9 may be seen to mature into wisdom's esteemed spouse in 31:10-31, to develop "from receptive child to responsible adult, from dependent to patriarch" (W. P. Brown, "The Pedagogy of Proverbs 10:1–31:9," in *Character and Scripture: Moral Formation, Community, and Biblical Interpretation*, ed. W. P. Brown [Grand Rapids: Eerdmans, 2002], p. 153).

the "wife of one's youth," the fool seeks what personified folly promises: the opportunity to "consume" each other until satisfied. Neither party regards the other as a person of wholeness and identity; rather, the other is a means to one's own pleasure and excitement. Metaphors underline this consumptive element. Folly invokes language of eating and drinking, the satiation of appetites, as a euphemism for sexual intercourse when she invites the fool to follow her: "Come! Let us drink our fill of love-making; let us together taste love" (7:18).[45]

The parent likens folly to fire — an enduring symbol of the suddenness, intensity, and power of erotic passion to devour a person. One who "goes into" her and "touches" her will surely be burned (6:27-29). And folly's house and path are compared to Sheol, the dark, silent, and dusty underworld to which the deceased descend after death (5:5; 7:27; 9:18; e.g., Isa. 38:10-11; Job 17:13-16; Ps. 31:17). Sheol was notoriously ravenous for human life. Biblical writers drew on depictions in Canaanite mythology of deified Death as an insatiable monster — one lip touching the underworld, the other the heavens, the tongue to the stars. In Proverbs, the greedy want to swallow their victims alive and whole like Sheol (1:12), and Agur, the sage of Proverbs 30, observes that Sheol never says "Enough!" (30:15-16; cf. Isa. 5:14; Ps. 73:9; Hab. 2:5). Folly is likewise insatiable — "many" and "numerous" are her victims, warns the parent in 7:27. Ironically, the fool's desire to consume ends up consuming him.

Strikingly, fools soon surrender their agency, becoming not the subject of verbs (as are the wise) but the objects of them.[46] The object of the fools' desire — foolishness — lingers near street corners, "lying in wait" for them like an animal on the hunt (e.g., Ps. 10:9; Lam. 3:10), an army ready to attack (e.g., Josh. 8:4; Judg. 9:34), and a street gang out to ambush the innocent for quick profit (Prov. 1:11, 18). With fluttering eyelashes, folly aims to "capture" the unsuspecting (6:25). She "stalks" them (6:26). And whereas the wise pursue and hold fast to wisdom, folly finds and seizes the fool, flattering him by making him think he alone is the object of her tenacious search — "I have come to meet *you* . . . to seek *your* face eagerly . . . and now I found *you*" (7:15). The flattery works. Her words "turn [the youth] aside"; her smooth words "shove" him. Folly is so compelling, the parent

45. Compare the adulteress who "eats, wipes her mouth, and says 'I have done no wrong'" (Prov. 30:20).
46. Cf. Nussbaum, *Upheavals of Thought*, p. 566. Compare O. Sigurdson's contribution in this volume: "Disordered desire means that we are no longer masters of ourselves, but the things we desire become our masters" (p. 37).

contends, the fool goes after her "suddenly" (7:22), without hesitation or protest.[47] In an instant, he is an animal (7:22-23) — an ox on its way to the slaughter, a stag that "bounds" toward the trap (the verb suggests movement that is unthinking, even joyful, cf. Isa. 3:16), and a bird that hurries headlong into a snare (cf. 1:17-19).[48] The fool hurries off to become "fresh meat" and does not know his wound is fatal.

The fools' unwillingness to take their moral agency seriously and their callous disregard for others — their longing simply to indulge their pleasure without a care for the consequences — imperil fools and their communities. "Just as they allow themselves to be used as objects by the buffeting winds of desire," so they end up buffeting themselves and others.[49] The fool loses everything (5:8-14). Gone is any wealth, the loss of which is particularly grave because the wealth goes to "others," "strangers," people not of one's family (5:9-10). Lost is any hard-earned honor. Imperiled is the fool's health — his "flesh and body consumed" (5:11). And certain are conflict and violence in the community. Even though personified folly has assured the fool otherwise, her husband's rage at the fool proves unrelenting; her husband shows "no restraint" and will accept no amount of compensation or "hush-money" (6:34-35). Arguably, the fool suffers a beating, and there are no indications of reconciliation. In the end, it is only in the waning days of the fool's life, in a moment of utter public humiliation and self-loathing, that the fool groans to speech and laments his errant passions: "*I* hated discipline . . . *my* heart spurned reproof . . . *I* did not listen . . . *I* did not incline *my* ear . . . Now *I* am ruined" (5:12-13). It is a moment of recognition, for sure. But one that comes far too late.

Conclusion

The parent's construction of erotic desire as integral to the moral life in Proverbs 1–9 invites us to reflect carefully about several matters as we en-

---

47. The term "suddenly" recalls earlier warnings about the calamity that descends on the wicked "suddenly" (6:15) and their equally "sudden" panic (3:25).

48. As the father lists them, 7:23a seems out of place. Why would a hunter shoot a stag with an arrow if it was already rushing into a trap? Most interpreters therefore read 7:23a as the conclusion: ". . . he does not know that it will cost him his life [until an arrow pierces his liver]."

49. In her analysis of Dante, Nussbaum uses this description for people who — like the fools in Proverbs — do not see the individuality and agency in others and do not respect their own (*Upheavals of Thought*, p. 566).

gage in moral formation and ministry. The parent advocates a holistic understanding of the human: he teaches to and for the whole person, and he resists distinctions and dichotomies between the rational, the emotional, and the passionate as he fosters certain beliefs in the youth. To educate, as Michael Fox insists, "more is required than sententious warnings and somber maxims or even a logical demonstration of cause and effect, for by themselves these are abstract and lack rooting" in people's experience.[50] It is not enough, then, to proclaim but not evoke, to teach but not enable affective participation, to appeal to the intellect and not care for the body. Proverbs reminds us that we are embodied creatures, and that the formation of moral, faithful individuals and communities depends urgently on our capacities to engage human pathos and cultivate passion.

Such work poses a considerable challenge for the Christian church, which has long been wary of desire, particularly erotic desire, in theology and practice. Compounding the challenge is the stranglehold on desire and its formation enjoyed by the consumer culture. As Wendy Farley rightly observes, "Christianity is in the strange position of condemning and denigrating minority sexual desires, maternal desires, and (in some cases) safe sex and birth control, while remaining almost entirely porous to consumerism."[51] Notably, the marketplace's construction of desire cultivates much of what the parent of Proverbs 1–9 describes as misplaced, foolish desire — namely, desire that is self-interested, appearance-oriented (even when that appearance proves misleading), insistent on immediate satisfaction, and heedless of consequences.

In the face of this, the parent of Proverbs 1–9 offers a model of theological-ethical discourse that urges the embrace of a wholly different understanding of desire: desire for knowledge and God that is sweet in its unquenched intensity, desire that directs our gaze outward for understanding and convicts us of our accountability and responsibility to the world we see, desire that fuels lifelong love stories. Moreover, by teaching this desire to his children early, and weaving it inseparably with ordinary decisions and practices (e.g., 1:10-19; 3:27-31), the parent lays claim to the immediacy and power of desire as inherent to "fear of the LORD." The wise and faithful in Proverbs 1–9 are not "objective" and removed, but people of passion, captivated by beauty and goodness, disgusted by wickedness, devoted to God, wisdom, and others. Such a relational portrait of what it

---

50. Fox, *Proverbs 1–9*, p. 349.
51. Farley, "Beguiled by Beauty," p. 132.

means to be wise challenges our cultural push for atomism, the view that every individual is a sovereign self, an unfettered agent who is by nature not bound to anything or any authority. Taking her stand in the heart of the city, wisdom calls us away from such folly, ushering us instead into a landscape of towering loves, fidelities, and profound responsibilities — a landscape that the ancient sages deemed ripe for human flourishing.

Desire and Justice: Levinas and Heschel on Human and Divine Pathos

Jayne Svenungsson

Although frequently accused of logocentrism, western philosophy and theology have never managed completely to do away with pathos, the unruly twin of logos. If logos marks order, sense, and clarity, pathos implies the rather unsettling condition in which something happens to the human self — a state of the soul aroused by something outside the self. Pathos, in other words, reveals the human self as defenseless passivity, as potential vulnerability. This, perhaps, explains why pathos has often appeared as something frightening, and why the early Greek philosophers took pains to define their task in terms of a rational exclusion of passions. For all their differences, both Plato and Aristotle, as well as the post-Aristotelian schools, tended to regard passions as weaknesses of the soul, something that had to be overcome in order to pursue right thinking (wisdom) and right living (morals).

Against this backdrop, there is little wonder that the same philosophers felt compelled to exclude passions and emotions from the nature of the Deity, the Supreme Cause of everything. Most famously manifested in Aristotle's Unmoved Mover, we find a God completely purified from pathos and needs, indifferent to everything except its own thinking activity. Although this conception of the divine is quite foreign to the Bible (at least the Hebrew part of it), both Jewish and Christian theologians have, throughout history, been inclined to merge this conception with the biblical one. Reaching its climax with the rediscovery of Aristotle in the High Middle Ages, Maimonides and Thomas Aquinas — arguably the two most influential thinkers of their respective traditions — stated clearly that passibility or needs must not be applied to God. To be entirely fair, however, it should be emphasized that this by no means compromised the strong conviction, shared by both philosophers, that the nature of the divine was inseparable from love and justice. Nevertheless, the scholastic rethinking of the notion of God certainly did pave the way for later rationalistic conceptions of the divine. Thus, in Newton's deism or Hegel's panentheism we reach the full-fledged manifestation of a Deity purified from pathos: God as a giant master mind in absolute control of the laws of the universe or of history.

There are yet other perspectives on this picture. If Ludwig Feuerbach was right in his conviction that theology is anthropology in disguise, one might conclude that the conception of the divine in ancient Greek thought to a large extent was the outcome of an anthropology that dissociated the higher rational activity of the soul from its lower faculties, tied to passions and emotions. However, as feminist and liberation theologians (in particular) have pointed out over the years, it is also true that anthropology is theology in disguise. Accordingly, it can be — and has been — argued that modern theistic and deistic notions of the divine have fueled and given legitimacy to modern liberal anthropology. Newton's self-sufficient God above joy and sorrow would, in other words, have his counterpart in Kant's autonomous subject, defined first and foremost in terms of its rational activity and moral decisiveness.

Looking at western philosophy in this light, one might conclude that as we reach modernity, logos has finally succeeded in quenching pathos. The perfect, impassible Deity is mirrored in the bourgeois man, taught to be rational, active, productive, and never to let passions affect his decisions or choices. Yet, this is not the entire story. Modernity has not been any more successful than antiquity in squelching pathos. It was merely subdued, by being transposed to the lower faculties of the soul — or to the lower representative of the two human sexes. Thus, if "man," more than ever before, lived up to the designation of being God's image, it was only by virtue of transferring, more consistently than ever, all the unwanted characteristics — sentimental emotions, uncontrollable desires, irrational passions — to the less perfect half of God's creatures. In this respect, modern anthropology (supported by theology and philosophy) only reinforced a dialectic at work already in antiquity, a dialectic according to which, on the one hand, the irrational, unruly nature of women justifies men's power over them, while, on the other hand, the very definition of women as more inclined to passion is part of the execution of precisely that (male) power. Hence the conclusion that logocentrism during the course of history has been inseparable from phallocentrism.

If logos has maintained its grip over pathos also in modern times, a considerable shift nevertheless occurs in the twentieth century. Although certainly present as an undercurrent within the modern project itself, a radical challenging of logos's incontestable priority over pathos breaks through the surface with the psychoanalytical and philosophical endeavors of — among many others — Freud, Heidegger, Foucault, Kristeva, and Derrida. To this line of prominent figures, who all sought to interrupt the monologue of logos, one could easily add the name of Emmanuel Levinas (1906-1995). Although the notion of pathos is not very frequently used by Levinas, it is fair to describe his philosophy as a thoroughgoing attempt to reverse the established order between logos and pathos. Leaning on Descartes's "discovery" of the idea of the Infinite in the core of the reflecting self, Levinas reveals the human subject as ultimately *passive:* the self is affected by an exteriority that unsettles its rational activity (logos) and utters itself as "extreme passion" (pathos).[1] This passion, furthermore, is construed in terms of a metaphysical desire, a desire precisely for the Infinite, which Levinas equally terms "God." However, this desire is always of an indirect character, as God, "the Desirable," has always already withdrawn, thus leaving space for and diverting our desire toward the other human being, "the undesirable *par excellence.*" By interpreting desire according to this scheme, Levinas makes two important philosophical gains. First and most importantly, given the strong ethical nerve of his entire intellectual enterprise, he manages to transform human desire for the divine into unconditional responsibility for one's neighbor. Second, and in line with Heidegger's critique of ontotheology, by which he was deeply influenced, the same move enables him to withdraw God from Being and thus to save God from idolatry.

Levinas's redefinition of human subjectivity in terms of passivity and vulnerability surely marks one step forward in challenging logos's dominance over pathos in western philosophy. It has, however, not gone unnoticed that when it comes to the divine, we are still left with a God completely purified from pathos. In his eagerness not only to save God from idolatry — from becoming a projection of human needs — but also, first and foremost, to save the other human being from being neglected, Levinas portrays God as a distant, anonymous "third," who neither desires

1. Emmanuel Levinas, *Dieu, la mort et le temps* (Paris: Grasset, Le Livre de Poche, 1993), p. 204; English translation: *God, Death, and Time,* trans. Bettina Bergo (Stanford: Stanford University Press, 2000), p. 174.

nor can be desired (directly) by human subjects. The critique of Levinas's construal of the divine as radical — according to some critiques even "violent" — alterity has, in recent years, been directed from various positions.[2] It is notable, however, that these critiques, despite their ideological diversity, to a significant degree share a tendency to contrast Levinas's unsatisfactory construal of divine otherness with a more satisfying "Christian" perspective. Be it the form of John Milbank's grand narrative of trinitarian harmony or of Gianni Vattimo's kenotic appraisal of divine immanence, the critique tends to repeat, on a subtle level, the supersessionist contrast between the harsh and distant Hebrew God and the Christian God of love and intimacy.

In what follows, it is my intention, too, to problematize Levinas's construal of divine otherness and, more precisely, the way in which he understands human and divine (absence of) desire. However, in order not only to avoid supersessionist tendencies, but also to challenge existing supersessionist interpretations, I wish to contrast Levinas's reflections on human and divine interrelatedness with the philosophical and exegetical reflections of another prominent twentieth-century Jewish thinker, namely Abraham Heschel (1907-1972).[3] Like Levinas, Heschel is deeply steeped in the Jewish prophetic tradition, refusing to sever the name of God from the idea of justice. Unlike Levinas, however, this prophetic conviction does not, for Heschel, entail that God can be approached only as absence, as the trace — left on the face of one's neighbor — of someone who has always already passed by. On the contrary, if there is a novelty introduced by the prophets in the history of religion, it is precisely the idea of "divine pathos."[4] The God of the prophets, in Heschel's reading, is thus

2. Cf., e.g., John Milbank, "The Ethics of Self-Sacrifice," *First Things* 91 (1999): 33-38; Gianni Vattimo, *Dopo la cristianità: Per un cristianesimo non religioso* (Milano: Garzanti, 2002); Phillip Blond, "Introduction: Theology before Philosophy," in *Post-secular Philosophy: Between Philosophy and Theology*, ed. Phillip Blond (London and New York: Routledge, 1998), pp. 1-66; Merold Westphal, *Transcendence and Self-Transcendence: On God and the Soul* (Bloomington and Indianapolis: Indiana University Press, 2004); Slavoj Žižek, *The Puppet and the Dwarf: The Perverse Core of Christianity* (Cambridge, MA, and London: MIT Press, 2003).

3. For a short introduction to the life and work of Heschel — with whom European readers may be less familiar — see Susannah Heschel, "Introduction," in *Moral Grandeur and Spiritual Audacity: Essays by Abraham Joshua Heschel*, ed. Susannah Heschel (New York: Farrar, Straus & Giroux, 1996), pp. vii-xxx.

4. The notion of divine pathos, at the heart of Heschel's interpretation of the prophets, is drawn from the rabbinic concept *zoreh gavoha*, denoting "a higher, divine need." See fur-

a God deeply involved in human history, a God who is passionately affected by human suffering and injustice. Correspondingly, the prophet is a person who is affected by this divine pathos and who shares God's deep concern for humanity, God's passion for justice.

By bringing the two philosophers into dialogue, I wish to question Levinas's conviction that the idea of a personal God, characterized by "divine pathos," is a mythological remnant that unavoidably leads us into idolatry. Furthermore, I want to challenge the assumption, also held by Levinas, that a God who not only can be desired by human beings but also is a desiring God necessarily puts us at the risk of disregarding our fellow human beings. Pushing this assumption to its limits, one can even ask whether the proposed redirection of the desire for God toward the other human being does not imply the risk of making the other person — the neighbor — an idol, and thereby deceiving him or her in a more intricate, but no less malign, way. Finally, I shall suggest that part of the problem with Levinas's assumption resides in his understanding of the nature of desire, more precisely, in his belief that there is such a thing as a nonerotic, "pure" metaphysical desire. I argue that in order to attain a richer understanding of divine-human (but also of intrahuman) interrelatedness, we have to recognize the unruly, erotic, or even "impure" nature of desire. In this recognition, I believe, lies the key to what I shall term, with inspiration from Heschel, a "theology of pathos."

Saving God from Idolatry

Ever since the early 1980s, when a celebrated work titled *God without Being* first appeared, the venture of rescuing God from philosophy's logocentric hold has been intimately linked to the name of Jean-Luc Marion.[5] What is thereby often overshadowed is the fact that the question of how to withdraw God from Being had, at this time, been preoccupying Emmanuel Levinas — Marion's former teacher at the Sorbonne — for at least a decade. One need only remind oneself of the statement, made in the very

---

ther Susannah Heschel, "Introduction to the Perennial Classics Edition," in Abraham J. Heschel, *The Prophets* (New York: Harper Perennial, 2001 [orig. 1962]), p. xviii.

5. Jean-Luc Marion, *Dieu sans l'être* (Paris: Quadrige/Presses Universitaires de France, 1982); English translation: *God without Being: Hors-Texte*, trans. Thomas A. Carlson (Chicago: University of Chicago Press, 1991).

opening words of Levinas's second major work, *Otherwise Than Being or Beyond Essence*, in 1974: "to hear a God not contaminated by Being is a human possibility no less important and no less precarious than to bring Being out of the oblivion in which it is said to have fallen in metaphysics and onto-theology."[6]

To be entirely fair, however, it should be recognized that Levinas did not, any more than Marion, announce his endeavor to withdraw God from Being in a vacuum; as indicated above, Levinas drew heavily on Heidegger's critique of ontotheology, first launched in the late fifties.[7] Like Heidegger, Levinas reproaches the western tradition for its repression of alterity. Still, while endorsing the critique of ontotheology, Levinas poses the question (implicit also in the quote above) whether "onto-theology's mistake [did not] consist in taking being for God, . . . rather [than] in taking God for being,"[8] whereby he exposes the incongruity between his own endeavor and that of Heidegger. While Heidegger's concern was to recover Being from its concealment beneath a highest being, Levinas aspires to something more radical, namely to uncover a way of approaching the divine beyond the realm of *both* beings and Being, i.e., beyond the ontological difference as such.

Although the repression of an alterity transcendent to Being lies at the heart of the western philosophical tradition, Levinas nevertheless admits that there have been important exceptions. Accordingly, in his earlier works, he recognizes Plato's placing of the Good beyond Being as a significant attempt to escape the logocentric reduction of sense to what is rationally graspable.[9] Ultimately, however, it is in the Hebrew, Talmudic heritage that he finds the answer to how to conceive of an alterity irreducible to "the Same."[10] Contrary to the Greek understanding of transcendence in

---

6. Emmanuel Levinas, *Autrement qu'être ou au-delà de l'essence* (La Haye: Martinus Nijhoff, Le Livre de Poche, 1978 [orig. 1974]), p. 10; English translation: *Otherwise Than Being or Beyond Essence*, trans. Alphonso Lingis (Pittsburgh: Duquesne University Press, 1981), p. xlviii.

7. See Martin Heidegger, "Die onto-theo-logische Verfassung der Metaphysik," in *Identität und Differenz* (Stuttgart: Neske, 1999 [orig. 1957]), pp. 31-67; English translation: "The Onto-theo-logical Constitution of Metaphysics," in *Identity and Difference*, trans. Joan Stambaugh (Chicago: University of Chicago Press, 2002 [orig. 1969]), pp. 42-74.

8. Levinas, *Dieu, la mort et le temps*, p. 141; Eng. trans., p. 124.

9. See especially Emmanuel Levinas, *En découvrant l'existence avec Husserl et Heidegger* (Paris: Vrin, 2006 [orig. 1949]).

10. In the 1950s Levinas encounters the Talmudic master nicknamed "Mr. Chouchani," and from this time onward the Talmudic literature has a decisive influence on his philoso-

terms of erotic ascendance to loftier realms, the Jewish tradition offers a more earthbound account: transcendence begins in the corporeality of human beings and is manifested in a horizontal movement toward another person. It is, in other words, in the ethical that Levinas finds the key to an alterity that is not reducible to ontology or the Same.[11]

Yet how does this relate to Levinas's ambition to save God from the idolatry of Being? To gain a full answer, we need to look closer at his notion of a "metaphysical desire," inherent in every human being. This desire, Levinas argues, has been revealed with unparalleled aptitude by Descartes. From his very earliest to his last works, Levinas never ceases to give tribute to Descartes for his "discovery" of the idea of the Infinite. More than any single event in the history of philosophy, this discovery has contributed to unsettling the dominance of logos: "In meditating upon the idea of God, Descartes sketched, with an unequaled rigor, this process . . . of a thinking going to the point of the breaking up of the *I think.*"[12] The idea of the Infinite marks, in other words, nothing less than the paradox of an idea that cannot be thought, which is precisely the discovery of something that escapes the structure of the *cogito cogitatum.*[13] Most importantly, however, this discovery is simultaneously a discovery of *desire* — for is not the very nature of (metaphysical) desire precisely a yearning for something that cannot be contained by desire itself, something that by definition always exceeds the desiring subject?

Thus, it is in the disclosure of metaphysical desire that Levinas finds the key to withdrawing God from Being. Yet some qualifications need to be made. Most importantly, if God is to remain uncontaminated by logos, desire must not be confused with need or erotic love. Although Levinas recognizes needs and erotic longing as essential to human life, he maintains that here we are still moving within the sphere of logos. Experiencing erotic desire (for another person or for God) is still an expression of the Odyssean longing for a return, where the desirable in the end is identified as a need to fulfill and thus is ultimately referred to representation, to the Same, to the ego. Metaphysical desire, on the contrary, is of a more

---

phy. See further Marc-Alain Ouaknin, *Méditations érotiques: Essai sur Emmanuel Levinas* (Paris: Payot & Rivages, 2003 [orig. 1992]), pp. 83-172.

11. Levinas, *Dieu, la mort et le temps*, pp. 195-200; Eng. trans., pp. 167-71.

12. Levinas, *Dieu, la mort et le temps*, p. 248; Eng. trans., p. 215.

13. While ascribing genius to Descartes for revealing the idea of the Infinite, Levinas seemingly overlooks the tensions and ambiguities inherent in that idea. See further F. LeRon Shults, *Reforming the Doctrine of God* (Grand Rapids: Eerdmans, 2005), pp. 18-22.

Abrahamitic nature. It denotes a desire that never reaches its final goal, a desire that increases the more the desirable is approached.[14] Nonetheless, it would be wrong to characterize such a desire in terms of lack. Only a being who is free, separated, and in need of nothing in relation to the infinite Other can experience metaphysical desire in the proper sense: "A desire without hunger, and also without end [*sans faim et aussi sans fin*]: a desire for the infinite *qua* desire for what is beyond being, which is stated in the word 'dis-inter-estedness.'"[15]

At this point, however, a critical question announces itself: For all the eloquent words about a desire *sans faim et sans fin,* how could we guarantee that our desire, in the end, does not fall prey to the temptation to grasp, define, and ultimately betray the divine? Levinas, it should be underscored, would be the first to admit that there are no such guarantees — on the contrary, both philosophy and theology have spent the last two millennia coming up with all the more sophisticated conceptual idols obscuring the divine.[16] This is what Heidegger detected with admirable precision, although he did not do much to alter the situation, apart from stating, somewhat cryptically, that if he were one day to write a theology, the word "Being" would not occur in it.[17] This is also the point at which Levinas, *pace* Heidegger, persists in his ambition to offer a way in which to withdraw God from Being. Yet this way is neither that of philosophy nor that of theology; it is, as indicated above, in the *ethical* that Levinas finds the doorway to a nonidolatric approach to the divine.

In what way does the ethical open the door to a desire for the Infinite beyond interest and eroticism? The answer, concisely, is that only the ethical offers a way in which God — the Desirable *par excellence* — remains transcendent in relation to desire. But how? By commanding the desiring subject to care for "the nondesired *par excellence*," which is one's neighbor. Expressed in more technical terms, what happens at this moment is that metaphysical desire, which is desire for the Infinite, is redirected toward the finite, whereby the Infinite escapes objectification. Through this "maneuver," desire is kept radically nonerotic, in the sense of no longer being driven by interests, e.g., expectations of reward or fulfillment of personal

---

14. Levinas, *En découvrant l'existence,* pp. 261-68.

15. Levinas, *Dieu, la mort et le temps,* p. 255; Eng. trans., p. 221.

16. Cf. Emmanuel Levinas, *De Dieu qui vient à l'idée,* 2nd ed. (Paris: Vrin, 1986), pp. 94-97.

17. Cf. Martin Heidegger, "Züricher Seminar" (1951), *Gesamtausgabe,* vol. 15: *Seminare* (Frankfurt am Main: Vittorio Klostermann, 1986), pp. 436-37.

needs. The desiring self, at this pre-philosophic, ethical level, is not even to be conceived of as an active subject with determined intentions and aspirations. Rather, the self finds itself in the accusative, as questioned or precisely *accused* by the other, called to be faithful to an engagement it has never committed itself to. Levinas summarizes:

> In this reversal and this referral of the desirable to the nondesirable, in this strange mission commanding the approach of the other person, God is torn out of the objectivity of presence and out of being. He is no longer an object or an interlocutor in a dialogue. His distancing or his transcendence turns into my responsibility: the nonerotic *par excellence!*[18]

One can ask, however, whether God is not still caught in ontotheology, despite this redirection of desire toward one's neighbor. After all, Levinas's "ethical turn" somehow presupposes that there is still a God there to command me to take ethical responsibility for the other human being. And, when it all comes around, in what way does this God differ from the God of, say, Maimonides, Thomas Aquinas, or Luther? Levinas escapes this objection by refusing to ascribe to God any presence or determination whatsoever. God is not the Thou of traditional theology, a Thou whom the human soul can desire erotically. Neither is God, as suggested by Martin Buber or Gabriel Marcel, the Thou hidden in the face of the neighbor, that Thou of which the neighbor is an image. The God beyond Being announced by Levinas can only be conceived of as an anonymous *third*, a "He" or "It" (French *Il*) who has always already withdrawn, but who has nevertheless left His/Its trace on the face of the other human being (who is the essential Thou):

> The God revealed by our Judeo-Christian spirituality preserves the entire infinity of his absence. . . . He shows himself only by his trace, as in Exodus, chapter 33. To turn to Him is not to follow this trace, which is not a sign; it is to turn to the Others who abide in the trace.[19]

Having reached this point, one can reasonably ask whether Levinas's concern is actually with God at all, and not rather with the neighbor *tout court*. Before drawing such a conclusion too quickly, however, it is revealing to look closer at some biographical details. As Catherine Chalier points

18. Levinas, *Dieu, la mort et le temps*, pp. 258-59; Eng. trans., p. 224.
19. Levinas, *En découvrant l'existence*, p. 282 (my trans.).

out in one of the most lucid studies on Levinas in recent years, it is of vital importance to see Levinas's notion of metaphysical desire against the backdrop of Mithnagdic Judaism, in which he was partly steeped through his Lithuanian background.[20] Mithnagdism, which had its most important representative in the Vilna Gaon (1720-1797), was first and foremost a countermovement to Hasidism and as such was deeply suspicious of spiritual experience as the primary source of knowledge of God. Against the religious fervor of the Hasidim, the Mithnagdim stressed the Talmudic study of texts and the importance of the observance of the Torah.

That Levinas shares these worries about religious fervor is clear in his sometimes adamant rejection of religious experience as a legitimate source out of which to speak of God beyond Being.[21] Yet here again, it is important to observe the exact motives for this rejection. Levinas is skeptical toward the individual's fervent devotion to God precisely because it tends all too often to divert his or her attention from the needs of the neighbor. However, the Talmudic tradition in which Levinas inscribes himself teaches that it is only through the acts of love and justice committed toward one's neighbor that God is to be ultimately sought. In the words of Chalier, the God at stake here is a God who commands his creatures to watch over his or her vulnerable fellow creatures, rather than to seek the enjoyment of pure divine presence.[22] Against this backdrop it also becomes clearer why Levinas so forcefully emphasizes that desire has to remain nonerotic, not only with respect to God, but also with respect to the neighbor: the command to care for our fellow human beings must never be dependent on our aspiration for reward of any sort; neither should it depend on whether the other person is amiable or pleasing. In other words, erotic or affectionate attraction must never be a condition for our acts of goodness and justice.

Levinas's discomfort with religious fervor likewise sheds light on his enduring suspicion of negative or mystical theology. Although, as I indicated earlier, Levinas was initially appreciative of the Platonic and neo-Platonic efforts to place the Good beyond Being, in his later philosophy he deconstructs this effort as merely another version of ontotheology: the

20. Catherine Chalier, *La Trace de l'infini: Emmanuel Levinas et la source hébraïque* (Paris: Cerf, 2002), pp. 18-19, 43-75. See also Aušra Pažeraite, "Levinas' Heritage in Lithuanian Rabbinic Thought," *Athens: Philosophical Studies (Athena: filosofijos studijos)* 2 (2007): 81-88.

21. Cf., e.g., Levinas, *Dieu, la mort et le temps*, pp. 246-51; Eng. trans., pp. 213-18.

22. Chalier, *La Trace de l'infini*, p. 57.

transcendent One of Plotinus is, after all, still a God that the human subject can come to *know* progressively through erotic ascendance. Culminating in the *unio mystica,* the mystic fusion with the divine, transcendence is once more turned into (the) immanence (of the subject), the Other into the Same.[23] Drawing on this tradition, Jewish and above all Christian mysticism has tended to favor the individual person's spiritual journey toward the divine, encouraging the exclusive rapport between God and the human soul. This, once more, makes Levinas hesitant, since the individual's quest for spiritual wellbeing all too easily brings the wellbeing of others out of focus. In the worst scenario, we risk ending up with religious loners who, under the pretext of seeking God devoutly, completely disengage their personal spiritual needs or convictions from the needs and convictions of others.

As I have argued elsewhere,[24] it is precisely here that perhaps the most important value of Levinas's reflections on divine alterity lies. By stressing that alterity or transcendence, if it is to remain truly transcendent, has to be construed intersubjectively, Levinas challenges the potential violence inherent in religious claims to having unmediated access to divine transcendence. For is not religious fanaticism and its various expressions (religious wars, terrorism, honor killing) precisely the result of an absence of the constraints placed upon us by the alterity of our fellow human beings? One can even argue that it is on this very particular level that the true pertinence of the philosophical critique of ontotheology reveals itself: it points to the danger that results when claims made on the divine reality are cut loose from the wider context of ongoing interpretative practices and are reduced to the logic or "logos" of a singular mind, prone to disregard or deny every claim that does not correspond to the convictions of this particular mind.[25]

Still, and finally, it should be asked whether this invaluable reminder

23. See, above all, Emmanuel Levinas, *Altérité et transcendance* (Paris: Fata Morgana, Le Livre de Poche, 1995), pp. 29-33; English translation: *Alterity and Transcendence,* trans. Michael B. Smith (New York: Columbia University Press, 1999), pp. 5-10.

24. Jayne Svenungsson, "Sacrifice, Conflict and the Foundation of Culture: A Response to Merold Westphal," *Neue Zeitschrift für Systematische Theologie und Religionsphilosophie* 50 (2008): 330-41.

25. Cf. Emmanuel Levinas, *Difficile liberté. Essais sur le judaïsme,* 3rd ed. (Paris: Albin Michel, Le Livre de Poche, 1976 [orig. 1963]), pp. 31-40; English translation: *Difficult Freedom: Essays on Judaism,* trans. Seán Hand (Baltimore: Johns Hopkins University Press, 1990), pp. 14-19.

of the inseparability of religious claims and ethical commitment, brought to the fore by Levinas, requires that we categorically leave the idea of a personal, desiring God behind, as well as the idea of a legitimate human *erotic* desire for the divine. In order to obtain at least a tentative answer, I shall now turn to the exegetically inspired philosophy of Abraham Heschel.

God as the Most Moved Mover

Before delving deeper into the often striking contrasts between Heschel's and Levinas's reflections on human and divine interrelatedness — contrasts that make Heschel an unusually stimulating conversation partner for Levinas — it is worthwhile to draw attention to some of the obvious common denominators between the two philosophers. First, and most importantly, both are profoundly steeped in the Jewish prophetic tradition, which refuses to address or even to conceive of God as separate from justice. In the words of Heschel:

> There are few thoughts as deeply ingrained in the mind of biblical man as the thought of God's justice and righteousness. It is not an inference, but an *a priori* of biblical faith, self-evident; not an added attribute to His essence, but given with the very thought of God.[26]

Or, in the words of Levinas:

> The fact that the relationship with the Divine crosses the relationship with men and coincides with social justice is . . . what epitomizes the entire spirit of the Jewish Bible. Moses and the prophets preoccupied themselves not with the immortality of the soul but with the poor, the widow, the orphan and the stranger.[27]

The notions of justice and righteousness at stake here — drawing on the biblical terms *mishpat* and *tsedakah* — have little to do with ethics in the formal sense. This captures another essential trait common to both philosophers. For, although a radical ethics lies at the heart of most of their writings, neither Heschel nor Levinas shows much interest in traditional moral philosophy. Justice must never be conceived of as an abstract prob-

26. Heschel, *The Prophets*, p. 255.
27. Levinas, *Difficile liberté*, p. 40; Eng. trans., pp. 19-20.

lem or a set of values; it is always played out on a particular, personal, or even carnal level: "Justice exists in relation to a person, and is something done by a person. An act of injustice is condemned, not because the law is broken, but because a person has been hurt."[28] In the same manner, Levinas stresses that the biblical notion of justice never begins in the empty construction of an ideal state; it is always fleshed out in a concrete world where there are wars, slaves, sacrifices, corrupted priests, material interests, jealousy, and crimes.[29]

Likewise, and in line with the conception of God first and foremost in terms of historical justice, neither Heschel nor Levinas shows much interest in the traditional philosophical way of posing the problem of God. I have already exposed at length Levinas's endeavor to withdraw God from Being, i.e., from western philosophy's numerous attempts to formulate proofs for God's existence — proofs that amount to nothing but conceptual idols. Before any proofs, confessions, or even words, "God," according to Levinas, comes to life in the human *witness:*

> The word God is still absent from the phrase in which God is for the first time involved in words. It does not at all state "I believe in God." To bear witness of God is precisely not to state this extraordinary word, as though glory would be lodged in a theme and be posited as a thesis, or become being's essence. As a sign given to the other of this very signification, the "here I am" signifies me in the name of God, at the service of men that look at me.[30]

Similarly, Heschel renounces speculations about God as a highest being and declares frankly that "[t]here are no proofs for the existence of the God of Abraham. There are only witnesses."[31] In other words, the idea of God, for Heschel as well as for Levinas, has little to do with timeless qualities of a supreme being and is, rather, intimately linked to concrete acts of justice committed by one human being to another.

Yet, at precisely this point where the thought of the two philosophers — who to my knowledge never refer to each other — seems to converge completely, a fundamental chasm reveals itself. As meticulously as Levinas spells out the God of the prophets in terms of anonymous absence, a trace

28. Heschel, *The Prophets*, p. 276.
29. Levinas, *Difficile liberté*, p. 156; Eng. trans., p. 101.
30. Levinas, *Autrement qu'être ou au-delà de l'essence*, p. 233; Eng. trans., p. 149.
31. Heschel, *The Prophets*, p. 27.

of someone who has never been present, Heschel imparts that "[t]he God of Israel is never impersonal,"[32] that God is above all experienced as an intense and overwhelming *presence*. Drawing on the very same prophetic heritage, they seemingly reach quite different conclusions when it comes to the question of the divine-human relationship, but also, I shall argue, to the understanding of desire. Why is this so?

An obvious answer would seem to lie in their biographical backgrounds. If Levinas, as indicated above, can be inscribed in the rationalistic tradition of Mithnagdic Judaism, Heschel hailed from a Hasidic family. He was, in other words, steeped in precisely that tradition of which Mithnagdism was a countermovement. This sheds light not only on the central role he ascribes to the idea of divine presence, but also on his positive evaluation of human experience of the divine. There is, however, yet another clue to their divergent conclusions, which can be attributed to their different methodological presuppositions. At a superficial glance, one is, once again, struck by the similarities rather than the divergences. Both Levinas and Heschel work, in a broad sense, within the phenomenological tradition, and they have important common influences in Edmund Husserl, Martin Buber, and Franz Rosenzweig.[33] Accordingly, they show little interest in psychological or ontological reflections on the question of God. Rather, although both philosophers certainly challenge the limits of phenomenology, they are to a significant extent faithful to the phenomenological definition of the task of philosophy in terms of describing the transcendental conditions for truth or meaning. Against this backdrop, both seem to agree that nothing can be said about the divine as such (about God's "being" or "essence"); a phenomenologically inspired philosophy of religion can only start in the *human,* in what is given as appearances to human consciousness.[34]

Yet, interestingly, they reach very different conclusions with regard to the outcome of the phenomenological analysis. Levinas, as we have seen, finds in human subjectivity at the most an experience of the *absence* of God; to the extent to which we can conceive of God at all, God remains the

---

32. Heschel, *The Prophets*, p. 28.

33. See further Norman Solomon, "Heschel in the Context of Modern Jewish Religious Thought," *European Judaism* 41, no. 1 (2008): 5-6.

34. Cf. Solomon, "Heschel in the Context of Modern Jewish Religious Thought," and further, Giuseppe Lissa, "Emmanuel Levinas: Pour une transcendence non idolâtrique," in *Emmanuel Levinas et les théologies,* ed. Danielle Cohen-Levinas and Shmuel Trigano (Paris: In Press Éditions, 2007), pp. 96-97.

great unknown, an infinite "illeity" that "overflows both cognition and the enigma through which the Infinite leaves a trace in cognition."[35] Heschel, on the contrary, finds an experience of divine *presence,* a strong intuition even of being an object of God's concern. While maintaining that nothing can be said of God as such — that both the premise of God's absence and that of his presence accordingly are beyond demonstration — he points to the inconsistency in the idea of God as the great unknown: "by attributing eternal mysteriousness to the ultimate being, we definitely claim to know it."[36] No one, in other words, could honestly claim to confess to a God defined in terms of absolute alterity, an idea that is either void of any content or, more likely, already subtly filled with mystical theological connotations. If, on the contrary, the phenomenological analysis clings consistently to what a religious consciousness *de facto* experiences, it is likely to find feelings of awe, praise, fear, and wonder, feelings that scarcely arise out of the assumption that God is devoid of life. Thus, if the only basis we have for our phenomenological analysis is how people throughout the ages have experienced the ineffable, i.e., as something more akin to a presence than to an absence, then this is where the conception of God as a religious problem should take its beginning.[37]

Heschel's Hasidic roots certainly offer a clue to his understanding of the task of religious philosophy. Yet, I maintain that it is the particular methodological path he follows that is most significant to an understanding of the very different conclusions he draws in comparison to Levinas. While Levinas remains more strictly within a traditional phenomenological framework — which also means that his reflections on the divine remain a rather abstract philosophical investigation — Heschel combines his phenomenological inspiration with the discipline in which he had his primary education, i.e., biblical studies.[38] Accordingly, when he seeks to elaborate a phenomenology of religiosity, he does not start in human consciousness in a general or formal sense, but rather in the particular con-

---

35. Levinas, *Autrement qu'être ou au-delà de l'essence,* p. 252; Eng. trans., p. 166.

36. Abraham J. Heschel, *God in Search of Man: A Philosophy of Judaism* (New York: Farrar, Straus & Giroux, 1955), p. 126. This critique has an interesting parallel in Jacques Derrida's problematization of the contradictory absoluteness of Levinas's notion of alterity in the famous essay "Violence et métaphysique. Essai sur la pensée d'Emmanuel Levinas," in Derrida, *L'écriture et la différence* (Paris: Seuil, 1967), pp. 117-228.

37. Cf. Heschel, *God in Search of Man,* pp. 125-35, and Abraham J. Heschel, *Man Is Not Alone: A Philosophy of Religion* (New York: Farrar, Straus & Giroux, 1951), pp. 25-34.

38. See further Heschel, *The Prophets,* pp. xxi-xxix.

sciousness of the pious person. And here the biblical material offers a bottomless resource. As indicated by the title of his perhaps most famous work, *The Prophets*,[39] it was, in particular, in the prophetic literature that he found the "material" for his phenomenology of the religious mind. (Interestingly, although no direct reference is made, this methodological path is not foreign to the one Heidegger follows in his early "phenomenology of religious life," drawing on close readings of St. Paul's letters.[40])

What, then, is revealed in Heschel's reading of the prophets? A short answer could be spelled out using the term "divine pathos." At the center of the prophet's consciousness is a strong awareness of divine attentiveness and concern:

> To the prophet, . . . God does not reveal himself in an abstract absoluteness, but in a personal and intimate relation to the world. He does not simply command and expect obedience; he is also moved and affected by what happens in the world, and reacts accordingly. Events and human actions arouse in Him joy or sorrow, pleasure or wrath. . . . This notion that God can be intimately affected, that He possesses not merely intelligence and will, but also pathos, basically defines the prophetic consciousness of God.[41]

The prophet, in his turn, is a person who discloses this divine pathos. An analysis of prophetic utterances shows that the prophet's fundamental experience is not only an urge to convey God's pathos to the world; he also experiences a strong fellowship or *sympathy* with this pathos. Yet, despite this closeness, the prophet does not claim to reveal truths about God's being or essence. The transcendent attentiveness of the prophet merely defines the limits of his understanding of the divine: "Overwhelmingly, mysteriously different from man, God was not [to the prophet] the object of imagination."[42] Still, the prophet insisted upon the ability to understand God's presence, expression, and manifestation. However, what is thereby revealed is precisely not God as an *object*, but rather as the supreme *Subject*:

39. *The Prophets*, first published in 1962, is an elaboration of Heschel's dissertation "Das prophetische Bewusstsein," completed in Berlin in 1932. Heschel escaped Europe eight years later and lived the rest of his life in the United States. See further Susannah Heschel, "Introduction to the Perennial Classics Edition," pp. xvi-xvii.

40. See Martin Heidegger, *Gesamtausgabe*, vol. 60: *Phänomenologie des religiösen Lebens* (Frankfurt am Main: Vittorio Klostermann, 1995).

41. Heschel, *The Prophets*, pp. 288-89.

42. Heschel, *The Prophets*, p. 620.

> To the prophet, God is always apprehended, experienced, and conceived as a *Subject,* never as an object. He appears as One Who demands, as One Who acts, Whose intention is to give righteousness and peace rather than to receive homage and adoration, Whose desire is to bestow rather than to obtain. In all the prophet knows about God, he never finds in God a desire that does not bear upon man.[43]

Clearly, the notion of God that Heschel infers from prophetic consciousness is very foreign to classical philosophy's idea of God in terms of passivity and impassibility. God is not the detached, unmoved Mover of the Aristotelian tradition, but, as Heschel expressed it, "the most moved Mover."[44] Although the term "desire" is not used very frequently by Heschel — the decisive term being "pathos" — God is repeatedly depicted as not only in need of humanity but also in need of being needed by humanity.[45] This leads us back to Levinas. Despite their common critique of the Greek notion of God in terms of a supreme being, Heschel's idea of a God who stands in a passionate relationship with humanity is, of course, also very foreign to Levinas's construal of the divine as completely devoid of desire. The contrast becomes even more striking when we recall that the divine, according to Levinas, even has to be *protected* from human desire — shielded by an "It," that anonymous third which finally escapes the economy of desire — if it is not to lose its alterity. The divergence between the two philosophers can hardly be more aptly expressed than when Heschel, concluding his study on the prophets, states: "God is never an 'it,' but is constantly given as personal spirit, manifesting Himself as subject even in the act of thought addressed to Him."[46]

Yet, in order to do justice to Levinas, we should remember the prime motive behind his reluctance toward the idea of a personal God whom the human being can desire directly: by encouraging immediate devotion to God, one tends to divest religion of its moral imperative. This prompts us to pose the question of whether Heschel's strongly personal God, who makes the person who seeks God experience himself or herself as "a divine secret," does not run the risk precisely of betraying this moral imperative. What happens to the unconditional responsibility toward our vulnerable fellow human beings — that responsibility which lies at the root of every word

43. Heschel, *The Prophets*, p. 621.
44. Cf. Susannah Heschel, "Introduction to the Perennial Classics Edition," p. xviii.
45. Heschel, *Man Is Not Alone*, pp. 241-48.
46. Heschel, *The Prophets*, p. 622.

Levinas has written on divine alterity — when so much focus is placed on the immediate relationship between the individual person and God?

To obtain an answer, we need to return to what I stressed at the outset of this section: for Heschel, as for Levinas, there is no reflection on God that does not already imply a reflection on justice. In other words, the God whose presence the prophets feel so intensely is *a priori* defined as justice, which also amounts to stating that the divine pathos in which the prophets share is nothing more, but also nothing less, than a burning passion for justice. Righteousness and justice, in this perspective, are the very essence of God's part of human life, God's stake in human history:

> Justice is not an ancient custom, a human convention, a value, but a transcendent demand, freighted with divine concern. It is not only a relationship between man and man, it is an *act* involving God, a divine need. . . . It is not one of His ways, but in all his ways.[47]

This essential trait of the Hebrew Bible is also well illustrated in Christine Yoder's engaging reading of Proverbs 1–9 in this volume. As Yoder points out, the path to wisdom conveyed by the author is intimately linked to a desire for righteousness, even to the extent that the terms "wise" and "righteous" ultimately become interchangeable. This places in a different light the concern that erotic desire for God or for wisdom may foster exclusivity and betray the concern for our common good. For if desire for divine wisdom is always already intertwined with desire for righteousness, then this desire, to the contrary, turns one outward and compels one to act with compassion and justice. Serving God, in other words, becomes inseparable from serving one's neighbor. Even more so, oppression and injustice committed toward our fellow human beings are ultimately regarded as humiliation of God: "He who oppresses the poor shows contempt for their Maker, but whoever is kind to the needy honors God" (Prov. 14:31).

Thus, to conclude, emphasizing the intimate relationship between the singular human being and God does not, for Heschel any more than for the biblical narratives on which he draws, entail a betrayal of one's neighbor, precisely because such a betrayal would simultaneously be a betrayal of God and thus undermine the very intimacy of the human-divine relationship. In other words, a person who desires God without desiring justice is simply not desiring God. Rather, that person is adoring an idol.

47. Heschel, *The Prophets*, p. 253.

Theology, Pathos, and Desire

In the early 1990s, David Tracy published a celebrated article titled "The Return of God in Contemporary Theology."[48] In a tone reverberating with the pathos of the prophets, he announced that, with postmodernity, "theos" had finally returned to unsettle the dominance of modern logos — that specific horizon of human understanding which for centuries had taken pains to classify, categorize, and finally fetter the divine to a number of well-defined "isms": theism, deism, atheism, panentheism. Today, almost two decades later, few people would contest that theos in several respects has indeed returned to unsettle logos, although, for good reasons, many of us are not unconditionally enthusiastic about it. All too often, it seems, the "God" who has returned in the postmodern world holds more traits of the arbitrary violence of ancient pagan deities than of the peaceful God of love and mystery conceived of by Tracy.

Is it possible today to announce an unsettling of logos, a critique of a certain repressive rationalism, without this resulting in an indiscriminate appraisal of theos, of any claim to divine revelation with all it can entail? I believe the answer is yes, and in the remaining sections I will suggest that the key to this affirmative answer can be spelled out in the notion of pathos. As Tracy rightly pointed out, good theology is in need of both theos and logos; poor or excessive theologies have often been the result of an overemphasis of either one or the other pole. What I wish to add is that theology is also in need of pathos. Theology requires both theos and logos — but both are empty and potentially dangerous when purified from pathos. This is what I have briefly tried to spell out in the introduction of this chapter: by placing God above joy, suffering, and empathy, large parts of the western theological tradition have contributed to sanctioning an ideal of human conduct in terms of self-control, restraint of emotions, and disinterestedness — an ideal that, needless to say, has been strongly gendered. In order to effect a more radical break with this paradigm, it is not sufficient to call out for more theos to unsettle logos. What is needed is more pathos, what Heschel even termed a "theology of pathos."[49] Such a theology would, above all, imply a stronger recognition of *desire* — human as well as divine — than most theology has allowed throughout the ages. Only in this way

---

48. David Tracy, "The Return of God in Contemporary Theology," *Concilium* 6 (1994): 37-47.

49. Heschel, *The Prophets,* pp. 285-98.

will we finally be able to obtain a richer and truer understanding of human and divine interrelatedness, but also of human interrelatedness.

Still, the question lingers: Does not the proclamation of a God who desires humanity, who is moved and affected by human deeds and prayers, undermine decades of philosophical struggle for liberating God from Being, from anthropomorphic projections of all sorts? If we had the opportunity to consult Levinas, his answer would most probably have been in the affirmative, echoing his strong rejection not only of religious philosophical speculation but also of religious experience as a source of knowledge of the divine. However, I believe Heschel offers a good case for answering in the negative. From their common phenomenological platform, both Heschel and Levinas, as we remember, challenge the philosophical reduction of God to Being, to an object accessible to human thought. Still, this does not lead Heschel to efface God from the human mind altogether, positing God as present only as absence, as a trace left on the face of the neighbor. Rather, it is by *reversing* the order between subject and object that Heschel succeeds in withdrawing God from the conceptual traps of metaphysical philosophy:

> To the philosopher God is an *object*, to men at prayer He is the *subject*. Their aim is not to possess Him as a concept of knowledge, to be informed about Him, as if He were a fact among facts. . . . The task is not to know the unknown but to be penetrated with it; *not to know* but *to be known* to Him.[50]

What Heschel seems to be suggesting here is that the "thinking" of God that takes place in prayer is possible only when this thinking is already part of God's thinking of us. To the extent to which we set God apart, as an object for our thought, we lose God and are left with an idol. If, on the contrary, we surrender our attempts at reification of God, we realize that it is only by conceiving of our thinking as already part of God's thought of us that we can think of God in the first place. In other words, just as in thinking about ourselves the object of our thought is never detached from the subject, so in thinking of God we realize that the subject cannot be detached from its object.[51]

Interestingly, the line of thought that Heschel here follows is not altogether foreign to the path that Jean-Luc Marion stakes out (following

50. Heschel, *Man Is Not Alone*, p. 128.
51. Heschel, *Man Is Not Alone*, pp. 126-29.

Levinas!) in order to detach God from Being. Although within a stricter phenomenological framework, Marion also proposes a reversal of subject and object as the key to approaching God beyond Being. He achieves this reversal by, famously, positing the "icon" as a phenomenological counter-concept to the idol. Accordingly, whereas the idol marks the unblurred projection of the subject's intentions onto that which appears to it, the icon marks an inverted intentionality. In the encounter with the icon, the subject's intention is interrupted by a different intentionality; it is, in other words, overwhelmed or saturated by intuition. In this account of the phenomenality of the icon, Marion draws explicitly on Levinas's notion of the face, where the face precisely marks an inverted intentionality, consisting in the gaze of the other that precedes and disturbs the intention of the self. However, whereas Levinas restricts the "epiphany" of the face to the neighbor, pushing God into the background as an anonymous third (although nevertheless part of the "epiphany"), Marion uses the icon to describe the phenomenality of an immediate divine epiphany. Still, if this epiphany is to remain an epiphany in the iconic sense, and not be reduced to an idol, we must resist the temptation to fix what appears (the *noema*) with our intentions. This is possible only by renouncing cognitive claims and predicative language altogether. Rather, it is through the nonpredicative language of prayer and praise that a possibility is opened for the subject to approach the divine without reducing it to an object of our thought.[52]

By construing the divine-human relationship in terms of doxological desire, I believe both Heschel and Marion indicate a way to retain divine otherness without letting it slip into absolute or violent transcendence (the fear of Vattimo and others), but also without "domesticating" it by turning it into a well-defined philosophical concept (the worry of Levinas). Furthermore, as Heschel suggests, it is precisely by conceiving of our desire as already part of God's desire, of God's pathos, that we manage to keep this balance and that there is, in the first place, such a thing as a "God who comes to mind."[53]

52. See further Jean-Luc Marion, *Dieu sans l'être;* and "In the Name: How to Avoid Speaking of 'Negative Theology,'" in *God, the Gift and Postmodernism*, ed. John D. Caputo and Michael J. Scanlon (Bloomington: Indiana University Press, 1999), pp. 20-53.

53. Cf. Levinas, *De Dieu qui vient à l'idée.* Paradoxically, I believe Levinas comes close to the same line of thought in his recurring "meditations" on Descartes's idea of the infinite as an idea that cannot be thought but nevertheless incites a desire in us. Also, although the scope of this chapter does not allow me to develop this any further, I believe a similar argu-

Redirecting Desire — But Saving Whom from Idolatry?

There is, however, yet another objection lingering. If the relationship between God and a human being can be conceived of in terms of mutual desire, we risk overemphasizing the significance of the individual's spiritual experiences at the expense of the command to serve one's neighbor. This is, as we remember, the second reason — besides concern about idolatry — for Levinas's skepticism toward an immediate desire of the human soul for the infinite other. This is also the reason why he proposes a redirection of our metaphysical desire toward the finite other, the undesirable *par excellence*. However, in light of the prophetic heritage that both Levinas and Heschel share, this skepticism is justifiable only insofar as it neglects the very essence of this heritage. In other words, to the prophetic mind, God's pathos is unconditionally tied to justice, which is why desiring God is inseparable from desiring justice and wellbeing for one's neighbor.

One can push the argument even further. If the reason to be cautious regarding human erotic desire, which causes the need to shield God from it, is its potentially possessive character, its yearning for immediate union with the desirable, one could ask whether we should not be just as careful — or even more careful — about redirecting our desire toward our neighbor. In other words, are we not just as likely to turn our fellow human beings into "idols," in the sense of making them targets for our sometimes unreasonable needs and wishes?

Levinas would, of course, respond to this objection by underlining that true desire, also for one's neighbor, ultimately has to be *nonerotic*. Yet, this is precisely where my strongest objection comes in. For is there, and has there ever been, such a thing as a *nonerotic desire?* I refer not primarily to the seeming contradiction that resides already at the verbal level (*desire* being the common English — and French — translation for *eros*), but above all to the actual logic or economy of desire at the concrete phenomenological level: Would desire even be desire, were it stripped of its yearning for union with the desirable, or, at the very least, for some kind of response or recognition from the other? In other words, however much we may wish to stipulate such a thing as a pure, disinterested, and utterly unselfish desire, I doubt not only that we are capable, as finite beings, of

---

ment could be set forth from Michel Henry's notion of auto-affectivity. See further Bernard Forthomme and Jad Hatem, *Affectivité et alterité selon Lévinas et Henry* (Paris: Cariscript, 1996).

bringing forth such a desire, but also that this would be something enviable. Desire, by its very nature, is dynamic, unruly, even *impure:* it is seldom free from egoistic motives, from aspirations of affirmation and reward, and it never runs entirely free from the risk of forcing the other into one's own sphere of power and influence. Yet this is only one side of the coin. Desire is also, often simultaneously, selfless, compassionate, and a true longing for the other for his or her own sake. In sum, desire is filled with *pathos,* to the extent even of sometimes becoming *pathological* and thus harmful, either to the other (possessive desire) or to ourselves (self-sacrificial desire).

Wendy Farley brings this latter aspect to light in an insightful way, while simultaneously indicating some of the shortcomings of Levinas's construal of desire in terms of an unconditional responsibility for the other person. As Farley rightly points out, desire always vacillates between the risks of turning into egocentrism or self-abnegation. Levinas, of course, is well aware of the former risk. It is hardly an overstatement to claim that his entire philosophical impulse is directed against violent egocentrism and its totalizing outcomes on the cultural and political stages of history. However, one can ask whether Levinas does not take his caution against egocentrism to an extreme, reflected in his — with few exceptions — negative metaphors for authentic ethical existence, such as being "accused," "obsessed," or "held hostage" (that these terms are furthermore linked to "motherhood" hardly renders them less problematic). Although it should be remembered that Levinas's argument is played out on a strictly phenomenological level — analyzing the transcendental conditions for responsibility, rather than actual moral experiences — the adequacy of his analysis nevertheless risks being undermined by his inability to distinguish violent egocentrism from appropriate self-affirmation.[54]

If, on the one hand, Levinas's construal of desire seems to possess too few resources to prevent authentic ethical existence from turning into self-abnegation, one can, on the other hand, ask whether it offers enough resources to prevent desire from becoming possessive. More precisely, one can ask whether Levinas's strategy of redirecting the desire for God toward one's neighbor — of inserting a "You" between the I and the absolute "He/It" *(II)*[55] — does not risk placing too much weight on the other human be-

---

54. See Wendy Farley, *Eros for the Other: Retaining Truth in a Pluralistic World* (University Park: Pennsylvania State University Press, 1996), pp. 90-99.

55. Levinas, *En découvrant l'existence avec Husserl et Heidegger,* p. 301 (my trans.).